FYI

FYI

FOR YOUR INFORMATION

Unexpected Answers to Everyday Questions

based on the award-winning ABC-TV program

with HAL LINDEN

EDITED BY NAT BRANDT

WITH THE FYI WRITING STAFF
  Elaine Brown
  Mary Ann Donahue
  Joseph Gustaitis
  Linda Kline
  Lou Potter
  Miriam Schneir
  Ed Tivnan
  Robin Westen

M. EVANS AND COMPANY, INC.   New York

Library of Congress Cataloging in Publication Data

Main entry under title:

FYI: unexpected answers to everyday questions.

Includes index.
1. Questions and answers. I. Brandt, Nat. II. FYI
(Television program)
AG195.F9   1982   031'.02   82-13846

ISBN 0-87131-393-6   HARDCOVER

ISBN 0-87131-391-X   PAPERBOUND

M. Evans and Company, Inc.
216 East 49 Street
New York, New York 10017

DESIGN BY RONALD F. SHEY

Manufactured in the United States of America

9 8 7 6 5 4 3 2 1

Foreword by Hal Linden

She smiled at me coyly and asked, "I've seen all your *Barney Millers*, but you know what I remember you best from?" At this point, I began to compute her age.

I had done about eighteen Broadway shows, ranging in longevity from *The Rothschilds* (one and a half years) to *The Sign in Sidney Brustein's Window* (four days) to *The Love Match* (closed out of town) to *Pleasure Dome* (closed in rehearsal), and I had discovered that since my TV prominence, people took a perverse pride in having been there for the flops. You could usually tell by their age which closing night they had witnessed. With her it could have been any of them, from *The Education of Hyman Kaplan* (twenty-eight performances—it opened the night Martin Luther King, Jr. was assassinated) to *Illya Darling* (about a year—it opened right after the New York Blackout of 1967) to *Something More* (two weeks—no disaster accompanied its opening, though you couldn't tell by the reviews). I waited. Which of my (innumerable) sterling performances was my most memorable?

Her eyes twinkled. "You're the man who told me where to press for menstrual cramps."

The fact is the lady's response was not unusual. I receive more mail about *FYI* than about *Barney Miller*. And if my objective as an actor is to give insight into relationships so that my audience can filter those insights into their own relationships, why not do it directly with information? And why not utilize my training and experience as an actor to deliver that information so that it is received as organically as possible?

When I was first asked to do *FYI*, I was skeptical. The more an actor is accepted as a personality, the less he is accepted in roles that violate the public's perception of that personality. But after reading the first fifteen scripts, I realized how important this series could be to so many people, and I wanted to be a part of it. And I'm glad I did. I now feel that relieving that woman's menstrual cramps is at least as important as getting a laugh.

By the way, in answer to one of the most frequently asked questions, I do not write *FYI*. That is done by a fine staff of writers, organizing the work of a brilliant staff of researchers. My function, besides delivering the message, is to act as a kind of ear of last resort. If it's not totally clear to me, I figure it won't be totally clear to everyone, and the spots are reworked to eliminate the lack of clarity. In the process, I have learned an amazing amount about nutrition, urban homesteading, allergies. For example, did you know . . . ?

HAL LINDEN
Los Angeles

Preface

On January 14, 1980, *FYI* starring Hal Linden went on the air on the ABC Television Network. It was a miniprogram, 45 seconds of information following three of ABC's most popular soap operas. For the first few weeks, viewers didn't quite understand what the show was all about; it was too new and different. What were we selling? Who was the sponsor? Was it possible that the concept of nonprofit had invaded daytime television?

Indeed, *FYI* was not sponsored, it was totally paid for by ABC, it was in the public interest, and it was a brand-new concept in daytime television, providing information on health, psychology, family life, and economics that was positive and helpful to persons of all ages in their daily lives.

FYI won its first EMMY award after just two months on the air. (It has since won three more.) Even more gratifying, *FYI* worked: Viewers began to write, at first a few at a time, but then by the hundreds, asking questions, telling us their problems, asking for help, and, most important, telling us how *we* had helped *them*. And in all the letters, one theme was repeated over and over: How about a book?

FYI owes a great deal to the leaders of ABC Daytime—Jacqueline Smith, Jo Ann Emmerich, and Christy Welker—who, with their inspiration and dedication, helped get *FYI* started, and to Jackie Smith and Jean Arley, who keep it going with their continued support and integrity. I hope you will note the list of staff and consultants at the back of the book who have worked tirelessly to make *FYI* possible. And my special thanks to Susan Garbarini Fanning, who was there when it all began; to Jean Barish for helping to check the manuscript; and to Sharon Fisher, who worked so long and hard to get the manuscript finished in time.

But most of all, my thanks and the thanks of the entire *FYI* staff go to our 60 million viewers who asked for this book.

YANNA KROYT BRANDT
Producer, *FYI*

Editor's Preface

When I first saw *FYI* on television I was struck by the simplicity of the messages it conveyed. To be sure, the information was written to be *heard,* not read. But the messages were not only brief but also occasionally naive—or so it seemed to me at the time. I wondered if it was possible to convey such information accurately in so brief a time. I questioned whether those "studies" anonymously quoted were grounded in scientific approach or methods.

My skepticism evaporated as I began to work on the book. What had seemed to me simple was in actuality a reflection of the ability of *FYI*'s staff writers to turn the most complex issues into clear, meaningful words and sentences that viewers, like myself, could readily understand. I saw firsthand the incredible amount of writing, rewriting, checking and rechecking that went into each message, first by the researchers and writers, then by the consultants, and finally by outside experts.

The book is an expansion and elaboration of the television program. When possible we have tried to explain the methodology and findings that led to the conclusions cited. When the conclusion is controversial we've indicated that. We've also cited many of the sources for the material. However, the main thrust of the book is—as is true of the television program—the transmission of vital, beneficial information for daily living in the clearest, most understandable way. I believe we have succeeded.

NAT BRANDT
New York City

How to Use This Book

The *FYI* book is very much like the television show. As you leaf through it, you may find advice on how to sleep better following a question about buying land for a few dollars an acre. The information is unexpected, surprising, and we hope enlightening. For those who want specific information about a particular topic, there is a detailed index at the back of the book. In addition, a comprehensive source list of books and organizations to contact if you need further information about a subject follows the questions. So whether you are reading for pleasure and serendipitous discoveries or are in search of the latest information about nutrition, you can find what you're looking for.

Is there a way to cheat the Tooth Fairy?

There is. If your tooth has been accidentally knocked out, speedy action is the key to saving it. A tooth replaced within thirty minutes has a high percent chance of survival. But after a two-hour wait, the success rate drops dramatically, and by the next day, it's definitely too late.

Dentists advise rinsing the tooth immediately but gently in tap water. Do not scrub the tooth at all. Ideally it's best to place the tooth back in the socket, holding it there with the tongue. If that's too painful, wrap the tooth carefully in a wet piece of gauze and hold it under your tongue. Then get to the dentist immediately.

The dentist will in most cases stabilize the tooth in position. This is done by attaching the damaged tooth to the adjacent ones with a wire band or by bonding. It is important for the tooth to be in place securely for a few weeks—long enough for the fibers on the surface of the root to reattach themselves to the socket.

By the way, the procedure works for children as well as adults. In children under nine, natural regeneration can leave the tooth as good as new because the roots are not formed yet and, as a result, will not suffer permanent damage. The tooth grows back into its socket and remains alive.

In older children and adults, the nerves in the tooth cannot survive the trauma. Root canal work has to be done, the canals cleaned out and filled. But the original tooth will be back in place, continuing to function normally for years.

What's the safest blood to take if you need a transfusion?

Your own. It's the best and most reliable blood—and it's possible to donate your own blood for your own use at a later date under a program now practiced at nearly two of every three hospitals in the country.

All hospitals, of course, have a rule that before any operation can take place blood of the patient's type must be on hand in case a transfusion is necessary. Such blood usually comes from donors, and in spite of tests, minute incompatibilities can sometimes go undetected. That can be dangerous, causing adverse reactions such as fever, chills, and rash. Cases of hepatitis even may occur in spite of careful testing, but they are rare.

Now, a majority of hospitals offer patients the option of donating their *own* blood well ahead of a scheduled operation—six to eight weeks is recommended. One method may require the patient to make weekly donations, one pint at a time, for three weeks to the blood bank. The blood is labeled with the patient's name and stored for the operation.

What if the operation is delayed? Some blood banks are equipped to freeze blood for up to seven years. But if it turns out *you* don't need the blood, you can donate it to the bank's supply, where it will be kept on hand for another patient with the same blood type. And you'll get "credit" at the blood bank for yourself, a relative, or a friend.

If you want to receive your own blood you'll undergo the same routine tests that any donor candidate does: a blood test for anemia, blood typing, and tests for hepatitis virus.

And don't worry about being weakened by giving blood. Doctors point out that the normal body restores its blood levels rapidly after a transfusion.

What's the easiest way to catch a cold?

By shaking hands with someone who has one. A recent study indicates that washing the hands may do more to stop the spreading of a cold than stifling a cough or sneeze does.

The same study (conducted at the University of Virginia School of Medicine) also shows that it's not just person-to-person contact that spreads cold-causing viruses. Contact with objects— a telephone or a table top—previously touched by a cold victim can cause you to come down with the sniffles. The cold viruses aren't short-lived either. They can retain their infection-spreading potency for up to three hours after they've dried. Don't rub your nose and eyes. They are sources of mucus that are loaded with cold viruses.

Togetherness may not be the best idea if your partner has got the sneezes. One research team studied married couples in which one partner had a cold. The healthy spouse caught the other's sniffles 38 percent of the time. In each case, the original cold was moderate to severe. Milder ones didn't get transmitted.

The next time someone in your household catches a cold:

☐ Have them cover those coughs and sneezes.
☐ See that they wash their hands frequently and thoroughly.

Why doesn't the Sandman come?

Probably because you've made it difficult for him. What position you sleep in, what you sleep on, what kind of snack you eat, and what exercises you do before bedtime, all will influence whether you have a good night's sleep or toss-and-turn insomnia.

The solutions are easy and clear, and one of them is not to take a sleeping pill or to up the dosage if you're already taking such drugs. Although Americans take more than a billion prescription sleeping pills a year, studies show that the effectiveness of the pills quickly drops off. After two weeks, they are of relatively little use against insomnia. Moreover, research has proved that the pills can cause a decrease in physical and mental capabilities—and may be addictive.

The first step to better sleep is to check your posture. The best sleeping position is the so-called fetal position, on your side (it doesn't matter which side), with one or both knees drawn up. Sleeping on your stomach can be a cause of lower back pain, and sleeping with your arms or hands tucked under your head may cut off blood circulation and place stress on the arms, shoulders, and upper back.

Select your mattress carefully, lying on it for a few minutes before you decide whether to purchase it. Choose one that's comfortable but also firm. It should provide well-balanced support for your spine.

If you find yourself waking several times during the night, suffering from head pains, or if you have a splitting headache when you get up in the morning, it's possible you're a victim of a common condition that doctors call "turtle headache." It's caused by pulling the bedcovers turtlelike over your head while sleeping. This restricts the brain's supply of oxygen. The severest pain is usually felt in the frontal area. The cure is exactly what you would expect: Don't keep your head under the covers. In most cases this should solve the problem at once.

Exercise before bedtime can be an aid to sound sleeping, but the type of activity is what counts. Vigorous exercising—tennis, running, bike riding—done late in the day tends to lengthen the time it takes most people to fall asleep. Studies show that static exercise—push-ups, weight lifting—two hours before bedtime may make sleep come more swiftly.

A glass of warm milk before bedtime may aid in inducing sleep. Scientists have confirmed that the warm milk Grandma used to recommend contains a sleep-inducing natural amino acid called tryptophan. And if you feel like having a bedtime snack, try nuts, chicken, turkey, cottage cheese, or tunafish along with your warm milk. They all contain significant amounts of tryptophan.

Nicotine, by the way, is a stimulant. Research shows that heavy smoking can increase the time needed to fall asleep by up to 45 percent and also affect the quality of the sleep.

What about counting sheep? Another old wives' tale? Not really; psychologists say it works. Visualizing the sheep occupies the right, or creative, side of the brain, while the counting process keeps the left, or rational, side busy. With both sides of the brain humming away you're prevented from dwelling on problems and unpleasant thoughts that might keep you from a good night's sleep.

How can a pet help you live longer?

The simple act of relating to a pet has much the same effect on your system as meditation. It reduces your body's manufacture of adrenalin, which in turn causes the heart to pump with less force. Petting an animal lowers your blood pressure and calms you down.

According to a study by the American Heart Association, pet owners are more likely to survive during the first year after a heart attack than those who don't own pets. And it is not just true of heart-attack patients. *All* pet owners recovering from *all* types

13

of illnesses do better than patients without pets.

The patients' pets weren't just puppies either. Cats, birds, gerbils, even snakes do the trick.

Most gerontology experts agree that pets are especially good medicine for the elderly. Pets provide companionship, promote a sense of self-worth, and give their owners a sense of feeling needed. They can encourage the elderly, who commonly skip meals, to pay more attention to their diet. As one researcher pointed out, "If you're feeding a pet, you're more likely to fix something for yourself."

And a dog can help to increase a senior citizen's exercise program by requiring daily walks. A dog can also encourage socializing; dog owners seem to enjoy a natural affinity when they meet in a park.

If someone you know has been seriously ill, or you have an elderly friend or relative living alone, why not consider getting them a pet? It just may help them live longer.

Is there a painkiller that isn't habit forming?

There's now a way to control pain without drugs, without side effects, and without the danger of addiction. It's called TENS, for transcutaneous electrical nerve stimulator. TENS is a small, battery-operated generator with electrodes attached to it. The low-voltage electric current blocks pain pathways between the brain and the site of the pain.

Doctors aren't sure exactly how TENS works, but studies have found that it provides safe relief for more than half of all acute pain sufferers. It's especially helpful for home treatment of the chronic pain associated with backaches, migraines, and arthritis.

Doctors also prescribe TENS for the pain that results from surgery or from injuries. It has the advantage of providing relief without making a patient drowsy or causing other side effects. And because the patient's system isn't overloaded with drugs, it may mean faster recovery.

TENS is about the size of a cassette tape, so it's small enough to carry with you. Two or more electrodes are placed on the part of the body that's in pain. When the switch that activates the generator is turned on, a pulsating current passes through the painful area, producing a mild, tingling sensation.

Relief can last for hours—even days. But most persons who have chronic problems find they get relief they need by using TENS an hour at a time, six times a day. It doesn't interfere with work or other routine activities. And it can be safely used for months, even years, at a time.

A doctor's prescription is needed to order TENS. The monthly rental runs between $60 and $100. (If you decide to buy, the cost is about $500 to $600.) But the cost is usually covered by medical insurance.

A caution: Any new pain is a warning signal, so check with your doctor if one occurs.

If you suffer from chronic pain and the pain is keeping you from functioning normally, ask your doctor if TENS might work for you.

Can a pan of water prevent snoring?

When the lights go out and we tuck into bed, a cacophony of grunts, snores, howls, and hoots echoes through bedroom walls all across the country. One out of eight Americans—25 million of us in all—are snorers. If you've ever tried to sleep next to one, you know it's no joke. If you're the snorer, you know how embarrassing and frustrating it can be.

Why do we snore? Probably because an airway to the lungs is partly blocked. As the lungs try to draw in enough air, the effort causes a vibration against the soft palate. The force of the vibration determines the strength of the snore.

But don't despair. There are several ways to prevent snoring:

☐ Adjust your sleeping position to discourage breathing through your mouth. Sleep on your side with your forearm under the chin, so that you're pressing your mouth shut. If you must sleep on your back, put a small pillow under the nape of your neck to elevate your head.

☐ Try to increase the humidity in your bedroom. When the room is too dry, membranes get swollen and cause snoring. Usually a pot of water placed by the radiator will do the trick.

☐ If you're overweight, lose those extra pounds. Fat can also impair breathing.

☐ Don't drink alcohol before going to bed. Alcohol acts as a depressant and relaxes the muscles of the respiratory system so that breathing may become more difficult.

If you're the unfortunate partner of a snorer and you're determined to put an end to the nocturnal noise, try waking and pushing the person into a corrective position every time the snoring starts. This takes persistence, but eventually a full night's sleep may be your reward. And, of course, there are always earplugs.

One note of caution: If none of the preventives works, the snoring can be the sign of an obstruction in the nose. See an ear, eye, and throat specialist. The doctor might prescribe medical treatment such as nose drops or antihistamines.

Is there a way to heal a stubborn broken bone?

Yes. A new technique, electrotherapy, is proving very effective in treating this painful problem.

Electrotherapy was tested on 400 patients who had fractures that hadn't healed in more than two years, despite bone grafts. Within twenty-four weeks, 85 percent of the bones had healed.

The procedure employs devices called bone-growth stimulators to generate electrical currents that cause new bone material to grow over the break. Although researchers aren't sure why the technique works, they think that the electrical jolts may rouse bone-producing cells into action.

The results don't seem to be affected by either the number of previous bone grafts undergone by the patient or by the length of time the bone has been broken. Bone formation usually begins within twelve weeks after electrotherapy has started. Each treatment takes about twenty minutes and can be performed in a doctor's office under local anesthetic. The cost is a fraction of what it is for bone-graft surgery.

The healing also appears to be permanent. Patients who were treated with electrotherapy in its experimental stages in the mid-1970s have not reported any posttreatment difficulties.

There are three types of stimulators licensed for use in the United States. Two of the systems involve implanting electrodes in the bone. In one method they remain permanently, in the other they're removed after treatment is completed. The third method uses coils placed outside the cast. The coils generate an electromagnetic field, and the treatment takes place while the patient sleeps.

Specialists foresee the use of electrostimulators also in treating bone infection. Electrotherapy has also shown some promise in treating osteoporosis, a condition that causes the bones of older persons to become brittle and break easily.

What should come first in first aid for athletic injuries?

Even some doctors admit confusion when it comes to treating certain injuries. Which is more advisable—applying heat or cold?

According to physicians and physical therapists at the Hershey Medical Center in Hershey, Pennsylvania, the answer is cold.

By applying ice (or extreme cold) to injuries such as contusions, a ligament sprain, a muscle strain, even fractures, you control the hemorrhaging and swelling that takes place beneath the skin. This may be critical in rehabilitation and return of the patient to normal physical activity, once the injury has healed.

Cold causes blood vessels to constrict and diminishes the flow of blood within the damaged area. It also slows the metabolic process within damaged cells, lessening their immediate need for oxygen and other nutrients, thereby reducing the process of swelling.

On the other hand, heat will do just the opposite. It increases the blood flow and cellular metabolism that produce inflammation and swelling.

Whatever the injury may be, the Hershey medical team suggests that cold be applied immediately, preferably in some type of ice pack, and held in place with an elastic bandage for at least thirty minutes. Never apply ice directly to the skin, because a kind of "burning" may result.

Ice is a natural painkiller and can also be used in packs or

17

compress form to relieve painful symptoms of neuralgia, arthritis, sore muscles, and toothaches.

Therapists recommend a cold foot bath to relieve swollen feet and ankles, cold compresses to soothe a headache, and a comfortable cool bath to help stimulate the body from head to toe and restore a feeling of vigor.

If you find yourself in need of or administering first aid, remember: Heat may aggravate the situation, cold never does.

Is a stroke unpredictable?

No. Doctors have discovered that many of the half-million persons who suffer strokes each year had warning signals weeks or months beforehand. The signals are called ministrokes. If you learn to recognize them and know what action to take, you could avoid a stroke or save a loved one from one.

The word "stroke" means a sudden, powerful event, such as the "rupture or obstruction (as by a clot) of an artery of the brain." On the other hand, ministrokes, also called TIAs (transient ischemic attacks), may last from as little as a few seconds to as long as several hours. No permanent brain damage occurs, and the clotting can actually dissolve itself when blood flow is restored. The TIAs start unexpectedly and consist of a variety of temporary symptoms. These may include any one, or several, of the following: temporary blindness or blurring of vision; numbness or paralysis of one side of the body, the face, or an arm or leg; slurring of speech or inability to speak at all; dizziness, fainting, or a feeling of disorientation, and failure to recognize familiar persons and objects.

TIAs can occur when individuals are awake and active. It's easy to confuse them with an ordinary dizzy spell and to ignore them because they pass so rapidly. But if you or anyone you know experiences one or more of these symptoms, you should suspect a ministroke. This is especially true if you or the individual has a history of high blood pressure, heart disease, previous stroke, or is over the age of sixty-five. However, although older individuals are far more likely to be victims, young persons and children sometimes suffer strokes, too.

Immediately report the symptoms to a doctor. He will check

blood pressure, listen with a stethoscope, and examine neurological signs. Sometimes X-rays, including a CAT scan, are needed to confirm a diagnosis. (A CAT scan, or Computerized Axial Tomography, allows doctors to see a cross-sectional view of the brain.) If the doctor finds that the blood supply to the brain has been partly blocked or slowed, there are several possible remedies—aspirin or other anticlotting agents, changes in diet, modified exercise levels, and a rethinking of one's life-style (which will undoubtedly preclude smoking and unlimited drinking). In some cases, surgery may be recommended.

One recent analysis of a group of individuals who sought medical advice immediately after detecting signs of a ministroke indicated that no major stroke occurred afterward in 97 percent of the cases. So the warning signal flashed by a ministroke can in a sense be a stroke of good luck.

Can you take the surprise—and inevitability—out of a heart attack?

Yes, because many heart attacks do not come by surprise at all. They often give out warning signals one to two weeks beforehand—repeated, brief episodes of uncomfortable chest pains, occasional skipped heart beats, shortness of breath, or dizziness. Some people may mistake these symptoms for indigestion or heartburn and ignore them. But if you pay attention to these warning signs and see your doctor promptly, you may be able to prevent the heart attack altogether.

It's likely that more than 1 million Americans will suffer a heart attack this year. Most victims will be over forty-five years old, and the number of women who will be affected is on the rise. Medical science has made tremendous advances in the control of heart disease, but, according to experts, the best treatment is prevention.

Not only do many people ignore early warning signals of a heart attack, but it's quite common for many individuals to delay, sometimes as much as three hours or even a day, getting help when they are in the throes of a full-fledged attack.

The warning signals of a major heart attack are uncomfortable pressure, fullness, squeezing, or pain in the middle of your

19

chest; pain that spreads to your shoulders, neck, or arms; and dizziness, fainting, sweating, nausea, or shortness of breath.

Not all these symptoms are present at one time, so it's best not to take chances if any occur. The American Heart Association advises to get help immediately if you experience any of them for two minutes or more. Call an emergency rescue service or, if you can, have someone drive you to a hospital. It's wise to know which hospitals in your area offer twenty-four-hour emergency cardiac care, and to keep a list of emergency numbers next to your telephone at home, at work, and in your purse or wallet.

It's common for many individuals to deny they are having a heart attack, and to ignore the warning signals that occur early on. But don't be one of them. Play it safe: Get to a hospital, contact your doctor. By recognizing the early warning signals and seeking immediate medical attention, you can not only prevent a major attack, you can save your life.

Is fresh air bad for you while you're sleeping?

It can be, particularly in wintertime, despite the adage that fresh air is good for you.

The body slows down during sleep, the heart beats less rapidly, and blood pressure, pulse, and breathing rates all decline. Cold air entering through open windows makes it more difficult for our slowed-down systems to retain body heat and maintain a proper temperature.

Open windows in subfreezing temperatures can cause humidity problems, too. When the air is cold, it contains only a small amount of water vapor. When such freezing air flows into a room, it causes the humidity level to go down. And this is uncomfortable for breathing passages. So it's best to air out rooms in the daytime. You can close the windows before retiring and give the humidity levels a chance to climb back to the comfort level before you turn in.

If you're a city dweller, there's also air pollution to consider, and sometimes that can be reason enough to keep those windows shut.

Is "senility" curable?

First of all, "senility" doesn't exist as a disease in its own right; it's just an inexact term for a collection of symptoms. Geriatricians now recognize that confusion and disorientation—the symptoms usually associated with the term—may be due to a wide variety of underlying conditions, ranging from inadequate blood circulation in the brain to depression, infection, or a side effect of medication. And it's neither inevitable nor hopeless; one out of five cases is treatable now, and as we learn more about brain chemistry, that percentage will undoubtedly increase.

Elderly patients may appear confused because they are suffering depression, metabolic disorders, poor nutrition, infection, allergic reaction to medication, loss of hearing, or vision impairment. These are not senility. Once the underlying problem is treated, the symptoms completely disappear in many cases.

A task force of the National Institutes on Aging suggests that an elderly person who begins to show signs of mental deterioration should see a doctor immediately, preferably a geriatrics expert specially trained in the problems of the elderly. The doctor should take a very detailed medical history from either the patient, a relative, or a close friend, including a comprehensive list of all the drugs the patient takes. The patient should have a thorough exam with blood, urine, thyroid, neurological, psychological, and intellectual tests.

It's likely the problem will be treatable. About 90 percent of all men and women over sixty-five—and many well into their eighties and nineties—have no serious mental deterioration. A change in diet or medication, a hearing aid, antidepressant drugs, even exercise may be suggested by the doctor.

Not long ago, doctors believed that confusion and disorientation were inevitable aspects of old age. Now they suspect that these symptoms result from a change in brain chemistry, and they are employing several drugs to treat it—and to prevent it from occurring at all. One of the drugs is Hydergine, a combination of three dihydrogenated ergot alkaloids.

Although there are several theories about the causes of changes in mental function in old age, no conclusive evidence singles out any specific one. But whatever the cause, patients taking Hydergine show significant improvement. In a number of separate studies, patients were able to remember important dates, telephone numbers, take the initiative to socialize, and care more about their appearance and health habits. Their concentration also improved, and they were less depressed. In one study, after fifteen months on the drug, patients showed an average increase in intelligence. Doctors aren't sure how Hydergine works, but they suspect that it stimulates the arousal and awareness areas of the brain.

If you're looking for a geriatrics specialist, contact a major medical center or a local agency for the aged.

Need a knee injury keep you down?

No. A new diagnostic and surgical procedure called arthroscopy offers the possibility of quick, inexpensive relief for some of the thousands upon thousands of persons who suffer from knee ailments and similar disabilities.

With Americans taking to the athletic fields and jogging paths in record numbers in recent years, the incidence of knee injuries has soared to the point where they now represent the number one sports complaint. When required, standard knee surgery can be complicated, is often only partly successful, and includes an extended recuperation period, normally from four to six weeks. On the other hand, with arthroscopy some patients with minor tears in cartilage, for example, can be operated on under local anesthetic and have the condition repaired and be back to work as early as the following day.

The key to the technique's success is the arthroscope, an optical instrument that's inserted into the knee through a tiny incision. This opportunity for visual inspection has greatly improved the orthopedist's ability to accurately diagnose knee conditions. In a few cases, surgery can even be performed through the incision with the use of the arthroscope.

Surgeons are now using arthroscopy to remove loose particles from knees and to correct dislocated kneecaps without costly hospital stays. The number of doctors using this procedure, though still limited, is growing. The next time your knee acts up, ask your orthopedist about arthroscopy.

Rub ice on my hand for a toothache?

When you've got a toothache, holding an ice pack on your cheek may reduce the swelling but it won't take most of the pain away. Incredibly, the safest, most simple drug-free way to relieve toothache pain is to rub ice wrapped in gauze into a muscle in your hand.

In one study at McGill University in Montreal, the majority of patients found that the ice massage reduced the intensity of their toothache pain dramatically.

To find the right spot to place the ice, follow these instructions:

☐ Use the hand that is on the same side as the tooth pain.

☐ Locate the muscle on the side of the hand that bulges when you press your thumb against your forefinger. It's the "hump" that forms in the "V" where the fingers meet.

☐ Now open your thumb. The area to be massaged is where the "hump" was. This area is called in acupuncture the "hoku" point, which the Chinese have known about for at least 5,000 years.

☐ Massage the hoku point with the ice wrapped in gauze for seven minutes. (If your hand starts to feel numb, remove the ice.) The seven-minute ice massage should give you between fifteen minutes to a half hour of relief from pain. That's enough time to get you to the dentist pain-free or to ease the discomfort after a root canal or extraction. You can repeat as needed.

What sex differences will mittens and socks cover up?

The fact that most women experience the cold more than men do, especially on their hands and feet. The male body simply copes with extremes of temperature—both cold and heat—better than the female body.

In 1979 Dr. Richard L. Bruce of the Altitude Research Division of the U.S. Army Research Institute of Environmental Medicine reported that, because of differences in physiological factors such as body mass, body fat, and body surface, women have less tolerance than men for both severe cold and heat.

Physiologically speaking, the bigger the body mass, the more heat the body produces. On the average, a woman's body mass is about 20 percent less than a man's. But her body surface is not reduced proportionately, and this gives her a larger surface-area-to-mass ratio than a man has. What this all amounts to is that a woman will begin feeling the cold before men.

It's true that women generally do have more body fat than men, but the layer of fat that provides extra insulation is not present on either hands or feet—prime risk areas for frostbite. Because of their physical makeup, women also do not generate as much heat from exercise or shivering as men do.

Under heat stress, women do not, on the whole, fare much better. According to the study, when women are exposed to extreme heat they experience a greater increase in heart rate than men do, lower rates of sweating (which, of course, is the body's way of trying to cool itself when overheated), higher skin temperatures, more storage of body heat, and a greater susceptibility to dehydration.

Experts advise that, in cold weather, a woman should wear 30 to 40 percent more insulation than a man, particularly mittens, socks, and boots—and, when it is very warm, minimal clothing made from natural fibers. Synthetics, such as polyester, don't breathe enough and end up conserving too much body heat during summertime.

For men only: What's the benefit of an annual checkup?

The key word is "annual." According to the latest medical recommendations, an annual physical for men under the age of forty may not be necessary or desirable. Indeed, there may even be some disadvantages.

For one thing, a doctor's clean bill of health can provide a false sense of security. As one extensive study found, taking exams and tests does not automatically prevent anyone from developing medical problems. More importantly, the "yield" or likelihood of finding something significantly wrong each year in healthy men under forty was so low as to make the expense and bother unjustifiable.

But a healthy or symptom-free man should not eliminate scheduling a physical from his calendar altogether. Many medical experts advise a man between eighteen and thirty-nine to have a complete checkup every five years, and a man over forty every one to three years. However, he should see the doctor immediately if something is bothering him—pain, persistent cough, or shortness of breath, for example.

The checkup should include a blood-pressure measurement, eye and ear exams, height and weight checks, urinalysis, cholesterol and other blood tests, and rectal and testicular exams.

It's also important for a man to see his doctor and his ophthalmologist periodically for specific purposes. Here's a suggested list of guidelines for the most important of these:

Men of all ages	Blood pressure once a year
Under 40	A tetanus booster every 5–10 years
Over 40	A glaucoma test every two years, a rectal and prostatic examination every three years
Over 65	Flu shots each year, in the autumn
Any age	Test for venereal disease every two years

For women only: What's the benefit of an annual checkup?

Two of the major illnesses that plague women are highly curable if they're caught early: cancers of the cervix and breast. An annual gynecological checkup can detect the early stages of these illnesses so they can be treated before they do serious harm.

Yet more than half of all women fail to have a yearly gynecological examination. If you're a woman who is among this majority it's important that you see the gynecologist once a year from now on.

The examination will include a Pap smear to detect cancer of the cervix. The same examination will be used to check out the possibility of infection in the vagina.

The gynecologist will also examine the breasts for possible signs of abnormality. If you're a woman between thirty-five and forty, the American Cancer Society now advises that you have a baseline mammogram. This will provide a point of reference in case you develop a problem in the future. At this point no safe statement can be made about mammograms. Medical experts advise that you follow your doctor's recommendation regarding the procedure.

The gynecological checkup should include a pelvic examination and a urine test for diabetes and kidney problems. If you're over thirty and are considering becoming pregnant for the first time, the pelvic exam should include a check for endometriosis, which can be cured if detected early.

As for a general health checkup, an annual physical may not be necessary for women under fifty. (See the explanations offered in the previous entry, "For Men Only: What's the Benefit of an Annual Checkup?")

As with a man, this doesn't mean a healthy or symptom-free woman should eliminate scheduling a physical from her calendar altogether. Many medical experts advise women between eighteen and thirty-nine to have a complete checkup every three years, women between forty and fifty every two years, and those over fifty every year. However, a woman should see the doctor immediately if something is bothering her, such as pain, persistent cough, or shortness of breath.

The general checkup should include a blood-pressure check, eye and ear exams, height and weight checks, urinalysis, cholesterol, and other blood tests.

Again, as with a man, it's also important for a woman to see her doctor and her ophthalmologist periodically for specific purposes. (Follow the suggested guidelines in the previous entry.)

Can lab tests lie?

When we get the results of lab tests, we assume they're correct. And most times they are. But it's important to be aware that mistakes may be made and can have a significant influence on the treatment a doctor prescribes.

Studies show that the most common errors are made in tests done for diabetes, kidney function, VD, and pregnancy. Mistakes also show up on Pap smears.

In a study conducted by the Centers for Disease Control (a branch of the U.S. Public Health Service), a blood sample sent out to 700 laboratories across the country was inaccurately analyzed in one out of every five instances. A blood urea nitrogen test used for diagnosing kidney function was in error 15 percent of the time.

What's more, experts estimate that 2 million lab mistakes are made in the country's 100,000 laboratories every day.

Some tests are made inaccurate by medication a patient is taking. For example, large doses of vitamin C can cause inaccurate reading of urinary glucose. It can also cause inaccurate results in tests used to detect occult (hidden) blood in the stool. A birth-control pill can be a contributing factor to an abnormal Pap smear. In fact, if you're taking any prescription or nonprescription drugs be sure to tell your doctor. A past history of various diseases may cause abnormalities in some test results used in routine screening. A good physician will always want to know (1) what medications you're taking, and (2) what diseases you've had in the past, before ordering certain lab tests.

However, the majority of errors are probably the result of poor laboratory management. Fewer than a dozen states require lab workers to be licensed.

If a test return, whether positive or negative, makes you suspect it's inaccurate, have a second test done. In the case of a serious disease, it's a wise rule of thumb to repeat some tests anyway.

_____

Is there an alternative to X-rays?

Yes. X-rays used to be the primary way that doctors could see inside the body to diagnose illness, but now there's a new technology that is safe and better for diagnosing many problems. It's called ultrasound, and it uses sound waves instead of radiation to create a picture.

The sound waves bounce off organs and tissues, then send back echoes that are turned into an image that looks similar to an

X-ray. But a sonogram, as the picture is called, shows the soft tissue more clearly.

For women who develop breast problems, ultrasound can reduce the need for a biopsy. One recent study found that it screens breast problems accurately 95 percent of the time. And it's superior to mammograms for women under fifty.

Ultrasound is particularly meaningful if a woman develops a lump during pregnancy, when it is particularly important to limit radiation exposure. A sonogram can determine whether the lump is benign and, if it is, the woman can wait until after the baby is born to have it treated.

Ultrasound is also used to diagnose tissues in other parts of the body—the eyes, abdomen, heart, bladder, and prostate. And a new ultrasound technique called endosonoscopy can probe inside the body and discover minute tumors that might be missed by less sensitive methods.

It's important to remember that ultrasound doesn't replace other diagnostic methods. X-rays are still the best means of diagnosing many problems. The most reassuring news is that these two methods now provide complementary information that adds up to a more complete picture of what's going on inside the body.

What new dental technique is so easy and cheap you'll ask for it?

It's called bonding, and in most cases it can be used to restore chipped, irregular, or stained teeth and fill unsightly gaps quickly and painlessly, without the expense and time of capping, and without drilling or anesthesia. And it can be done at one sitting, too.

With capping, one tooth may require four or more sittings. The dentist drills and files away healthy as well as unhealthy enamel, then cements a gold or porcelain crown on the remaining stump. It's a costly and time-consuming process, and can be painful as well.

Bonding, on the other hand, generally requires only a single appointment. The dentist uses a mild acid to clean the affected tooth, then coats the tooth with a clear plastic. A matching tooth-colored paste is applied and molded into shape. As soon as the paste hardens, it is contoured and polished. The entire process costs only about $100 a tooth; capping can run three to four times as much.

Bonding is especially useful for children who fall and chip their teeth. Most dentists usually prefer not to give children caps anyway because their teeth aren't fully developed.

With bonding, you may need some minor repairs after four to five years. Which is one reason that it's important to choose a dentist who is thoroughly familiar with the procedure. There are now 40,000 dentists trained in this procedure, which requires great skill. Discuss bonding with your dentist. It's a small price to pay for attractive-looking teeth.

An annual checkup for my medicine chest?

If you're like most people, your medicine chest is in your bathroom and it's full of half-used prescriptions and over-the-counter medications that are years old—a hazard to you and your family. Many drugs have a limited shelf life and deteriorate after a few months. They then become ineffective and, in some cases, toxic.

Take immediate action: Flush all those old medicines down the toilet, and clear off all the shelves.

Now, you're ready to start from scratch. Reserve the bathroom cabinet for the essentials you need to keep on hand for common ailments, skin problems, first aid, and poison emergencies. Set up a separate cabinet in your bedroom or a hallway for medications that are affected by heat and moisture, and be sure it's placed high up out of a child's reach. Set aside each shelf in this cabinet for a separate purpose so that in an emergency you won't have to lose time searching for the medicine you need. For example:

Shelf No. 1: Common Ailments—Aspirin, decongestant, antacid, paregoric, laxative, eardrops, a fever thermometer.

Shelf No. 2: Skin Problems—Hydrocortisone cream, calamine lotion, sunscreen lotion, insect repellent.

Shelf No. 3: First Aid—Antiseptic cleanser, antibiotic and burn ointments, rubbing alcohol, petroleum jelly, bandages, cotton balls, gauze, an elastic bandage, prepared eyewash, mercurochrome, and tweezers.

Shelf No. 4: Poison Antidotes—Activated charcoal, epsom salts, and syrup of ipecac.

Tape a list of emergency telephone numbers inside the cabinet for your doctor, local pharmacy, hospital, and poison control center.

If poison is accidentally swallowed, call Poison Control at once before taking anything. But if poison gets on the skin, don't wait to call. Shower immediately with lukewarm water for at least fifteen minutes. Poison in an eye must be flushed out without delay. Run a steady stream of water across the eye for at least fifteen minutes. Hold the lid wide open to be sure you wash the poison out of the corners of the eye. Afterward, get to your doctor or hospital emergency room at once.

Many medications carry expiration dates on their labels, but it's wise anyway to label each one you bring home with the date of purchase before storing it. And remember: A year from now give your medicine chest another checkup.

What's the most important part of a medical checkup?

It's not any of the tests, and it's not the physical examination: It's your own medical diary, the complete history of not only your health from birth to present, but also all the information you have on the health of your parents, aunts, uncles, brothers and sisters, and cousins. This information is vital because so many conditions tend to run in families.

Bring your medical diary along each time you have a checkup. You may not remember the type of rare virus that laid you up when you were in high school—but if your parents kept a medical diary you'll be able to look it up. You may not remember the name of the drug that caused you to break out in a rash—but it'll be in your diary. It's never too late to start a diary. By asking family members or asking the family doctor to check records, you will be able to reconstruct your medical history.

To keep a record for yourself and every member of the family, purchase an inexpensive notebook for each of you. Chart all the important information: blood type, allergies, vaccinations, childhood diseases, adult illnesses, the date and purpose of X-rays and surgery, and any medications that have been taken. Also

30

include living habits: whether you jog, play tennis, or are sedentary; whether you smoke and drink, and what kind of diet you follow.

And keep your medical diary up-to-date. Record the results of each medical checkup: your blood pressure, height, weight, cholesterol level, and other relevant information. Write down any instructions your doctor gives you so you can refer to your diary between visits. Each time there's a health change, remember to add the new information.

Of course, your medical diary will only protect your health if you see your doctor as regularly as your age and physical condition require.

Any advances lately in cataract surgery?

New technology is making great strides in helping persons with cataracts to see better sooner.

Four hundred thousand persons undergo cataract surgery each year. Cataracts—the clouding of the lens that blocks the passage of light rays into the eye—are one of the leading causes of blindness. Currently, eye surgery has advanced far beyond the time when it was almost mandatory for doctors to wait until a person's vision was reduced virtually to minimal light perception before operating.

With modern surgical techniques and instruments, cataract surgery now is safer, hospitalization is short, and visual recovery can be rapid. Some of the key factors include better instruments and operating microscopes, improved suture material, and smaller incisions for faster healing. There have also been improvements in cataract spectacles and contact lenses. Some contact lenses can be worn for extended periods of time.

One surgical technique involves the insertion of an artificial plastic lens—intraocular lens implant—into the eye after the affected natural lens is removed. The implanted plastic lens rests inside the eye close to the position previously occupied by the cataract. Unlike a contact lens, which sits on the surface of the eye and can be removed by hand, the implanted lens is designed to remain in the eye permanently. It can provide vision that most closely resembles that of a normal eye, and will give people the ability to see without glasses or with thinner glasses than they would otherwise need.

There are several different techniques for removing cataracts from the eye. The intracapsular type removes the entire cataract; the extracapsular type leaves the back portion of the cataract in the eye. The latter can be done with simple instruments by hand or with an ultrasonic machine. The options allow the surgeon to tailor the operation to the needs of the individual.

If you have symptoms of blurry, distorted, or double vision, or increasing nearsightedness, see your doctor. If you don't have symptoms, have a thorough eye exam once a year anyway for your own protection, especially after the age of forty. There's no reason why your world should be out of focus.

Are you afraid of your doctor?

Many patients are, or stand in awe of him or her, and, as a result, they're not getting the quality of medical care they should. Studies tell us that the better the communication between doctor and patient, equal to equal, the better the health care the patient will get.

Sometimes patients hesitate to question their doctors for fear they will get angry or feel insulted. Surveys show, however, that most physicians respond positively to direct requests for information.

There are ways by which the patient can help improve the communication process. Go to the doctor's office prepared with detailed information on your personal and family medical history. List your symptoms in the order in which they appeared and describe them as precisely as possible—their location in your body, their frequency, their effect on your everyday activities.

It's very important that you speak directly about what's troubling you. Don't let fear, pride, shame, or embarrassment prevent you from giving the facts. Make sure the doctor hears you out.

Always ask about the course of treatment your doctor recommends. Is it the only one dictated by your specific complaint? If there are alternatives, ask the physician to spell out the pros and cons of each.

32

When diagnostic testing is required, determine why the tests are necessary, what can be learned from them, and how much they will cost.

If medication is prescribed, make certain that you are well briefed on dosage levels and possible side effects. Check if less expensive generic drugs may be substituted for brand-name drugs.

This may sound like a lot of asking and questioning, and some patients fear they'll appear to be questioning the doctor's authority. Nonsense! That's what you're there for—to learn everything you need to know—and no good physician will resent it. After all, the word "doctor" comes from the Latin for "teacher."

Finally, if you have persisting communications problems, or if you leave the physician's office unsatisfied by the answers you've gotten about an important problem, don't hesitate to seek a second professional opinion. After all, it's your body and your health. You owe it to yourself and to your family to get the best possible care.

A laugh a day is good exercise?

It's true. We all know that a good joke, a funny book, or a silly movie makes life's problems easier to bear. Now researchers are finding that laughter can do a lot more than cheer you up.

In a recent study, one thousand persons aged seventy-five and older were asked the secrets of long life. Up near the top of the list, along with family and friends, they put a good laugh.

Laughing is not only good for the soul, it's also good exercise and a way to fight illness. When you laugh, you exercise your heart, your lungs, even your adrenal glands. You breathe deeper and get more oxygen flowing through your body, which is important because many serious illnesses deplete the body's supply of oxygen. There's also evidence that laughter stimulates the production of substances called endorphins, which are the body's own natural painkillers.

Ready for another tickling finding? Laughter can even help learning. Recently, researchers studied one hundred and forty kindergarten pupils and first graders. They divided the children into four groups and showed each group identical educational films. Two of the groups also saw funny cartoons and puppet skits along with instructional material. Those who saw the humorous bits paid closer attention, and, when they were tested on what they remembered, they scored significantly higher than the other children.

Do the new ways to cure stuttering really work?

Yes, a variety of innovative techniques offer sufferers complete relief.

Stuttering is a puzzling and ancient affliction. The Greek orator Demosthenes had it, as did Charles Darwin and Thomas Jefferson. Among the many varied causes that have been suggested over the years are childhood emotional conflicts, defective hearing, and the lack of calcium in the diet. Whatever the cause may be, more than two million Americans of all ages stutter. After years of unsuccessful speech therapy, many have become discouraged about ever overcoming the problem. For them, speaking to strangers or answering a telephone remain nightmares. However, the recently developed techniques succeed in most every case.

One of the new therapies uses a recording machine. Stutterers hear their own speech fed back to them through earphones at a delay of milliseconds. By controlling their rate of speech, they can gradually eliminate the echo effect—and the stutter. Treatment duration varies from two weeks to a year or more, with children progressing the most rapidly.

Another highly successful new method of treating stuttering aims at relaxing the vocal cords and keeping them vibrating. The stutterer exhales gently before beginning to speak and maintains the flow of air directly into the first spoken word or phrase. This prevents the vocal cords from tensing up and "locking," and the stuttering decreases greatly within two days. With diligent practice and follow-up for about two years, an individual may be free of symptoms. A cure rate in excess of 90 percent has been reported.

If your child stutters, ask your doctor about these new techniques.

34

Getting older, sleeping less, but worrying about it more?

Stop worrying. We're all expected to sleep less as we get older. It's a natural part of the aging process.

Research shows a clear relationship between age and sleep habits. The newborn infant sleeps up to eighteen hours a day. As the child grows older, sleeping gradually drops until it reaches the adult level sometime between the ages of ten and twenty. A very slight decline continues, however, throughout the course of one's life.

Not only does the length of time spent sleeping change but also the patterns of sleep are realigned. Instead of going to bed at midnight, the older person may turn in at ten, and rather than rising at seven or eight in the morning, be wide awake by sunrise. An older person may wake up and go back to sleep several times during the course of the night and take quite a few short naps during the day.

Scientists say that as we age our brain activity becomes less synchronized. This diminishes the quality and efficiency of our sleep periods. The older person feels less rested because his or her Delta activity or "Deep Sleep" time has decreased.

It's important to understand these changing body rhythms. Sleeping less is perfectly normal, and sleeping pills should definitely not be taken to counteract it. In fact, studies show that older persons are especially prone to the sleep-distorting effects that the pills can cause.

Is there an easy cure for migraines?

Yes: Check your diet. The food you eat could be the cause of those excruciating, long-lasting attacks.

Until very recently doctors generally believed that migraines were triggered by stress and tension. Medication seemed to be the only source of relief. The drugs, however, proved ineffective in many cases and often produced discomforting side effects.

35

Now researchers report that food allergies may well be the reason for many migraines. In one study, the removal of certain foods from the patients' diets reduced or eliminated migraines in 70 percent of the sufferers within two weeks. The treatment was found to be effective even in chronic cases, including patients who had not been free of headaches for years.

Sufferers—there are 30 million in the United States alone— were usually found to be allergic to several food groups. Cereals, milk, rice, eggs, fish, chocolate, tomatoes, oranges, and cheese headed the list of most frequent offenders.

In light of these findings your doctor may want to put you on an "elimination diet." You'll drop the suspect foods one by one until the cause in your particular case is pinpointed. It may take some time, but the results will almost certainly justify the effort.

Is self-hypnosis hocus-pocus or panacea?

According to both the American Medical Association and the American Dental Association, hypnosis is a legitimate contribution to the treatment of dozens of problems related to high blood pressure, abnormal heart rhythms, seizures, dental anxiety, asthma, backaches, overweight, stuttering, drug dependence, warts, phobias, smoking, migraine headaches, insomnia, alcoholism, childbirth, arthritis, mental depression, nail biting, shyness, fatigue, hiccups, procrastination, itching, even bed-wetting.

Obviously hypnosis has come a long way since the fourteenth century, when the Roman Catholic Church used it to exorcise the devil. Indeed, a recent survey shows that a third of all medical and dental schools in the United States currently offer courses in hypnosis. And hypnotherapy is used in treating more than half the patients at the pain clinic at the Walter Reed Medical Center.

If you're highly motivated, there's an excellent chance that you can learn to hypnotize yourself. Between 70 and 90 percent of all individuals have the capacity to hypnotize themselves.

You'll need training by a hypnosis professional. One or two lessons should be sufficient. It's not difficult, but you must make sure you see a reputable, licensed hypnotist. Ask your physician to recommend one, or send a stamped, self-addressed envelope to either one of the following organizations:

The Society for Clinical and Experimental Hypnosis,
129-A Kings Park Drive,
Liverpool, N.Y. 13088.

The American Society of Clinical Hypnosis,
Suite 218, 2400 East Devon Avenue,
Des Plaines, Ill. 60018.

The hypnotist will teach you how to make yourself relax and eliminate all unnecessary messages that are flooding your mind. You will learn, instead, how to concentrate on one clear thought. The idea, generally speaking, is to visualize—in slow, successive stages—how well you can feel without a particular problem, and all the things you can do as a result. In a sense, it's akin to positive thinking.

Contrary to popular myth, hypnosis does not put you in a sleeplike trance. Dr. Herbert Speigel, a Columbia University professor and an expert in the field, calls hypnosis "the opposite of sleep." Brain scans show that while under hypnosis, the mind is attentive and alert, even though the body is totally relaxed. You remain in control at all times.

What do bug bites, sunburns, and poison ivy have in common?

Milk, ice, and salt. The itching they cause is treatable by a folk remedy that doctors still recommend.

Along with dry skin and allergic reactions to some soaps, bites, burns, and poison ivy can drive you up the wall with itching. If you scratch, you'll only make matters worse. Scratching will further aggravate the nerve endings in the skin, causing you to itch even more. Continual rubbing or scratching can result in hardening or leatheriness of the skin, or can abrade the skin's protective top layer.

To take the itch away:

Fill a quart bottle half with ice and half with milk. Add two tablespoons of salt. Wet a cloth with the mixture and apply it to the affected area for twenty minutes three or four times a day.

The milk-ice-salt solution should provide you with substantial relief. For added comfort, dermatologists suggest that you:

- ☐ Get rest and relaxation. Fatigue and stress increase itching.
- ☐ Avoid wearing rough fabrics.
- ☐ Don't use harsh or highly fragrant deodorant soaps.
- ☐ Don't drink any beverages with caffeine or alcohol.
- ☐ Relieve dry skin by soaking in a tub and trapping the moisture with a skin emulsion. Use only a super-fatted soap for washing.

Are you ever too old to learn?

No. In fact, older folks have certain advantages young 'uns don't. And studies show that, contrary to popular belief, learning capabilities do not disappear with age. The secret is to keep the brain active.

Many persons think that aging somehow causes the brain to slow down and the memory to fail, making it harder to learn and acquire new skills. But scientists who study aging have found that the human brain remains capable of learning until very late in life—even into the eighties and nineties. The memory of an eighty-year-old can be as sharp as that of a twenty-year-old. Studies indicate that the elderly have a good facility for remembering but that they require more time to recall facts and incidents.

The studies also indicate that fading memory can, and does, occur if the brain lacks intellectual stimulation. Like the body, the brain requires exercise to keep fit. That's why it's important to keep the mind active by taking up a new hobby, attending adult education classes, or doing something such as taking piano lessons. Piano teachers report that an oldster can learn in six months what a child might take a year to learn. Adults may not have the quick fingers, but they grasp musical concepts much more quickly. Adults can also learn new languages fast, because they have greater patience and motivation, and their attention spans are longer than a child's.

If you're a senior citizen, your memory and your mind don't want to retire from life any more than you do.

Can a stiff upper lip conquer a leg cramp?

Sure. Pinch your lip. You may get rapid relief from the painful spasm.

Muscle cramps, particularly in the legs and feet, are a source of serious and recurring discomfort for many people. Researchers say a quick pinch of the upper lip—a technique known as acupinch, which is related to acupuncture and acupressure—has proved to be up to 90 percent effective.

The method, discovered by Milton F. Allen, a chronic sufferer of muscle spasms and now Director of the Acupinch Outreach Center in Atlanta, is simplicity itself. At the first sign of any muscle cramping, immediately compress the area above the upper lip and under the nose between your thumb and forefinger. Maintain a constant pressure for twenty to thirty seconds, longer if necessary. The pain should subside and the muscles relax within moments of the pinch.

Although doctors are at a loss to explain the reasons for acupinch's success, they agree that it works. Their opinion is substantiated by the experience of many athletes and team trainers.

If the cramps persist and recur frequently, see your doctor.

Can anger help fight cancer?

There is some interesting evidence that it does just that. In a recent study of patients with breast cancer, doctors found that those women who were visibly angry about having cancer—they openly resented the disease—seemed to survive longer than patients who tried to cope with their cancer by showing a brave face to the world. The doctors hypothesized that by releasing their anger, the angry cancer victims may have also provoked changes in their body chemistry that helped fight the disease.

The feeling of anger, as everyone has surely noticed, produces a great deal of energy. Irate persons may slam doors, scream obscenities, even hit each other. But when individuals repress their anger, hold it in, those feelings may find some other

39

form of expression. Often, according to psychologists, repressed feelings are associated with elevations in blood pressure, or headaches, or ulcers.

In a study by the University of Michigan, researchers confirmed that persons who constantly repressed angry feelings tended to have higher blood pressure. However, those who expressed their anger and openly discussed their feelings seemed to avoid high blood pressure—even when they lived in areas with such stress-inducing factors as high crime and unemployment.

The Michigan study pointed out that when we get angry, our bodies get ready for action: Adrenaline is released; blood sugar increases for more energy; blood pressure goes up; the heart beats faster; the senses sharpen. All that is normal and fine, provided there is an outlet for the body's emergency preparations. But when all this preparation results in no real release, physical symptoms may appear. Tension, the most common cause of headaches, is often caused by repressed anger. And when the circulatory system is maintained in a state of, as it were, "red-alert," persistent elevation of blood pressure may occur.

Doctors have long counseled ulcer patients to show their anger. That's because inhibited anger has been identified as a common factor associated with gastrointestinal disorders, in particular ulcers and colitis.

Let the world around you know when you are angry, no matter what the cause. But don't go out of control: Open hostility, verbal abuse, or violence will not do anyone any good. When you express your anger, make it constructive. Discuss why you are angry. It is the best way to eradicate the cause of your fury.

Why worry if you're over forty and don't wear glasses?

Because even if you've never had an eye problem in your life and think a trip to the eye doctor would be a waste of money, you might be one of the 800,000 Americans who suffer from undetected glaucoma. This disease is responsible for 12 percent of all cases of blindness.

Glaucoma, which can be inherited, results from abnormally

high pressure inside the eye. The disease has an insidious characteristic: There often are no symptoms in its early stages, and many sufferers do not display the aching eyes, dull headaches, blurred vision, or appearance of halos around lights that are indicators of the disease. Decreased peripheral vision—a common symptom—usually means that the condition has already progressed to a serious degree.

A device called a tonometer is used to test for the illness. It's placed against the cornea and registers the amount of pressure built up inside the eyeball. It's not an infallible method, so the ophthalmologist may conduct further examinations to check the retina and the section of the eye chamber where the iris and cornea are joined. The tests are routine and fast.

Glaucoma is treatable through medication in 90 percent of all cases if it's discovered at an early stage. If you are over forty years old—when glaucoma normally strikes—a yearly eye exam should be a must.

What can stop me from reading my morning newspaper in the morning?

An allergy. If you're one of the 70 million Americans who has some type of allergy, you might find that the reason for it is inside your home—maybe inside your daily paper. Ten years of investigation by a team of scientists indicates that items such as carpeting, wallpaper, household cleaners, and newspaper ink might be the cause of your allergy.

If you're feeling uncomfortable in your own house, see your allergist. He'll scratch your skin with a battery of possible household allergens. After twenty minutes, he'll be able to tell if you've had an allergic reaction. Many allergists now arrange for home visits to check for possible allergens that could have been overlooked.

Dust is one of the major causes of allergy, and carpets love to hold onto dust. Even after they're freshly vacuumed, they still contain an incredible amount. Carpets generate their own house dust when normal wear causes the fabric to break up and pollute the air with microscopic particles.

If you discover that you're allergic to your carpet, get rid of it

41

if possible. Throw rugs, on the other hand, can be washed frequently enough so that they don't provide a cozy home for house dust.

Wallpaper can also contribute to allergies. It may flake, causing irritating cellulose particles to permeate the air. In addition, many wallpaper pastes contain unlabeled antiinsect and antifungal chemicals.

Toxic vapors from cleaning agents such as laundry bleach, scouring powders, window cleaners, room deodorants, and furniture polish are also common allergy provokers. Make sure to use rubber gloves when you're cleaning, to keep the windows open, and to shower when you're done.

Many people find the ink in newspaper print especially troublesome. Experts suggest placing the newspaper in the sun for a few minutes to dry the ink, or reading it later in the day. Reading the news first thing in the morning can make you sick in more ways than one.

Can cheese cut cavities?

Yes, if it's Cheddar cheese, which has a decay-slowing (cariostatic) effect on human teeth.

Until recently, most of us knew four ways of fighting tooth decay—using a toothbrush, flossing, avoiding sugar, and drinking fluoridated water. Even so, it's frequently been a losing battle, especially with children, 90 percent of whom develop cavities by the age of seventeen.

The cheese connection was made by scientists at the National Institute of Dental Research. They found that Cheddar cheese counteracts the negative effects of cavity-causing foods. But in order for the cheese to do its job, it needs to be eaten immediately following the intake of such foods. Apparently—the scientists haven't pinpointed the reason yet—the cheese either has a negative effect directly on the acid that causes the decay or on the bacteria that produce the acid. One of the main bacteria that is responsible for decay is called *Streptococcus mutans* or *S. mutans*. The bacteria do their damage by creating acid that dissolves away the tooth.

The scientists at the institute came up with another startling discovery. Contrary to what's been thought all along, foods with large amounts of sugar may not be our worst enemies when it comes to tooth decay. In other words, the amount of sugar in a particular snack is not the critical factor. According to their findings, potato chips can be more cavity-promoting than caramels; cream-filled cookies do more harm than a plain chocolate bar, and some of the worst offenders are certain fortified low-sugar breakfast cereals. In addition, the frequency of eating sugars or starches, not the kind of sugar, is most responsible for the rate of cavities.

What could sugar possibly cure except a sweet tooth?

Hiccups. Reach for the sugar bowl if you want a sweet and quick solution.

Hiccups usually are a minor, short-lived annoyance, but a persistent case can cause the sufferer a great deal of distress.

Recent studies show that swallowing a teaspoonful of ordinary granulated white sugar (dry—not dissolved in water) can often stop an attack of hiccups in a matter of minutes. The sugar treatment has been found effective in up to 95 percent of the cases in which it was tried, including test subjects who had been hiccupping for as long as six weeks.

Researchers haven't been able to figure out why the remedy is effective, but they think that the sugar granules may irritate the throat in such a way that the nerve impulses that cause the hiccups are interrupted.

Regardless of the reason, the treatment works. If the hiccups reappear—as sometimes happens—just repeat the dose.

Should anyone ever have a routine X-ray?

"Routine" means without a specific clinical reason. And the answer is no, according to the Food and Drug Administration, not even "routine" chest or dental X-rays. In fact, the FDA discourages any routine X-ray without clinical evidence of its necessity, because every X-ray you have adds to your total radiation exposure.

The FDA recommends the following precautions:

- ☐ Don't decide on your own that you need an X-ray.
- ☐ Don't insist on an X-ray.
- ☐ If your doctor or dentist orders an X-ray, ask if it's really needed for diagnosis or treatment, but—
- ☐ Don't refuse an X-ray if your doctor explains why it's needed.
- ☐ Tell your doctor or dentist about any similar X-ray you've had; perhaps, if it can be located and reviewed, it may obviate the need for a repeat.
- ☐ Ask for gonad shields to protect reproductive organs if you're still of reproductive age.
- ☐ Tell your doctor if you are, or think you might be, pregnant. If the X-ray is not an emergency, reschedule it after the birth of your baby.

Record all X-rays by writing down the date, the type of X-ray examination, and the name of the doctors who ordered them. This will help you keep track of radiation exposure, as well as reduce the expense of repeat X-rays.

The FDA has a free, wallet-sized X-ray record card available for use when visiting a doctor or a dentist for the first time. Enter any new X-ray on it as soon as it has been administered. You can get the card by writing to:

X-Rays,
Food and Drug Administration,
HFX-28,
Rockville, Md. 20857.

X-rays can save lives. They're an important diagnostic tool in preventing permanent injury and needless death, but unnecessary X-rays may present health hazards that can and should be avoided.

Anything new a diabetic should know about?

Yes. For one, there are now "do-it-yourself" testing kits that allow a diabetic to monitor blood-sugar levels at home—or anywhere, for that matter.

These tests are performed by placing a drop of blood on a specially prepared strip or tab that is then "read" by a small meter usually no larger than a portable radio. The home monitoring system has a high level of accuracy and reduces the need for frequent visits to the doctor's office, diabetic clinic, or out-patient department of a hospital.

Patients utilizing a testing kit—there are several such systems on the market—are taught by their doctors how to recognize the need to change their insulin dosage or adjust their diet or physical activities if test results vary. It's best to discuss with your doctor which one to buy to determine if it suits your particular needs. The equipment is expensive and may cost between $340 and $600. (The equipment cannot be leased, but some medical insurance companies are covering the cost.)

Research has demonstrated that maintenance of normal blood-sugar levels is particularly important to expectant mothers who are diabetic. This may also be true in the prevention of eye, kidney, and nerve damage, complications often associated with diabetes.

Home monitoring of blood-sugar levels is particularly recommended for insulin-dependent diabetics whose condition was diagnosed in childhood; adult diabetics who require insulin; diabetics who are diet-controlled; and pregnant diabetics. Blood-sugar levels are especially important to the last group because control of blood sugar lessens their risk of delivering infants with birth defects.

Scientists continue to research the possibilities of transplants and an insulin pump that will deliver a continuous supply of insulin to the body.

Keep in touch with the American Diabetes Association for up-to-the-minute news on treating diabetes. If there is no local chapter in your area, write to its national headquarters at 2 Park Avenue, New York, N.Y. 10016.

Is there hope for the hernia sufferer?

New surgical techniques cut the postoperative period from a few weeks to but a few days. That's a boon if a patient ordinarily can't find time for the operation. And it's less expensive.

The techniques, which are available at most major medical centers, use a special suturing method to overlap the tough tissues surrounding the groin muscle. This results in a much stronger repair than the standard procedure, in which tissues are sewn together edge to edge.

Hernias often recur after surgery, but physicians using the new procedures say they cut the recurrence rate to a very low 1 percent.

The operation is performed under a local anesthetic. The patient is completely conscious and able to cooperate with the surgeon by coughing and straining so the strength of the repair can be tested even before the wound is closed. By using a local rather than a general anesthetic, the chance of complications is reduced and the cost of the operation is held down.

Many patients leave the hospital immediately after the operation, others require a two- or three-day postoperative stay. Normal activities can generally be resumed immediately after discharge, but the patient is cautioned to refrain from vigorous sports—tennis, jogging, skiing—until about a month afterward.

Half a million persons undergo hernia operations in the United States each year. Now surgeons can have many of them quickly back on their feet.

What's the long and short of back pain?

It's quite possible that either one of your legs is too long, or the other is too short. Seriously, unequal limb length is quite common and it is one cause of backache that is easily corrected but often overlooked.

The difference between the length of the legs of most persons is only about an eighth of an inch, but it can be as much as half an inch. The greater the difference, the more your body must compensate by making adjustments in various joints. Although these adjustments may be very slight, they can throw your posture off and put a good deal of stress on the side with the longer leg. In addition to lower back pain, possible effects include foot difficulties, aches in the joints, and headaches. If uncorrected, unequal limb length can even lead to arthritis.

If you have such symptoms, you can try a few simple tests to see if one of your legs is significantly longer than the other. Observe yourself as you walk toward a full-length mirror. Do you have a shoulder that seems to sag and a hip on the same side that's slightly raised? Is one pants leg a fraction longer than the other? Look at your shoes. Do the heels show uneven wear? Or sit on a straight-backed chair with your feet on the floor and your heels, knees, and thighs together. Place a carpenter's level across your knees. The bubble is supposed to be right in the center; if it isn't, that's a sign that you're off-stride.

Children, joggers, dancers, salespersons, and others who are on their feet a lot are especially susceptible to recurring pain from legs of unequal length. The easiest way to test a child is to have the youngster sit on the floor, back flat against a wall and legs extended. A parent can then tell whether the knees, ankles, and heels of both legs are aligned.

The customary remedy for this condition is to have a professionally fitted orthotic device placed in the shoe of the short leg. Don't add only an insert in the heel of the shoe because this puts a strain on the ball of the foot. The proper corrective device will give one leg a little boost and your entire body a lift.

Is all depression in the mind?

No. In many cases, depression is a problem with the body. Loss of appetite, decrease in energy, disinterest in sex, insomnia, oversleeping, and decreased ability to concentrate—all may be indications that a person is depressed. But why is another story altogether. The problem may not be psychological. It could, instead, be a result of biochemical changes in the body. And now there are two new tests that can help determine the cause of the illness.

The DS (dexamethasone suppression) test measures the level of the hormone cortisol, which is known to be excessively high in some persons who suffer from depression. The DS test helps doctors to design a specific treatment that can correct the physiological root of the illness, and return the patient to normalcy by controlling the excess flow of cortisol.

The TRH (thyrotrophin releasing hormone) test measures the level of hormone produced by the thyroid gland. The thyroid is a gland located in the neck that is regulated by the pituitary gland in the brain. The pituitary gland is, in turn, regulated by the hypothalamus. The hypothalamus, which is also located in the brain, releases TRH. Some persons who suffer from severe depression have low thyroid levels. In one study at Fair Oaks Hospital in New Jersey, the TRH test accurately identified cases of major depression 92 percent of the time.

If the TRH test response is low, drug therapy is usually administered until the TRH test response returns to normal and the depression lifts.

When a doctor knows the cause of biochemically induced depression, it can help him or her to design an early, specific, and successful treatment. If the depression has persisted for a long time, it may have led to secondary psychological problems—insecurity, maladjustments, feelings of inadequacy at both work and home—that require psychotherapy.

Depression does not have to be an ongoing condition. And don't assume it's all in your head. There's a good chance there may be a biochemical imbalance in your body that can be treated.

What's the big deal about shoveling snow?

It's strenuous exercise, and most individuals don't know how to do it properly. It's no mere coincidence that news stories about increased numbers of heart attacks often follow severe winter storms. For people who are not fit enough or accustomed to such activity, shoveling snow can be dangerous, even fatal.

Physicians report that exercising the arms while standing still—the movement required for shoveling snow—places a greater demand on the muscles of the heart than exercise performed while lying down. Furthermore, exercise in an upright position may cause "pooling" of blood in the feet and legs, which results in a slower return of blood to the heart. This makes the heart pump faster, adding to the strain already present. Moreover, breathing the cold air outside may constrict blood vessels and contribute to the load on the heart.

So what should you do when the front steps and drive are covered with snow? A few precautions can help minimize the risks:

☐ Before and after shoveling, avoid heavy meals, alcohol, and caffeinated beverages.
☐ Before going outside, do a few warm-up exercises.
☐ Don't overdress, but do cover your nose and mouth with a scarf.
☐ Always use a short-handled shovel with a small scoop.
☐ Lift small loads only.
☐ Alternate fifteen-minute periods of shoveling with fifteen minutes of rest—indoors. Pacing yourself is especially important for anyone over forty.

Experts advise that elderly persons or those with a history of hypertension or heart disease should avoid shoveling entirely.

Will a color-blind person ever appreciate a rainbow?

Yes. Color blindness can't be cured, but now, thanks to a simple new device, the majority of color-blind individuals may be able to widen their career horizons as well as enjoy more colorful lives.

One out of every twelve males (but only one in every 250 females) is color-blind. But the term "color-blind" is misleading, because most sufferers are not really blind to colors, but rather have deficiencies in their perceptions of certain hues. The commonest form of color blindness is the "green-weak" defect, in which the individual perceives the green range of the spectrum only dimly. Others have "red-weak" defects. For a small group of persons, red, orange, green, and yellow all appear the same.

The new device is a hard, red-tinted contact lens called the X-Chrom lens. It is worn over either eye, but not both, and can bring improvement to all but the completely color-blind, those who see the world as almost totally gray. The lens can be made with a corrective prescription if necessary. Because of its ruby-red color, it is noticeable when worn by blue-eyed people, but almost invisible on those with dark eyes.

Recent tests have found the new lens effective in increasing the range of visible colors. This is possible because when light waves reach the retina a physical-chemical reaction occurs. The X-Chrom lens alters the wavelength, changing the reaction in such a way that a wearer can perceive a color not previously distinguishable. After being fitted with it, many persons who formerly could not distinguish varying shades of the same hue were, depending on their defect, able to identify them. For example, some could distinguish red and yellow traffic lights, and many found the lens a useful device to aid in the performance of tasks requiring the ability to discriminate different colors.

It's surprising how many jobs rely on the ability to identify different colors. Not just obvious occupations, such as artist or textile designer, but many others—computer technician, photographer, laboratory analyst, printer, beautician, electronic specialist. And the ability of color-blind persons to discriminate colors well enough to perform the tasks required by these jobs may well be improved by the red-tinted lens.

The lens does not cure color blindness. And because it is a filter and cuts down light, it may not be effective at night, and may cause vision problems when driving after sundown. That's a question a prospective user should discuss with the eye doctor. But the lens can be a real help to many of the 10 million Americans who are color-blind. And who knows? It may open your eyes to some new opportunities.

Is it flu or food poisoning?

Holiday mealtime may provide pleasant moments, but it can provide some very unpleasant ones as well. Stomach and intestinal upsets attributed to flu or virus are often caused by improper handling of festive foods.

The U.S. Department of Agriculture recommends that extra

caution be taken at holiday time, when meals are served in larger quantities from kitchens much busier than usual.

When planning your guest list, try to decide how many people you can serve, safely. How much space you have to keep food stored properly is as important as table space and serving areas. Perishable foods should never be kept at room temperature for more than two hours. When meat, poultry, and dairy products remain at room temperature too long, food bacteria can multiply in dangerous numbers.

Certain traditional holiday foods require special attention. Bacteria thrive in foods such as turkey stuffing, cream pies, and eggnog.

Food experts say the safest way to cook a turkey is to roast the stuffing and the bird separately, because bacteria thrive on the ingredients of a stuffing and the moist, warm interior of the turkey.

For cooks who insist that their turkey must be stuffed before it's roasted, here are a few precautions:

☐ Prepare stuffing in advance, refrigerate, then stuff the turkey just before it goes into the oven.

☐ Thaw frozen turkey in the refrigerator. (A frozen bird may be thawed outside by placing the turkey in a watertight package and submerging it in cold water. Or, wrap the turkey in two closed paper bags and thaw overnight.)

☐ For holiday buffets, keep servings small and replenish when necessary directly from stove or refrigerator.

☐ When hot dishes are prepared well in advance, refrigerate while still hot, then reheat thoroughly before serving. This is particularly true for sauces and gravy.

☐ If you're preparing meringues, soft custard, or pudding for dessert, be sure the eggs are fresh, clean, and unbroken. Cracked eggs are another source of food bacteria.

☐ Promptly refrigerate all foods that you plan to serve another day.

If you're wondering what to do for a Fourth of July or Labor Day picnic, the most important point to remember is to store all cold cuts, salads, and sandwiches made with mayonnaise in a cooler with ice or in a reusable cold pack. That holds true also for any foods made with milk or eggs.

Guess what doctors now say about swimming after eating?

Chances are you've always been told, "Don't swim after eating. Wait an hour, or you'll get a cramp." The advice is one of the most widely believed bits of folk wisdom around. Except that it's not wise. It's not even true. The fact is, it is far better to swim on a partly full stomach than on an empty one.

When you feel hungry, it means that your body needs refueling, muscles included. The myth was probably based on the observation that digestion draws a large amount of blood to the stomach, decreasing the supply to the muscles. It does take time for the body to completely convert food into glucose, the form in which muscles can use it. But some of the glucose becomes available right away. By the time you've finished your picnic and are ready to swim, your energy-starved muscles will already be sufficiently fortified to perform normally.

The real enemies of athletes, as every long-distance swimmer and runner knows, are fatigue and cold. These two conditions can cause severe cramps because of spasms in the muscles and the arteries. But far from avoiding food, distance swimmers take nutrition while in the water to help ward off a cramp.

This does not mean it's advisable to jump right in after a heavy banquet, especially if the repast included wine or other alcoholic drinks. Such a meal makes most people drowsy, slows reflexes, and dims general alertness. But if you're hungry, eat a moderate meal first, then take the plunge. That way fatigue won't cramp your style.

What's fishy about lowering your blood pressure by staring into an aquarium?

Nothing at all. It may sound fishy but, according to a University of Pennsylvania study, you can actually reduce your blood pressure by staring into one. In fact, fish watching can provide relaxation benefits equal to biofeedback and meditation.

In the study, subjects read aloud for two minutes from academic textbooks (a standard method of inducing stress) and alternated between a twenty-minute period of looking at a wall and a two-to-twenty-minute period of looking at a fish tank. The tanks contained either fish and plants or just plants.

As expected, blood pressure rose during the textbook reading. It fell during wall watching, and surprisingly dropped even further when the subjects looked into a fish tank only. But by far the most significant drop in blood-pressure level occurred when the subjects stared into a fish-filled tank.

For the few subjects who suffered from high blood pressure before the experiment, fish watching was even more effective.

Simply stated: When you look at a fish you relax.

When's a good time to be pushy?

You've got the chance for a promotion and are about to see the boss. Your palms become moist, your tongue seems mired in sand—and are those your knees giving way? What you've got is what actors call stage fright. But don't be flustered. There is a way to regain self-control—acupressure.

Acupressure is based on the Chinese therapeutic technique acupuncture. Instead of pins inserted in the body, acupressure entails stimulation of strategic body sites. To relieve stage fright, simply place the tip of your thumb or index (first) finger a hand's breadth below your collarbone on the right side of your chest. Push in or press down strongly, vibrating slowly in doing so; then rotate your finger rapidly, always clockwise.

Acupressure can be used to relieve not only stage fright but also a variety of problems ranging from tired eyes and hiccups to menstrual cramps.

The pressure point for an aching eye is the inside corner of the *other* eye.

For tired legs, there's the so-called coolie's point—halfway between the knee and the ankle on the outer side of the leg and in back of the thin, long fibula bone that's also on the outer side of the leg.

For an upset stomach caused by overeating, massage points are located on the outer side of each leg in a hollow in front of the fibula; in massaging, cross your hands so that the left hand is rotating on the right leg and the right hand on the left leg.

To get over an extended bout of hiccups, ask someone to massage a point at the lower tip of one of the shoulder blades and two finger widths from the midline of the seventh vertebra of the spinal cord.

To relieve menstrual cramps, rub the area an inch to the right of the spine, about midback. The pain should subside within thirty seconds and disappear completely after three or four minutes—and not return for three to six hours.

If these simple home remedies don't work and the symptoms persist, then, of course, it's best to seek professional help.

Does the first visit to a dentist have to be traumatic?

It doesn't, not if you choose a dentist who is an expert in treating youngsters—and knows how to make the visit as pleasant as possible. A child's lifelong response to dentistry may be affected by what happens. Some 10 million youngsters grow up so afraid of the dentist that they never seek any treatment at all as adults.

Periodic checkups for a child should start soon after the first molars are in, which usually occurs between the ages of about two and three years old. Select a dentist who has had extra years of training in the new specialty, the care of children. They're called pedodontists and they know how to get youngsters to relax. Their offices are decorated with bright posters and filled with toys and picture books. They and their assistants often wear street clothes rather than uniforms. Their voices and manner are calm and cheerful.

The basic approach of the pediatric dentist is to "tell, show, and then do." This means they tell the child what is about to happen so that the youngster will be less worried. Many use slides, pictures, and films to explain the treatment. Often they enlist the help of an older sibling as a model. Studies show that this can be especially effective in reassuring a youngster on a first visit.

It's best not to offer a treat for good behavior—the child is likely to suspect that something unpleasant is about to happen. Also, during the examination, let the dentist take over. Sit quietly in the waiting room, unless your presence is requested. An adult's anxieties are easily communicated to a youngster. If you bring two children to the dentist's office for treatment, let the younger child go first. Dentists report that both children tend to be more comfortable that way.

Can you talk a child to sleep?

Yes. There's a simple technique called "toe-to-head relaxation" that children, overactive ones included, seem to enjoy. And once they get the hang of it, they can do it on their own.

Bedtime problems are the number one complaint that parents voice to pediatricians. Child psychologists believe the reason is that children, particularly those between two and five years old, are so strongly attached to their mothers that they're reluctant to be separated from them, even to sleep alone. The relaxation technique is reassuring because the mother stays and comforts the youngster until sleep takes over.

First, try to get the child to play quietly in bed for about fifteen minutes. Then tell the youngster to lie down with arms at the side. Explain that you're going to make the child's body feel droopy and sleepy.

Beginning with the toes and working up to the head, help your child to relax each part of the body. Repeat the following phrase in a soothing monotone:

Your toes are droopy

Your toes are droopy

Your toes are droopy

Your toes are droopy

Your toes are droopy

Your toes are droopy

Touch the toes to assure the child that they feel heavy. Now say "Your feet are droopy" six times, in the same soothing monotone. After two or three body parts, repeat the idea that the parts that you've made droopy are still at rest.

Work up the body from the toes, to the feet, to the legs, back, tummy, chest, fingers, hands, arms, shoulders, neck, chin, lips, eyes, and forehead.

By the time you reach the eyes, they should be closed. If not, gently tell your child to shut them. You'll be surprised how much an overactive youngster welcomes sleep.

After you use the toe-to-head method regularly, your child will memorize the routine and eventually be able to fall off to sleep without help.

P.S. The technique also works for adults.

Does your "marine," by chance, drink milk?

If your child is a "marine"—a bed wetter—and does indeed drink milk or eat certain foods, you may find that the two may be linked. And avoiding the milk or foods may scuttle the bed-wetting.

Pediatricians used to believe that children over three years old who were persistent bed wetters had either a physical defect, an infection, or emotional problems. Examinations rarely disclosed physical abnormality or infection, so parents were advised to ease up on the troubled youngster and to be encouraging and supportive. Physicians could suggest little more. It was a psychiatric puzzle with few, if any, solutions.

Now, however, according to a long-term study of 500 youngsters who suffer this uncomfortable and embarrassing problem, many cases may stem from an allergic reaction to common foods. Pinpointing the offending food and eliminating it from the child's diet brought relief from bed-wetting in about four out of five instances.

The study points out how in an allergic youngster the bladder swells, just as the lining of the nose and the sinuses swell in a hayfever victim. The walls of an affected bladder are less elastic than normal, so the organ is able to hold less. The bladder shutoff valve, the sphincter, also becomes inflamed and incapable of performing its function adequately.

You may need your child's cooperation to identify the allergy-causing substances. A great many foods are eliminated from the daily diet for about a week, and antiallergy medication is often given during this time. The child then gradually adds new foods one by one, and keeps a journal of bed-wetting occurrences, until the food that triggers the bed-wetting is discovered.

In 60 percent of the cases of allergic bed wetters who participated in the study, cow's milk—whole or skim—was found to be the culprit. Other foods implicated were corn, wheat, eggs, chocolate, and citrus fruits.

Bed-wetting is a problem that may erode a youngster's self-confidence and often interferes with social life by inhibiting the child from taking part in activities such as camping and sleepovers. If your child is one of the many who suffer from bed-wetting, discuss the question of a possible allergy with your pediatrician. If an allergy does not prove to be the cause, you may be reassured to know that in 75 percent of cases, bed-wetting disappears by itself by the time the child is three years old, and in 90 percent, by the age of five.

The relationship between bed-wetting and allergies is controversial. Some pediatricians dismiss it as insignificant, without sufficient substantiating research. But common sense would dictate that because it is fairly simple to check out, it is certainly worth a try.

Why sit backwards in a car?

For safety's sake—not, of course, for the driver, but for an infant. According to the National Safety Council, babies are safer when riding backwards in the front seat in a special car carrier. That way, a parent can keep an eye on the child and comfort the tike when need be. And using the proper safety seat also keeps baby from fretting and getting car sick.

Safety seats come in a variety of models. They are relatively inexpensive, but before you buy one, make sure it fits properly in your car. Not all designs fit all car models.

The kind of seat you choose will probably depend upon the age and weight of your child. For example, if your child weighs under twenty pounds, one kind of safety seat cradles him or her in a semierect position and secures him or her with a harness. Another type, for a child over twenty pounds, is padded with a slightly flexible safety shield.

The American Academy of Pediatrics offers a free guide to safety equipment, "Family Shopping Guide to Infant/Child Restraints." For a copy, write:

Child Safety,
American Academy of Pediatrics,
P.O. Box 1034,
Evanston, Ill. 60204.

One warning the guide emphasizes is never to hold an infant on your lap. If an accident occurs, a child—who weighs much less than you do—is more likely to be tossed around and hurt. Up to 80 percent of injuries to infants can be avoided, the experts say, if a safety seat is used. At last count, thirteen states mandated the use of such seats in carrying small children—Florida, Kansas, Kentucky, Massachusetts, Michigan, Minnesota, New York, North Carolina, Rhode Island, Tennessee, Virginia, West Virginia, and Wisconsin.

The way to keep older children safe is with a safety belt in the back seat.

Do honey and babies mix?

Absolutely not. And if you're tempted to sweeten your infant's food with honey to make it more palatable, don't. It could be dangerous. Research shows conclusively that honey fed to an infant either directly, diluted in formula, or spread on a pacifier can pose a serious threat to the baby's health.

Honey can cause infant botulism. It's produced by a strain of the *C. botulinum* bacteria that contaminate improperly canned foods.

Honey contains a certain strain of spore that children under a year old are highly susceptible to. The temperature used to process honey is not high enough to kill these *botulinum* spores. And doctors hypothesize that infants don't have the immunological ability to nullify this particular strain.

In an investigation by the California State Department of Health, 300 different brands of honey were tested. Spores were discovered in a random 10 percent of them.

You should take your baby to the pediatrician if the infant becomes noticeably lethargic, cries weakly, has difficulty swal-

58

lowing or sucking, and has not had a bowel movement in several days. These are the symptoms of infant botulism. Although not all cases of the illness are honey-related, experts estimate that a third of all cases are honey-linked.

The Centers for Disease Control, the American Medical Association, and the American Academy of Pediatrics have all issued warnings about the hazards of honey for babies. The safety of honey as a food for older children and adults, however, is totally unquestioned.

What's a leading cause of burns in young children?

Bath water. Partly because few parents realize that water that feels warm enough for them can be too hot for a youngster.

The skin of young children is thinner and more sensitive than that of adults. What would be considered a second-degree burn in a grown-up would penetrate deeper and therefore be a more serious burn for a child.

In many homes, tap water is hot enough to inflict extensive damage to a child's vulnerable skin. Recent research based on hospital records in New York State showed that half of all tap-water burn victims were preschool children. Many of these youngsters had been in a bathtub or a sink of hot water. In other cases, the children were left alone in a tub and turned on the hot-water faucet themselves.

One solution is to set your water heater at no more than 120 degrees Fahrenheit. That's hot enough for any household use, including a dishwasher, though many manufacturers preset thermostats at unnecessarily high and potentially dangerous temperatures. Then, too, never place a toddler in a tub before first testing the water with your wrist. It should feel lukewarm. And don't leave the child there unattended.

Naturally, beware of leaving pots of hot liquids on the stove when children are around. Turn handles so they cannot reach them. Make sure that the child's high chair is set a distance from coffee or other steaming dishes. And don't hold baby on your lap when you're drinking or serving hot beverages or soups.

Minor burns, including sunburn, can be treated by gently bathing with cool water and covering loosely with a pad of gauze.

But take a child with a serious burn to the hospital *at once*. Serious burns are difficult and painful to treat, and children are especially susceptible to infection. The best advice, of course, is to prevent burns by keeping your child out of hot water.

Is a chubby baby cute or fat?

Both, but especially too fat. Your roly-poly infant may be so adorable that you can't help but beam at the little folds in those chubby thighs, but if the baby's thirty-five pounds by the age of one, or at least ten percent above average weight, the child is overweight. And unless the baby is put on a diet now, there's a good chance he or she will grow up with a weight problem—and have to diet throughout life.

There are many ways parents can safely control their baby's weight. To begin with, don't be in a rush to put your infant on solid foods. The American Academy of Pediatrics strongly recommends keeping baby on milk with supplemental vitamins, breast milk, or infant formula, for the first four to six months.

When your baby acts full, don't try to forcefeed what's left in the bottle. Overfeeding can make the child's stomach bigger and eventually the appetite will grow well beyond what is nutritionally necessary.

If your baby is overweight, restrict milk intake to no more than sixteen to twenty-four ounces a day. If the baby is still on formula, water it down. After the first year, switch to low-fat milk.

Once a child is on solid foods, don't overdo breads, red meat, or cheese. Instead, substitute low-calorie, high-protein fresh foods such as fish, poultry, and green vegetables. For dessert, offer fruit.

Don't rely exclusively on canned and processed foods. They're not always as nutritious as their fresh counterparts, and many are high in calories, salt, sugar, and questionable additives.

Experts also suggest that you don't reward or punish your baby with food, or give gifts of edibles. A Christmas stocking stuffed with candy canes is a no-no. Fill it with a ball or push-and-pull toys instead, because exercising is as important for toddlers as adults. Encourage your baby to move around, play ball, crawl on the floor, chase the cat. Don't leave the child in a restrictive playpen for too long a period of time.

Studies have confirmed that adults who were overweight as babies have more fat cells than adults who weighed normally when they were young. Once fat cells are formed, they can be shrunk by dieting—but never lost.

Should you hassle a teenager about beddy-bye time?

Yes, if his or her sleep pattern is unregimented. Growing boys and girls do need sleep in order to grow properly, but it's the regularity of the sleep pattern that's important, not the number of hours spent sleeping. The amount of sleep time varies from teenager to teenager. But whether a youngster sleeps six, seven, eight, or nine hours, it should be about the same number of hours every night.

The hormones that help the body mature show a marked increase during regular periods of sleep, particularly so during the teenage years. In fact, sleep researchers now believe that youngsters who fail to follow a consistent sleep schedule may run the risk of suffering abnormal growth patterns and delayed puberty.

It's also not a bad idea for adults to keep to as regular a sleep schedule as possible. Studies show that even grownups can be disturbed and disoriented when their normal sleep patterns are interrupted.

Do pacifiers harm or help?

Help. Most babies have a natural sucking urge. That's why doctors recommend that parents let their children suck their thumbs. Now research indicates that not only is thumb sucking good for children, but that pacifiers may be just as beneficial.

New pacifiers shaped like a human nipple help a baby to exercise the muscles in the tongue and cheeks, and to develop the swallowing reflex needed for chewing solid foods. They may also help to prevent orthodontic problems from occurring in the

61

future. Many times crooked teeth in adults are caused by an imbalance in the pressures of the muscles that guide teeth into position or hold them in position. Sucking pacifiers helps to strengthen jaw muscles, which helps teeth to erupt more evenly and straight.

For premature infants, pacifiers may be particularly important. In a new study, high-risk infants given a pacifier while being fed intravenously developed more muscular coordination and stronger sucking reflexes after only two weeks. As a result, they gained weight faster because they were able to begin oral feeding five to six days sooner than babies who had not been given a pacifier. They were also allowed to go home from the hospital about one week earlier than average.

Don't worry that pacifiers are habit forming. Most children either kick the pacifier habit or, unlike thumb sucking, lose it by the time they're two.

When's the worst time to use the Heimlich maneuver for a choking victim?

When the victim is five years old or younger and choking on a piece of food or a foreign object such as a tiny toy caught in the windpipe. The abdominal thrusts that are the key to the Heimlich maneuver can injure a child's internal organs, especially the liver.

Choking—the second major cause of accidental deaths in the home for children under five—is responsible for between 400 and 500 deaths every year. Most times, the youngsters choke on ordinary objects left around a home—earrings, buttons, tacks, erasers, and the like—or on foods such as nuts, popcorn, raw carrots, and celery stalks. Recently the U.S. Consumer Product Safety Commission mandated the recall of more than 20,000 teddy bears because "a substantial percentage" of the noses and eyes pulled off easily in testing.

Rule One: When your baby is able to crawl around the house, make a careful check beforehand to be sure that nothing's within reach.

Rule Two: Always feed the child in an upright position and never leave the youngster alone during the meal.

Rule Three: Don't let the child talk with a full mouth because even foods that are soft can cause aspiration if he or she suddenly laughs.

Rule Four: If choking does occur, do not try to do anything if the child can still speak or breathe. And don't ever hold the child upside down by the heels—that could worsen the situation. The child will probably cough up the obstruction.

Rule Five: Do not try to remove any obstruction by putting a finger in the youngster's mouth unless you can see the object. The windpipe of a year-old infant, for example, is not wider than a pinkie, and what doctors call a "blind finger sweep" can push the object even farther back.

Rule Six: Instead, if the choking victim is an infant, straddle the child over your forearm, head lower than the trunk, and with your other hand strike the back of the infant between the shoulder blades four times—firmly but, of course, taking into account a baby's size. If that doesn't dislodge the blockage, turn the infant over and in rapid succession administer four blows to the chest. However, the chest thrusts should not be attempted unless you have had prior training from a pediatrician.

Rule Seven: If the child is older, follow the same procedure but drape the youngster over your knees or let the child lie on the floor. Either way, the head should be kept lower than the body.

Rule Eight: If the procedures fail, rush the youngster to a hospital emergency room or to a doctor. But don't let the situation get that far: Keep the child out of harm's way by keeping out of arm's reach anything that can harm him or her.

What serious problem in children is frequently ignored?

Their hearing ability. Most parents take it for granted, unaware that, by the age of five, one out of ten children has a hearing problem that may affect the ability to speak as well as to learn. Hearing specialists report that more than half of all children experience occasional hearing loss before their third birthday.

A simple, painless test can help avoid speech and learning disabilities as a child gets older. By using a device known as a tympanometer, a hearing specialist can determine if the space behind the eardrum is blocked with fluid or mucus. Such blockage sometimes leads to "conductive hearing loss," a condition that causes sound to be perceived as though it's being filtered through water. The test can be performed on children as young as seven months old.

Because there's no health code requiring tests for deafness among infants and small children, it's up to parents to be on the lookout for symptoms that might indicate deafness. If there's a history of early hearing loss in the family, heredity is a possibility. A jaundiced baby may suffer hearing loss, as well as babies whose mothers contracted German measles during pregnancy. Premature babies and those underweight at full-term birth may also have their hearing affected.

The following is a series of questions, the answers to which may suggest a temporary or permanent hearing loss. Does your child:

☐ have frequent colds?
☐ breathe through the mouth?
☐ pull at an ear?
☐ turn up the TV set louder than playmates?
☐ seem prone to allergies?
☐ run a frequent mild fever?
☐ speak in an unusually soft voice?
☐ appear listless, inattentive, or unresponsive to loud noises?
☐ lag behind in speech and learning development?

If the answer is yes to any of the above and your doctor hasn't recommended a hearing test for the child, suggest an appointment with an audiologist.

Does the child with asthma have to sit on the sidelines?

Not any more. Doctors are now convinced that regular exercise combined with special breathing techniques may actually *reduce* the frequency and severity of asthma attacks. For two million American schoolchildren, the days of restraints on vigorous exercise are over.

In a recent two-year study, children with asthma participated with healthy classmates in a supervised daily program of general-fitness exercises that included three to five minutes of deep breathing. The well students gradually progressed to more strenuous exercising for longer periods of time. The asthma sufferers were encouraged to join in as much as they could. They ended up being absent from school far less frequently because of asthma attacks than a similar group of asthmatic children who had not exercised.

Information about supervised instruction in deep-breathing techniques is available from the American Lung Association. This program of exercises helps children to control wheezing and other breathing problems and often increases their self-confidence dramatically. Sometimes a family doctor will recommend that a child take medication in conjunction with the course.

Don't be surprised if your child is asking to play baseball before long. Of course, you'll want to notify the team coach beforehand of the child's asthmatic condition. Help your child to recognize his or her physical limitations and to react appropriately to any sign of trouble. You can also guide your youngster to a sport that will not aggravate the illness. For example, swimming may be a better choice than soccer played in a meadow of pollen-laden wildflowers.

What's a common reason for early school woes?

The child can't see. One out of every five preschoolers has a visual disorder of some kind. The youngster may not be aware of it and hence won't complain about it, so it behooves parents to get their children to an eye doctor early on because almost all learning during childhood involves vision.

Most optometrists and ophthalmologists recommend a complete eye examination for every child between the ages of three and four and again at five or six, when the child is learning to read. There are some pediatric ophthalmologists who believe every child should be routinely examined at one year old. If there is a suspicion of a visual problem or a family history of problems, you should definitely have your child examined before age three.

The key to responsible eye care is a complete examination by an eye doctor who specializes in testing children—a pediatric ophthalmologist. Many pediatricians have received little training in vision, and for even specialists such as ophthalmologists, optometrists, and neuro-ophthalmologists, diagnosing the visual problems of infants and toddlers is a difficult job. Because children too young to talk are unable to tell the doctor what they can or cannot see, and because there are few objective tests available, a successful examination rests heavily on the doctor's own experience in testing children under three.

Moreover, some childhood visual defects present no obvious symptoms—distorted vision in one or both eyes, for example, or farsightedness and nearsightedness. Only special tests will turn up such problems.

Not only are visual disorders often difficult to detect, but also they are sometimes misdiagnosed as a physical, mental, or psychological problem. For example, infants who are extremely nearsighted may never grab for toys or try to crawl or stand; a pediatrician might wrongly label such a child retarded. And how many bright, talented children have been forever turned off by school because their teachers have tagged them stupid, lazy, or troublemakers when their only failing is that they're having trouble seeing the blackboard?

A complete examination by an eye-care specialist can avoid such unnecessary anguish for children—and their parents.

Whoever heard of a child with high blood pressure?

High blood pressure, it turns out, isn't only a grown-up's problem. Nearly two million American youngsters suffer from hypertension. Ninety-five percent of them go untreated, and the problem can set in at a much earlier age than previously believed—as early as three years old.

Current research indicates that unless preventive measures are taken, children who have continued high blood-pressure readings will probably maintain them as they grow older. And one in seven adults—some 23 million Americans—suffer hypertensive conditions that markedly increase the possibility of strokes and heart attacks. In fact, hypertension by itself is responsible for more than 20,000 deaths each year.

Parents should be aware that blood-pressure readings are a necessary part of a child's continuing health-care program. A reading should be taken at least once a year beginning at the age of three. Continued monitoring of a child's pressure is particularly important if there's a family history of hypertension or if the youngster is overweight.

The pediatrician will probably take three readings about five minutes apart and average out the results. These multiple readings are necessary because a child's pressure tends to fluctuate a great deal. The averaging process also takes into account the stress that youngsters often feel when they visit a doctor's office.

Medication usually isn't prescribed for children with elevated blood pressures. Scientists just don't know enough about the long-term effects of antihypertensive drugs on children's growth and development patterns. Instead, treatment usually involves dietary management, including reduced salt intake, weight control, and, in the case of teenagers, more exercise.

What can a black eye hide?

Black eyes are almost an inevitable part of childhood. A miscalculated snowball or a scrap with a friend can bring your youngster home with a whopper. Most parents think it looks a lot worse than it is, so they just apply ice and forget about it. Don't. Prompt attention to a black eye can help prevent permanent damage.

Medical experts caution that black eyes can be the sign of a much more serious injury. A black eye should be treated with the same concern as if your child had come home with a broken leg.

Contact your pediatrician immediately. If the pediatrician is not available, then take your child to a hospital emergency room. A doctor should examine both eyes for any vision problems. If one is found, the most likely next step will be referral to an ophthalmologist. The eye specialist may prescribe eye drops, salve, or an eye patch; in extreme cases, surgery may be necessary.

By performing a quick office procedure, the doctor will know if the black eye indicates that a facial fracture is involved. He'll simply prick the child's upper lip with a pin. If the lip is numb, it could be the sign of a facial fracture. X-rays will most likely then be recommended, as well as referral to a plastic surgeon, who is best qualified to treat a facial fracture.

How do you fight back against scoliosis?

Young victims of scoliosis—a lateral curvature of the spine—may be saved from years of using braces because of a new electrical-stimulation procedure. In recent clinical trials the stimulators were 80 percent effective in stopping curvatures from getting worse, and, in some cases, reduced the curvatures. Progress has also been made in treating adult sufferers through new exercise programs and improved surgical techniques.

Scoliosis affects some one million American youngsters, the great majority of them girls between the ages of ten and fifteen. The ailment, if uncorrected, can lead to degenerative spinal arthritis and disc disease, causing increasingly severe back pain and disability as the child grows older. The affliction can also have psychological effects, causing a sense of rejection and isolation in its young sufferers.

Although a growing number of school districts have instituted screening programs to identify scoliosis in children, parents are still advised to check for its symptoms:

Examine your child's back while she is standing up straight. Is one shoulder higher than the other? Does one hip seem more prominent? Does she lean to one side? When her arms hang loosely at her sides, is the distance between arm and body greater on one side? Next, have the youngster bend forward, arms hanging down loosely and palms touching at knee level. Can you see a hump in the back of the rib area or near the waist? If the answer to any of these questions is affirmative, you should consult your family doctor.

The new stimulation procedures—though still experimental—have been widely tested on children in Canada and Europe, and tested on a limited basis in the United States. One technique involves implanting a small receiver into the patient's back. Wires are connected from it to specific back muscles. A radio transmitter sends signals that cause the muscles to contract, pulling the spine back into place along the convex part of the abnormal curve. The device is designed to be used while the child is sleeping.

A second method achieves similar results but without any implantation. A battery-operated stimulator sends electrical impulses through wires to discs resting on the child's back. It's also used when the youngster is asleep.

While these devices are becoming more readily available, bracing and supplementary exercises will remain the standard methods of arresting scoliosis in children. Surgery is required in only one out of one thousand cases. The brace—a girdle-like device made of leather or plastic—is worn until the child's bone structure is matured in the late teens. It allows her to engage in most normal activities.

If your child does have scoliosis, contact your local chapter of the Scoliosis Society. It sponsors clubs that provide valuable psychological support in helping the youngster adjust emotionally to the brace.

Adults who have scoliosis got it primarily because their illness was undetected, misdiagnosed, or wrongly treated in childhood. Many of them believe that delicate spinal surgery is the only treatment for their condition. However, orthopedists have developed a rigorous system of daily exercises designed to arrest the curvature by helping to maintain body weight and spinal flexibility. The earlier the treatment is begun, the better the chance of success.

If surgery is needed, new techniques are available that reduce pain in the majority of cases and improve a patient's appearance most of the time.

Will baby fat disappear on a pleasingly plump lass?

It often will if she diets properly. But one third of all children who are 20 percent or more overweight will be fat adults. Most of them will be women because boys are more active and thus fat girls are more numerous than fat boys.

If you have a twelve-year-old daughter who's overweight, it's important that she want to lose weight. If she does, studies have shown that special hospital-based weight-control clinics designed for adolescents are effective in helping to take pounds off permanently. Almost every major hospital has a program that's reasonably priced, or free.

Doctors and nutritionists at the clinic work closely to design a diet individually suited for the preteen's life style. For example, if your daughter and her friends stop off for a slice of pizza after school, that pizza will be included in her diet.

The weight-loss plan is based on a complete physical examination, body-fat measurement, early growth patterns, and height projection. Most children who attend clinics have daily meal plans calling for from 1,300 to 1,600 calories.

Psychologists are usually on staff to talk to the children about the social problems they may be experiencing. And the group atmosphere helps too, because peers are able to share their emotions and experiences and support each other.

Once your daughter loses the desired weight, she'll attend a monthly maintenance meeting.

But if she'd rather not go to a clinic, you can help her at home by controlling the foods that are brought into the house. Obvious temptations—cookies, cakes, candies, sodas, and ice cream—should be strictly eliminated from your shopping list. Medical experts also advise that you avoid diet foods. They can symbolize an admission to your daughter that she can't control her own eating habits.

Suggest that she take her own lunch to school. A sample low-calorie fare might be a tuna-in-water or a turkey sandwich on wholewheat pita bread, with pickles or lettuce. No condiments. A fruit for dessert.

Finally, be open and discuss her overweight problem, but be sure to point out all the positive aspects in her development, such as academics or hobbies.

Do tomboys menstruate?

They often start later than average and their cycles can be erratic. The same holds true for young ballerinas and female athletes. A recent medical survey showed that over 80 percent of female college athletes who began strenuous training before puberty had either irregular periods or none at all as long as the vigorous activity continued.

Don't be concerned if your daughter gets her period much later than most girls her age. Researchers have found that a critical level of body fat is required for menarche and for the maintenance of regular menstrual cycles. They suspect that irregularities in female athletes may be the result of an excessive ratio of lean tissue to body fat, even in those women who are average or above average in weight for their height. They also believe that the tension and stress of competition has an effect, too, by increasing the secretion of adrenaline and other substances that control the release of female hormones.

If your daughter is in her teens and a little anxious because most of her friends are menstruating but she's not, assure her that there's no reason to worry. According to medical experts, there should be no long-term ill effects on her menstrual and reproductive functioning because of her athletic prowess. And they agree that she'll probably start menstruating by the time she's reached the age of sixteen.

What are common household poisons?

If you guessed ammonia, bleach, and other household cleaners, you were only half right. Some of the most widely ingested poisons are the least likely—cosmetics, shampoos, shaving creams, colognes, and lipstick. From a child's point of view, they're pretty to look at, usually easy to get to, and some look good enough to eat or drink. Thousands of children—80 percent of them under five years of age—are poisoned each year because the poisons are attractive.

Thanks to "Mr. Yuk" you can now teach your child about poison, even in the toddler stage. Studies have proven that Mr. Yuk program, sponsored by the National Poison Center Network, is effective in teaching children as young as two years old about poisons.

The program requires that you put Mr. Yuk stickers on all household poisons while explaining to your child what you're doing and why you're doing it. The stickers should be placed not only on all medications—including aspirin and vitamins—but also on shampoo, shaving cream, cologne, mouthwash, hair tonic, hair spray, hair color and conditioners, toothpaste, moisturizer, baby powder, astringent, facial cleanser, lipstick, nail polish and remover, makup, and deodorant. And, of course, on all those household cleaners, insecticides, and the like, even if you think the bottles are ugly and smell awful enough to ward off a child.

A set of Mr. Yuk "Under-Five Understanding Cards" is also effective in helping you to clearly explain to your child that certain items are poison, and that poison is bad.

Both a sheet of twelve stickers and a card set are available for $3.00, plus postage, by writing:

The National Poison Center Network,
Childrens Hospital of Pittsburgh,
125 DeSoto Street,
Pittsburgh, Pa. 15213.

In addition, the Poison Center Network recommends the following measures:

☐ Lock all poisons away securely. Commonly used products should be put on a high shelf, out of reach.
☐ Buy a bottle of syrup of ipecac. It's available at most pharmacies without a prescription. Ipecac is used to induce vomiting. But only use when vomiting is recommended.
☐ Watch your toddler closely, especially before meals. A substantial number of accidental poisonings take place when children are hungry.
☐ Post the phone number of the nearest poison center by your telephone. It's usually listed in the white pages under "poison."
☐ If your child should swallow a toxic substance, call poison control *immediately*. Eighty-five percent of all poisoning accidents can be effectively treated at home.

Since when are sneakers better than baby shoes?

Most experts now agree that hard-soled baby shoes are unnecessary and can even damage a baby's tender feet.

Stiff oxfords with arch supports and steel shanks hamper a

baby's mobility and may even delay walking. And when the feet are confined, important muscles may not develop properly. This is a particular problem if your baby has a tendency to toe-in or toe-out.

But according to a recent study, most parents don't ask their pediatrician's advice about baby shoes. Instead, they purchase expensive leather baby shoes on the recommendation of their shoe salesperson.

What's the alternative? Pediatricians advise rubber-soled sneakers with a canvas upper. The soft sole and porous cloth covering give a baby's feet freedom of movement so they maintain their natural flexibility. And sneakers fulfill the main purpose of shoes for baby: They protect feet from the cold and rain, and keep baby from getting hurt on dangerous objects on the ground.

But don't rush out to buy sneakers if your baby is still crawling. Until your baby begins to take steps, bare feet are just fine.

What can you do for the kid who's a klutz?

Help to develop coordination by having the patience and providing the support your child needs to kayo clumsiness.

All children between the ages of two to five love to run, jump, hop, leap, and skip around. But according to a thirteen-year Michigan State University study of 1,400 youngsters, by the time they're fourteen years old, 75 percent of them will drop out of the sports they once played.

One major reason is physiological development. In about one out of ten children, coordination lags behind, sometimes as much as two years. A seven-year-old can have the nervous system of a five-year-old. Such substantial differences in development can be confirmed by hand and wrist X-rays, as well as by microscopic examinations of a child's cells.

If your seven-year-old is throwing a ball like a child much younger, your child may begin to feel awkward and ashamed, a born loser. Worse, the feelings of incompetence can extend to other areas and seriously lower self-esteem in social situations and at school.

But a late-bloomer can catch up to peers. The following are

recommendations from the American Alliance for Health, Physical Education, Recreation and Dance, an organization specializing in the education of children and youth:

☐ Play with your child. To improve catching skills, throw a large, soft ball. As the child improves, use a smaller one. For practice in throwing skills, have the youngster toss a small sponge ball to you, one that fits into the child's hands. In other words, a large ball for catching, a small one for throwing.

☐ To develop eye-hand coordination, toss a balloon in the air. Have the child catch the balloon or tap it back to you.

☐ Be sensitive to your child's individual pace. Don't pressure or sports will become a chore. Build skills gradually.

☐ Discuss the problem with the child. Explain that sometimes boys and girls are a little slower than their playmates when it comes to sports. Assure your youngster that sports will get easier within a year or two.

☐ If your child has trouble with competitve sports, try swimming, sailing, horeseback riding, or dancing. After all, exercise is exercise, and it's important to have fun doing it.

Check with your school about special exercise classes. They're available in many communities. Or, enclosing a self-addressed, stamped envelope, write to the Alliance at:

1900 Association Drive,
Reston, Va. 22901.

The Alliance will tell you what classes are nearest your home.

In the meantime, if your child misses the ball, applaud the effort and you'll help to develop the spirit to keep on playing.

Can being a Rembrandt be hazardous for your child?

Yes, if the youngster is using the wrong kinds of art supplies, ones that may be harmful to the child's developing nervous system.

Your child might be especially artistic and spend hours

deeply absorbed in the process of creating masterpieces with paint, felt-tip markers, paste, and clay. Experts are advising that, without discouraging your Rembrandt, the following routine safety precautions should be followed:

- ☐ Purchase art supplies that have "child approved" labels and read "nontoxic."
- ☐ Help make your child's own paste with flour and water. Never use rubber cement. It contains a harmful ingredient called hexine.
- ☐ Give your child water-based paints.
- ☐ Supply Play-Doh rather than adult modeling clay.
- ☐ Make it clear that materials are not to be applied to the body, hands, or face. Or put into the mouth.
- ☐ Make sure the work area is well ventilated with an exhaust fan running and the window open.
- ☐ Make sure the area is also kept clean with a damp mop.
- ☐ When done creating, the child should wash hands thoroughly. Clothes should be changed, too.

By the way, it's a good idea for adult home hobbyists also to follow safety precautions because many materials that are routinely used are toxic:

- ☐ Don't eat or smoke while working.
- ☐ Wear a respiratory mask if particles are flying.
- ☐ Store materials carefully, labeling everything and securely covering all containers.
- ☐ Keep your work area clean.
- ☐ Once finished, shower and change clothing.

What's the best age for the potty?

Wait until your child's second birthday. By then, the child's nervous and muscular systems are likely to be developed enough to control elimination. In fact, research now shows there's a 90 percent chance your toddler will be toilet trained within a week or so if you wait until that second birthday.

If your child is showing absolutely no interest in toilet training, relax. Don't even try. There are several good reasons to wait until the child shows some interest in going it alone. First of all, there can be wide variations in age for a toddler's muscular and nervous development. Pushing your toddler into something before the child is physically ready is unnecessary and unfair. Moreover, after their first birthday, toddlers are inclined to want to be independent; with motor skills and curiosity rapidly increasing, one-year-olds are quite serious about rambling around their new world, indulging their curiosity and skills, on their own. Any parent trying to force an independent toddler into the bathroom before the child is ready is risking an emotional crisis.

How do you know when your child is ready? Keep an eye on the child during playtime because a good clue is when the youngster repeatedly put toys or twigs into pots, pans, cans, or sand pails, bringing them with a glow of satisfaction to a parent. Another clue: The child may suddenly start coming up to you for help after soiling a diaper. According to pediatricians, this is the child's way of saying, "I'm ready to comply with your wishes."

The next step, doctors advise, is to suggest that the child might want to use a potty for bowel movements. If the answer is a resounding "No," back off a bit and try again in a few weeks. By then, your child might have already decided to take the initiative and master toilet training within a few days.

Some parents have a problem deciding what kind of potty to use—one of those cute little chairs with a plastic container underneath that sits on the floor, or a small seat that fits on top of an adult toilet. The floor model has the advantage of being child-level, enabling the toddlers to accomplish toileting on their own. Then, too, pediatricians warn that many small children sitting on an adult toilet get terrified by the sight of their feces being flushed away; they think that a part of themselves is disappearing, and, worse, that the rest of themselves might be in danger.

Still, some children identify so strongly with adults that they insist on doing it the way the big folks do. So be prepared to be flexible. Also keep in mind that stressful domestic situations such as a move, a death in the family, a new sibling, or illness can sometimes delay the age at which the child is physically and psychologically ready for the complex tasks of self-control. Some children are not ready until age three or four. Others who seem to have mastered the potty can backslide during times of stress. Such behavior is normal and usually temporary.

Does breast milk supply everything a baby needs?

For the first six months, it does. But after that breast-fed babies frequently need more iron than their mother's milk provides—despite all its vitamins and minerals.

Studies show that as many as 15 percent of all one-year-olds suffer from iron deficiencies. For breast-fed babies, the percentage is higher than for bottle-fed infants. One third of these infants have been found to be iron deficient at age one.

The lack of iron can have serious effects on a baby's growth, temperament, and learning ability. So whether breast- or bottle-fed, by the age of eighteen months a child should be given a blood-count test by the doctor. The test will precisely determine the infant's iron needs.

If you're breast-feeding your baby, the American Academy of Pediatrics recommends that additional iron be added to the infant's diet once the child is six months old. For bottle-fed babies, use formula with iron or add foods containing iron at six months.

When is a teaspoon not a teaspoon?

If your child's prescription calls for a teaspoon of medicine and you use a household spoon, you could be risking giving your child a drug overdose. When a doctor says "teaspoon," that means five milliliters—no more, no less. Less than the right amount is not likely to do any good; too much, especially for a child under twelve, whose body is unable to neutralize or eliminate drugs as easily as an adult's, can be dangerous.

A recent study at the University of Missouri-Kansas City School of Pharmacy showed that when different persons poured a prescribed amount of medicine into a teaspoon, the amount varied as much as 100 percent. That means one person's "teaspoon" was actually half a teaspoon, while another's measured a teaspoon and a half. If a household teaspoon of medicine can be so far off the mark, imagine the damage a *table*spoon might do.

How do you get the *exact* amount your doctor is prescribing? Take a tip from him or her and the pharmacist: Use the proper utensil. Instead of reaching for the same spoon you stir your coffee with, pick up a calibrated measuring device on your next trip to the pharmacy. You'll find cups, droppers, cylindrical tubes, and oral syringes with precise calibrations that correspond to the amounts your doctor has prescribed. One of the most accurate and flexible measuring devices is the oral syringe, which is designed to expel the total dose of medication (certain medications are inclined to stick to a cup or tube). Syringes are available in a variety of sizes in both glass and plastic.

One other tip: When you buy your new measuring device, ask your pharmacist for a quick lesson in how to use it. Remember, precision is the goal.

Will your whirling dervish do well in school?

It wouldn't be surprising. Scientists find that what children love to do—spin on swings and merry-go-rounds—improves their balance, motor control, concentration, learning ability, and general well-being.

In a number of recent studies conducted over a three-year period at Ohio State University, children between the ages of two and six were given repeated "vestibular stimulations"—that is, they were spun around on a chair for about a minute twice a week.

To judge the effect of the spinning, the scientists used a measurement called the Motor Assessment Scale. The children, who were spun at about fifteen revolutions a minute, showed a marked increase in their motor performance, and measured more than three times the normal development rate.

Spinning, the researchers said, stimulates the inner ear's semicircular canals, which, along with a person's eyes, are responsible for equilibrium and motor control. The controlled spinning had a "miraculous effect," they declared.

The improvements your child makes may be minute—every youngster reacts differently—but encourage the youngster to spin. If just a toddler, you can begin spinning the child when as as young as thirteen months. But not by the arms—that's too dangerous. Embrace the child from behind under the arms. Then be careful not to let yourself get dizzy.

78

Is it possible—and necessary—for a toddler to have an eye exam?

It's possible, and it could be necessary. Most youngsters don't require an eye examination until they're three years old but there are important exceptions.

Some simple tests that a parent can do at home may help tell whether your baby has a vision problem:

☐ Cover each of the infant's eyes in turn. Does the child cry or seem disturbed at sightlessness in either one of them?
☐ Cover each of the child's eyes in turn and move a shiny object in front of the other. Does the free eye follow the object?
☐ Observe how the infant picks up small objects such as pieces of candy. Do you notice any difficulty in performing this task?

If difficulties show up in any of the tests, your pediatrician should be informed immediately.

In addition, if your infant makes a habit of squinting or tilting his or her head to one side, this might be an indication of strabismus, or "crossed eyes," a serious eye condition that specialists now say can appear in a child within the first year of life.

Strabismus occurs when the youngster's eyes are misaligned and can lead to blindness if not treated. The condition is often misdiagnosed or overlooked because specific vision problems are sometimes difficult to identify in children under three.

The deviation in the eyes is caused by muscle weakness in one of them. This results in double vision. Youngsters will compensate by blocking out the image transmitted by the weaker eye, often squinting or tilting the head. This compensation causes an increasing loss of vision in the underused eye. Children with double vision often have difficulty walking and may be overly fussy and easily irritated.

Almost all infants have eye-wandering or eye-crossing episodes during their first six months. These are normal and generally last only a few minutes. The strabismus child's symptoms, however, don't go away after six months of age. If either eye fails to track with a moving object, or if the child's eyes appear "crossed" or misaligned, see your doctor as soon as possible.

Your pediatrician should check for the condition anyway during the first year after the baby's birth. Some methods of treatment—patching the good eye to make the weak one work harder, and surgery to tighten the weak muscles—are more successful the earlier they are started.

So what's new about circumcision?

Although religious and cultural reasons still apply, the American Academy of Pediatrics reports that there are no valid medical reasons for circumcising an infant boy and that it should no longer be routine. It's the parents' choice.

Years ago, circumcision was chiefly performed for health reasons. Poor hygiene often led to infections under the foreskin of the penis. If a man with an infection had sexual intercourse with his wife, it was believed that she could develop cervical cancer. As a result, it was widely held that cutting away the foreskin reduced the risk of disease transmitted from husband to wife and made personal hygiene easier.

Several studies tested this belief. One found that Israeli women have lower rates of cervical cancer. This was primarily attributed to the fact that all Jewish boys are ritually circumcised eight days after birth. However, shortly afterward, a study conducted in Scandinavia, where circumcision is rare, demonstrated that the incidence of cervical cancer was the same among Scandinavian women as among the Israelis.

It wasn't until after World War II that circumcision became standard in this country. This was largely because of the increased incidence of penile infections that servicemen experienced while serving overseas, especially in the South Pacific. Army doctors subsequently performed innumerable circumcisions on G.I.s headed for the battlefronts. The rationale for them carried over when the G.I.s returned home, married, and became fathers of boys. The vets believed that circumcision was a worthwhile health step.

However, today, proper hygiene is no longer a major problem. It is simple to clean the uncircumcised penis to prevent irritation and infections.

After reviewing medical and scientific literature dating back a century worldwide, experts concluded that circumcision does not reduce the risk of cervical cancer in a woman. Optimal, life-long hygiene provides as much, or nearly as much, protection. Nor does circumcision—as some persons have also believed—adversely affect a man's sex life. A recent study of circumcised and uncircumcised males reports no significant difference in ejaculatory time or in sexual pleasure experienced by the two groups.

Does a fever go hand in hand with teething?

Yes—but. They often appear together, but the two don't mix. The fever is a symptom of something else. Teething can make babies cranky, but it can't make them sick. The long-held belief of mothers that teething causes infants to run a fever is a myth that doesn't stand up to scientific investigation.

Like many myths passed down from one generation of mothers to another, this one is based on erroneous observation of many, many infants. Very frequently, babies cutting teeth also become feverish, or develop a rash, a cold, or diarrhea. This is because about the same time their first teeth appear—at the age of six to seven months—infants are also losing the immunity to infection that they acquired from their mothers before birth. As a result, they are more susceptible to many more kinds of illnesses than they had been previously.

The myth linking fever to teething is a dangerous one. It sometimes causes parents to ignore a baby's elevated temperature until it reaches as high as 103 degrees Fahrenheit or more. One doctor reports that it's not unusual for a parent to telephone him about an infant with a high temperature but then to remark apologetically, "It's probably only teething."

The eruption of teeth is uncomfortable to babies, but does not cause severe pain. If your child evidences signs of extreme distress, or fever of over 100 degrees, or any other symptom of illness, do not delay seeking medical advice just because the baby also happens to be teething at the same time. After all, you'd never expect growing fingernails or bones to cause fever. Why should teeth be any different?

81

Can teenage acne be zapped?

In most cases, yes. A special panel of the Food and Drug Administration reports that benzoyl peroxide and sulfur are safe and effective in treating acne, and, most importantly, in preventing it. Both substances are available in medications that can be obtained without a prescription.

At the first sign of acne, apply products containing benzoyl peroxide, which can suppress an outbreak by preventing lesions from getting worse. This ingredient penetrates the skin and kills the bacteria that cause acne blemishes to occur. The medication should be applied not only to the face, but also to other areas where acne is most likely to appear, such as the chest, back, neck, and arms. However, benzoyl peroxide should be applied to the skin gradually; a common side effect is irritation, especially in the winter, because skin dries more easily then.

If your teenager already has widespread acne, advise the use of sulfur products. These heal pimples by drying them out and peeling them away.

Dermatologists advise against *prolonged* use of either benzoyl peroxide or sulfur. Use only when necessary. And some teenagers may be allergic to these products. So it's wise to check with your dermatologist before starting any new medications even though they are available without a prescription.

Can retardation in newborns be prevented?

In many cases, yes, because of four new, easy, and inexpensive tests that every newborn should have before going home from the hospital. They are:

PKU (phenylketonuria) test—This can detect an inherited metabolic disorder in which a food protein (phenylalanine) can't be broken down by the body because the infant lacks a specific enzyme. When detected early, a special diet that's low in phenylalanine can prevent brain damage, including mental retardation. Usually, in place of milk, the child will be immediately put on Lofenalac, a complete food that doesn't contain phenylalanine. Later, a diet will be recommended that is rich in natural, low-protein foods such as fruits, vegetables, wheat germ, and cereals such as oatmeal.

Hypothyroid screening test—This measures the infant's production of the thyroid hormone, thyroxine. Thyroxine is essential to normal growth, especially during the infant's first five months when brain cells are growing quickly. If any malfunction of the thyroid gland is discovered, it can be easily treated with thyroxine tablets.

Syphilis Test—This detects the venereal disease that may be passed on to the child from either parent. When diagnosed early, penicillin can cure the illness and prevent brain damage or other physical manifestations such as sores and rashes. (In addition, there is a test called Ellisa that can be given if the doctor suspects the baby has herpes.)

And for premature, low-weight, and other high-risk infants, add these tests:

Hypocalcemia Test—This checks the calcium level of blood in the infant. Low calcium levels may cause speech, learning, and hearing problems. Increasing calcium with supplements can prevent difficulties.

Bilirubin test for jaundice, HCT level for anemia, and blood-count and glucose-level tests—All are readily available, though all states do not require them by law. Check with your doctor to find out if the tests are standard procedure in your hospital. If they're not, arrange to have them done before you bring your baby home.

Are growing pains for real?

Yes, even though you may have thought "growing pains" was merely a fanciful expression. The leg pains often experienced by adolescent boys are all too real and can occasionally result in long-term difficulties, including tendonitis, sciatica, and backache. Fortunately, a little caution will go a long way toward lessening the pain and preventing lasting problems.

One kind of growing pain occurs in about half of all teenage boys during the growth spurt. Characteristically, the pain is felt in the knob of bone just below the knee and can be quite severe, though there is no deformity, stiffness in the joint, or limitation of movement associated with this complaint. It is known as the Osgood-Schlatter syndrome and the treatment is not complicated. Eliminating activities that exert stress on the knees—such as bicycle riding or basketball—leads to a full cure within several months. Even after he is free of pain, a boy should still take it easy for a few weeks to let the leg heal completely. Normal athletic activity then can be resumed.

A condition known as slipped capital femoral epiphysis is more severe, but far less common. This, too, usually occurs in adolescent boys who are growing rapidly, and many of whom are overweight. Such a boy will first experience pain in the lower third of one leg or both, even though the disease is in the hip. Movement of the joint becomes limited, and a pin must be implanted in the hip to restore activity. The boy must stop all sports for a time.

So, don't ignore your son's "growing pains." There may be a real medical problem.

What's an adolescent doctor?

A doctor for teenagers. The medical profession has finally recognized that pediatricians, general practitioners, and many other specialists are not prepared to deal with the dizzying array of medical and emotional problems faced by teenagers—problems quite peculiar to that age group. But a new breed has evolved, men and women interested in the emotional and physical complaints of adolescence who have continued their medical education for two to three more years to learn how to deal with teenagers. They're called "adolescent doctors."

Perhaps your thirteen-year-old son has complained about sitting in the pediatrician's waiting room surrounded by Tinker toys and squealing infants; maybe your daughter is none too keen about discussing her menstrual cramps or fears about sexuality with your gynecologist. Or how about the teenager plagued by depression who is sure everyone will think he's crazy if he goes to a psychiatrist? These are precisely the kinds of problems that adolescent doctors are trained to handle. Their interest is in the *whole* teenager; they are, as it were, full-service physicians, prepared to cope with all the skin, weight, gynecological, and psychological problems common to adolescence.

While many family doctors are inclined to shy away from the highly charged or embarrassing topic of adolescent sexuality, the specialist is prepared to talk to a teenager about such matters as venereal disease, pregnancy, and sexual anxiety. These physicians also offer many aspects of gynecological care, and they are trained to know when an adolescent's emotional well-being requires help from a psychotherapist.

To find an adolescent specialist in your area, send a stamped, self-addressed envelope to the Society for Adolescent Medicine, c/o Business Office, P.O. Box 3462, Granada Hills, Calif. 91344.

Should you let your baby grow up a lefty?

Why not? You can indeed force the child to be right-handed, but you shouldn't. Forcing a lefty to use the right hand can cause frustration, clumsiness, stuttering, and learning problems. According to current estimates, nearly one in three persons in the country would be left-handed if their parents had allowed them to follow their preference.

How can one tell which hand a baby favors? It's not always easy. One clue is that the right thumbnail of a child who is naturally right-handed often is broader than the left thumbnail. If your baby eats, plays, and reaches for objects with the left hand most frequently, you probably have a budding southpaw. When the child starts to draw and use tools, you'll have an even clearer indication of which hand is preferred.

The majority of children make a clear choice of one hand or the other by the age of six. If yours does not, you can gently nudge the youngster toward the right hand. But don't push too hard.

Some headway with the problem has been made in recent years. In 1970, about 12 percent of the population wrote with the left hand—six times more than in 1930, when the proportion was only 2 percent. But the bias still continues, and is reinforced by our language. The Latin word for left hand, for example, is *sinis-*

ter, which means threatening or evil. And you wouldn't want to dance with a person with two left feet, or receive a left-handed compliment.

The prejudice, of course, has no basis in fact, and numerous remarkable individuals have been left-handed—da Vinci, Bach, Michelangelo, Benjamin Franklin, Picasso, Babe Ruth, and Dorothy Hamill, to mention a few.

So, if your child seems to be left-handed, leave the youngster alone.

How can milk possibly be bad for a baby?

Putting your baby to sleep with a bottle of milk may do wonders for the child's disposition (and yours), but it can also ruin those new teeth.

Bottle feeding is the leading source of dental problems for children under the age of three. Whole milk is loaded with lactose (a form of sugar) and other carbohydrates that make a feast for oral bacteria, producing acid that will quickly begin to erode the enamel of the child's teeth and cause tooth decay. Although the dental profession has been warning parents about the problem for years, the incidence of "Nursing Bottle Mouth Syndrome," as dentists call it, remains at the same level year after year.

The prime sign of the syndrome is badly decayed upper front teeth, which are the most susceptible because the nipple of the bottle is positioned directly behind them. Back teeth are also vulnerable for those babies who are in the habit of falling asleep with a bottle in their mouth. Since the milk is no longer being swallowed, it is likely to rest in a pool in the mouth, producing acid that attacks the enamel.

Once decay sets in, professional care, especially for severe cases, can get very expensive. And that is most unfortunate because Nursing Bottle Mouth Syndrome is completely preventable.

Milk is not the only culprit. Apple juice is worse, while other juices that contain sucrose, dextrose, or corn syrup—all sugars—can also be destructive. Natural sugars are just as bad as store bought. Check the labels, and keep in mind that a baby's teeth have thinner enamel than permanent teeth and thus are especially susceptible to tooth decay. Even if your child doesn't take a bottle at night, slipping a quick bottle or cookie to keep the toddler occupied or quiet can be just as injurious.

How do you break the habit if your baby is already addicted to a night-time (or naptime) bottle? Ideally, according to dentists, you should feed the baby before putting him or her to bed instead of leaving the bottle in the crib. If that is not the case in your household, do not suddenly try to make your baby go "cold turkey" by snatching that bottle out of the crib. It will probably ruin the child's, and your, sleep. The trick is to gradually reduce the amount of sugary liquid over a period of days by diluting it with water. Keep this up until the bottle contains just water, which won't do any harm whatsoever.

But the best way to deal with the problem is prevention—adequate oral hygiene for your baby from the moment of birth in a hospital. Many parents do not realize that they can and should clean the mouth area before their baby's teeth have even surfaced. All it takes is a moist piece of cotton gauze or a wet washcloth after every feeding. When the child reaches the toddler stage, you can buy a toothbrush, child-size, with soft bristles. Make a game of brushing the child's teeth; the toddler will enjoy it, and meantime get into the habit of good teeth care.

When is a dentist a painter?

When the dentist is applying a transparent, plastic sealant that can prevent decay-causing bacteria from attacking the vulnerable biting surfaces of a youngster's teeth. This new method of cavity prevention can save children many agonizing hours in the dental chair.

Studies show that the sealant, which is recommended by the National Institute of Dental Research, can reduce childhood cavities by as much as 80 percent. The sealant, which can provide protection for up to five years, is first applied when the child is about eight years old. Should it come off for any reason, it's easily reapplied.

The procedure is painless and safe. The chewing surfaces are first cleaned with a mild acid to help the sealant stick. Next the teeth are painted with the substance in much the same way that nail polish is applied. Soon after application the sealant hardens to a glossy, transparent finish, leaving the treated teeth looking completely natural.

The sealant has other uses in addition to decay prevention. If a child has a chipped front tooth the dentist can recreate its natural shape by applying a similar tooth-colored material in layers— a much simpler and less expensive method than constructing an individually molded cap.

A youngster's braces can also be attached with the sealant, doing away with most of the unsightly bands. Dentists are also using the new plastic to splint loose teeth to firm ones.

_____

Does baby know best about burping?

Surprisingly, in many instances, you don't have to burp a baby at all. Although babies do swallow air while sucking, the amount varies from baby to baby. And some infants don't experience any discomfort from the swallowed air.

Pediatricians report that parents, especially first-timers, are so eager to burp their baby after feedings that they persist for half an hour, sometimes longer. Occasionally they're so anxious that they begin to thump a little too aggressively. The result: Baby is even more uncomfortable.

If a baby falls asleep or rests comfortably after feeding, is not colicky or agitated, many pediatricians advise parents to leave their babies alone. Don't burp.

When your infant does need a little help after feeding, here's how to do it:

Place the baby in a sitting position on your lap, facing away from you. Make certain the child is supported securely. Then gently massage, beginning in the lower back and pushing softly upward.

If your infant is colicky, speak to your doctor. A colicky baby may require a change in routine, such as more quiet periods or the use of mild heat from a hot-water bottle or heating pad. Make sure to wrap any heating device in a terrycloth towel to prevent the baby from getting burned.

As children grow older, their more active movements stimulate the burping process naturally.

88

Should you stop your child from thumb-sucking?

Don't bother. There is absolutely nothing wrong with thumb-sucking. In fact, it is quite normal. A baby's ability to eat—and thus survive—depends on an effective sucking reflex, and obstetricians point out that X-rays and sonagrams of babies still in the womb show them getting in practice by sucking on their thumbs there. Thumb-sucking may even be a normal exercise that helps develop some of the facial muscles used in pronouncing certain sounds.

Doctors now warn that trying to prevent thumb-sucking only increases the child's frustration and probably prolongs the habit. Infants vary in the amount of sucking they need, and before long they are likely to grow out of the habit, especially if they are well fed, emotionally content, and allowed to suck away in the early years.

What about buck teeth? Again, don't worry. Dentists explain that the main cause of protruding teeth is heredity. And though baby teeth might be moved by hard thumb-sucking, permanent teeth won't be, unless the habit persists beyond the age of three or four. At that time, the permanent teeth begin to be positioned, and intense, prolonged thumb-sucking can influence the bone structure around the mouth, causing the permanent tooth buds to be pushed forward. The eventual result is that when the large upper teeth erupt at about the age of six-and-a-half or seven, they may come in out of place or protruding. This is even more likely if sucking continues past seven, when the thumb can press directly on the permanent front teeth.

Happily, most children stop sucking their thumbs about the time they start school. If, however, your child is more than five years old and still sucking away, you should start looking for some psychological factor that may be causing it. Some likely possibilities:

☐ A new baby in the home. Orthodontists have noticed that sometimes an older child who has already broken the habit returns to thumb-sucking when a sibling arrives.
☐ Unreasonable demands. If a parent (or even an older brother or sister) sets expectations too high, the child may

protest by thumb-sucking, thus signaling, "I'm still a baby. Give me a break."

☐ Imitating other children. Your child may admire a friend in nursery school who happens to be a chronic thumb-sucker.

☐ Anxiety. Children are quite amazing at picking up emotional signals in the home. Quarreling, a recent move, a job change may cause thumb-sucking—just as the same sorts of tension can provoke an adult to biting fingernails, nibbling pencils, or smoking too much.

Any child pushing six or seven and still a chronic thumb-sucker is going to need some professional help to break the habit, especially if front teeth are being displaced. Some experts suggest that a trip to the orthodontist might do the trick. He usually shows the child plaster models of "ugly" and "pretty" teeth, asks if the child would like to quit, inquires whether the youngster's old enough to pull it off, and then asks the child to promise not to suck on purpose again. The orthodontist and the child shake hands on it, and the doctor asks the child to call in a few days to report on progress. This approach used along with other methods is very effective for children. The child appreciates not being treated like a baby and usually responds, within a few months, by becoming an ex-thumb-sucker.

Fortunately, however, most little thumb-suckers never get that far and quit the habit on their own.

Does your child's sleepwalking conjure up a nightmare of worries for you?

Don't worry, there's no cause for alarm. Many youngsters occasionally walk in their sleep.

Sleepwalking is ordinarily just another phase in the growing-up process. Because parts of the child's brain are immature, dreams can be stimulating enough to cause a youngster to take a nocturnal stroll. Researchers estimate that about 25 percent of all children will have one or more sleepwalking episodes between the ages of seven and twelve.

Don't wake the child up. A sudden return to consciousness

can be frightening and confusing. Often the youngster will return to bed unguided. If not, gently lead the way.

Most children soon outgrow the habit, but until they do it's a good idea to place gates on stairs and windows as a safety precaution.

Frequent sleepwalking episodes could have several causes. They may be an indication of an emotional disturbance, perhaps caused by stress at home, school, or even in a play situation. So parents should keep a sharp eye out for signs of tension. They might also be a sign of abnormal delay in the maturing youngster's nervous system. In any case, if sleepwalking persists, it should be discussed with your child's pediatrician, who might recommend evaluation by a child psychologist or neurologist.

Why is boiling a nipple passé?

Sterilizing baby's bottles and nipples by boiling is completely unnecessary and might even be harmful.

Boiling nipples may dangerously weaken the rubber. The possibility then arises that a zealous infant can chew through the damaged tip and bite off and swallow a sizable chunk of it. That could lead to choking.

Pediatricians suggest washing both bottle and nipples in lukewarm water, just like your dishes. Soap, then rinse well, and drain dry. Don't put the nipples in the dishwasher; the rubber will disintegrate. Inspect the nipples for wear regularly, and the bottles for chips.

It's natural for parents, especially first-timers, to worry when it comes to keeping their newborn's utensils sanitary. But as medical experts point out, germs are everywhere, even on the very hands that screw on the bottlecap. In addition, we've come a long way during the last two decades in vastly improving the sanitary conditions of our homes, so the threat of serious disease through contamination has been virtually eliminated.

Another note: When purchasing new nipples, read the package label carefully. Specially designed ones for premature babies are made of a thinner, more pliable rubber. Full-term babies have stronger sucking and biting action and can easily bite through the premie nipples.

What's the bottom line on cornstarch and diaper rash?

Don't use cornstarch for the rash; it may promote fungus. Forget about petroleum jelly, too, either for preventing diaper rash or for treating it; it keeps the air off the skin, predisposing it to yeast infection. Plain water is best for cleaning a baby's bottom.

The exact cause of diaper rash has not been scientifically established. Many experts believe that it may be caused when bacteria from bowel movements interact with urine to form ammonia, which is irritating to the sensitive skin of infants. The irritation is increased by infrequent changing and the use of plastic pants or tight, disposable diapers, both of which reduce air circulation.

The key to avoiding diaper rash is to keep the diaper area dry, clean, and well-aired. The best diaper for dryness, according to pediatricians, is the old-fashioned cotton type, which is very absorbent. In one study, researchers compared babies wearing cloth diapers with those in disposable ones and found that rashes were up to five times more common among the babies wearing the disposables. If you cannot face the prospect of washing all those diapers, use the loosest disposable diapers you can find. And don't ever use those plastic or rubber pants that go over diapers; they might keep the crib dry, but they also keep your baby's bottom wet and warm, the perfect environment for diaper rash.

Change your baby's diapers frequently and, when you do, be sure to clean the entire diaper area—buttocks, thighs, and abdomen—with water. (Mild soap may be used after a particularly messy bowel movement). Too much soap or frequent use of alcohol pads tends to remove the skin's protective barrier and cause unnecessary irritation. To help promote dryness, a thin film of cream with a zinc-oxide base is useful over the diaper area.

If a diaper rash does not respond to any of these treatments, check with your pediatrician.

Can orange juice ever be bad for you?

When you have to take penicillin. Orange juice is but one of many drinks and foods that are counterproductive with drugs—and sometimes harmful.

Here is a list of some of the many food-and-drug and drug-and-drug combinations to be alert to:

- ☐ Any kind of alcoholic beverage combined with certain medications is especially dangerous. Don't imbibe if, for example, you're taking antibiotics, tranquilizers, antihistamines, motion-sickness medication, aspirin, codeine, or sleeping pills. Alcohol can stimulate metabolizing enzymes and cause a medication to be chemically digested before it can work. Then, too, alcohol depresses the central nervous system and, if taken with another depressant, can cause an overdose or increased sedation.
- ☐ Tea and coffee contain tannins that can prevent the proper absorption of some drugs.
- ☐ Milk should not be taken with iron pills or with tetracycline because they bind with calcium and cannot be absorbed by the body.
- ☐ Like orange juice, acidic beverages shouldn't be mixed with penicillin because acid destroys the effectiveness of penicillin.
- ☐ Medications for diarrhea may block the effectiveness of other drugs.
- ☐ For a woman using a birth-control pill, regular doses of laxatives that contain mineral oil can block estrogen absorption and possibly the contraceptive effect.
- ☐ Tyramine counteracts the benefits of a class of drugs called monoamine oxidase (MAO) inhibitors, which are used to control high blood pressure and fight depression. Tyramine occurs naturally in Cheddar, Stilton and Gruyère cheese, in chicken liver, beer, red wine (especially Chianti), chocolate, avocado, soy sauce, raisins, and pickled herring.

The list of food-and-drug interactions is long, and it keeps growing as new medications are constantly added to the physician's arsenal. Before taking any new drug, it's wise to ask your doctor about foods or over-the-counter medications that should be used sparingly or avoided altogether. Or ask your pharmacist, who is trained to answer queries of this kind. The answers to a few questions can help the important medications do the job they were meant to do—and safeguard your health.

Can car sickness be patched up?

Yes. There's a new way to take medication that cuts down and even eliminates side effects. Instead of swallowing a pill or liquid, you wear the medicine on your skin. Medication patches look like dime-sized adhesive bandages with a concentration of medication embedded in the gauze. Minute amounts of the medicine seep through the pores in the skin into your bloodstream at a steady rate. A single patch can deliver medication for twenty-four hours.

So far, two drugs are available in patch form. Scopolamine for motion sickness is worn behind the ear. Nitroglycerin for the angina suffered by coronary patients is worn on the chest.

The patch is a remarkable advance in delivering drugs to your system. With the exception of time-released pills, the medicines you swallow give you a large dose immediately. But as the hours go by, less and less of the drug acts on your system, and, after a few hours, the medicine is used up. On the other hand, the patch releases no more than the smallest dose you need right from the beginning. And this same small amount continues to be delivered to your system for as long as twenty-four hours. Because of this, the unpleasant side effects some people experience are eliminated.

If you're using a motion-sickness patch, you'll have less tendency to get sleepy or nauseous.

If you're an angina patient, the benefit of a nitroglycerin patch is especially valuable. Angina is caused by the narrowing of the coronary arteries by atherosclerosis. The blood and so the oxygen supplied to the heart muscle suddenly decrease. When this happens, a coronary patient feels a recurrent, suffocating pain in the chest and shooting pain in the left arm.

94

The prescribed medication is nitroglycerin, which dilates the arteries around the heart. Until now, a combination of nitroglycerin tablets and ointment rubbed into the chest was the way the problem was treated. But as the action of pills and ointment wears off, a patient's arteries are in danger of constricting again.

A coronary patient can now wear a nitroglycerin patch continuously and receive a safe and steady dose of medication that keeps the arteries evenly dilated.

Researchers are currently working on patches for medications used for asthma and high blood pressure. And they're even trying to develop a birth-control patch.

Will you always be allergic to penicillin?

If you've been allergic to penicillin in the past, you and twenty million other Americans may think you won't ever benefit from its wonder-working properties. But recent studies indicate that as many as 75 percent of those who are certain they can't take penicillin have actually "outgrown" their allergy, or never were allergic in the first place. And this is important because penicillin is still the drug of choice to take for a whole host of illnesses.

Doctors are unclear about the reason that persons no longer demonstrate the allergy, but the phenomenon has been observed in several controlled experiments. Researchers think the explanation may lie in individual genetic and metabolic factors.

Many people are told in childhood that they're allergic to penicillin, a judgment generally arrived at because a skin rash developed when the antibiotic was administered. Doctors now believe that in some cases the rashes were caused by the disease under treatment rather than by the drug itself.

If your doctor recommends penicillin treatment, it may be worth taking two recently developed highly accurate skin tests that can determine if you're still allergic. A negative reaction to both tests indicates that penicillin can be administered at very little risk. These tests are only available at major medical centers.

One important warning: penicillin allergy is dangerous and should not be ignored or taken lightly. So, don't under any circumstances assume you are no longer allergic without taking these tests and discussing the matter carefully with your doctor.

Is it true what they say about copper?

Yes, there's some truth to the folk belief about copper relieving arthritic pain. Several new scientific studies show that taking copper pills or injections, or wearing a bracelet or anklet made of copper, actually helps ease rheumatoid arthritis for some people.

With the bracelet and anklet, the copper is absorbed through the skin. In recent studies, significant numbers of patients with arthritis said the bracelet did have therapeutic value.

Copper works because it has a unique anti-inflammatory, or antiarthritic, effect. Persons who suffer from rheumatoid arthritis experience a biochemical breakdown in the linings of the joints that the body is unable to repair by itself. The copper can help repair the tissue in damaged joints. It can decrease swelling, morning stiffness, and fever, and can increase mobility. In fact, adding copper to aspirin may make aspirin more effective in relieving arthritic pain.

Many people are unaware that copper is an essential element that our bodies need for the normal metabolism of all tissue. In other words, copper is just as important as the essential fats, amino acids, and enzymes that our bodies require to function properly. But copper should not be used excessively because too much can cause serious diseases of the liver, so check with your doctor. He can tell you the best way to use copper to relieve arthritis pain.

Does iced tea or coffee really cool you off?

Not much. Contrary to popular belief, neither iced tea nor iced coffee will really cool you off much because they contain caffeine, which constricts the blood vessels. Because of this effect, coffee or tea, either iced or hot, can cause you to become overheated, so it's best to avoid these drinks on hot days. But don't substitute a cola drink for them; colas also contain caffeine. Instead, drink water or a fruit juice.

Because heat and sun themselves affect your system, the drugs you take, plus summer weather, may add up to a dose of trouble. Some drugs cause, as a side effect, blood vessels to dilate, which can result in a person's body temperature dropping below normal in hot weather. Other drugs—like caffeine—constrict blood vessels, which can lead to overheating. If you're on any medication, ask your doctor if the weather exaggerates its side effects. Some antibiotics such as tetracycline or aureomycin contain chemicals that cause photosynthesis and cause a sunburn.

The effects of still other drugs may be influenced by *both* sun and heat. These include tranquilizers, antidepressants, diuretics, and anti-Parkinsonism drugs. They can aggravate a sunburn as well as cause your body to lose water and salt. As a result, you may become dehydrated.

In summary, the best advice is, if you're on medication of any kind—over-the-counter or prescription—double-check with your doctor and with the weather report to protect your health.

Venom for a bee sting? Isn't that a bit much?

Acute reaction to an insect sting by a bee, hornet, wasp, and certain ants is more common than realized.

For 1 to 2 million highly allergic Americans, an insect sting can cause a serious drop in blood pressure, blackout, or difficulty breathing. Doctors report that some deaths at poolside or on the golf course or tennis court, all of which were previously considered the result of heart attacks, may actually have been caused by stings.

A new immunization treatment recently developed at the Johns Hopkins University School of Medicine will counteract severe reaction in adults or children considered high-risk victims. The treatment is known as "venom therapy." The patient is injected with gradually increased doses of insect venom, until the allergy has been successfully "blocked" and acute sensitivity virtually disappears.

The National Institutes of Health warns, "Everyone is a potential victim." If you've ever experienced unusual itching, redness, or swelling from a sting, the next incident might be worse.

For individuals with high sensitivity, doctors prescribe emergency sting kits to prevent a serious reaction before medical aid can be summoned. The pharmacist who fills the prescription will explain each item in the kit, as well as when and how it should be used.

Susceptible persons should keep an emergency sting kit at home and carry another in their car or on their person whenever they expect to be in a situation where a sting can occur. It's also a good idea to wear emergency medical identification to inform bystanders that medical assistance may be necessary.

Here are a few precautions to help you keep from being stung in the first place:

☐ Never go barefoot or wear bright clothes outdoors. Instead, wear white clothing, long pants, and closed shoes (never sandals).
☐ For gardening, add long-sleeved shirts and gloves.
☐ Inspect plants closely before gardening.
☐ Do not use perfume or scented lotions on your body.
☐ Try to avoid eating or drinking outdoors.
☐ Move away slowly when a dangerous insect appears.
☐ Stay clear of outdoor trash cans.
☐ If out in the open and attacked by a swarm of bees or wasps, drop to the ground, lie face down, and cover your head with your arms.

For those less sensitive to insect stings, there's a new first-aid tip for quick relief. Wet the area of the sting and rub it with soluble aspirin until the sting is covered with moist, white powder. For prolonged relief once the skin has dried, moisten the powder and apply it again. Also, taken internally, aspirin will inhibit pain and inflammation.

What's better, a tranquilizer or a bike ride?

Try the bike ride. Studies show exercise is at least as effective as a pill in coping with stress. And you won't risk becoming dangerously addicted to a drug.

Fifteen million Americans take tranquilizers to treat problems ranging from insomnia to backache and, also, most often, stress. Women still outnumber men about two to one in taking tranquilizers, but the pills are becoming more widely accepted by men as well. According to the National Institutes of Drug Abuse, Valium is the most frequently prescribed tranquilizer, with at least 15 percent of all adults taking it regularly. Librium is also commonly used. Yet studies show that an average prescribed dosage—three pills a day for one month—may be enough to cause some persons to become addicted. And many individuals become addicted without even realizing it.

If your doctor prescribes a tranquilizer for you, be sure to ask why, for how long, and in what dosage—minimum or maximum—it's being prescribed. If the doctor suggests you use the tranquilizer daily for more than a month, and fails to warn you that it may be habit-forming, think twice about filling the prescription, because the Food and Drug Administration is now urging doctors not to prescribe tranquilizers for daily stress. Instead, talk to the doctor about alternative ways of dealing with any chronic emotional problem. There may be a healthier solution.

Several new studies indicate that exercise can be at least as effective as a tranquilizer in relieving mild stress. Exercise releases a chemical substance in the brain called endorphins, which act as a natural tranquilizer. Strenuous exercises—including running, bike riding, and jumping rope—relax your muscles and make you less anxious and uptight. Even walking helps. Exercise regularly, at least three times a week, and you may begin to feel more relaxed about yourself and make positive changes in your life, without any harmful side effects.

What's on your windowsill that can heal bites, burns, and other bothersome boo-boos?

The aloe vera plant. This remarkable plant has healing properties that can heal insect bites, minor burns, poison ivy rash, and athlete's foot, and can relieve summer sunburn and dry skin as well.

The reason: The fresh leaf juice of the aloe vera contains the drug aloin.

The Ancient Greek and Egyptian civilizations knew of aloe's medicinal powers, so it's not surprising that Cleopatra use aloe as part of her beauty regimen.

99

If you get a minor burn, treat it promptly. Break off the largest leaf of the plant and squeeze it gently, like a tube of toothpaste. It yields a sticky clear gel. Apply the gel directly on the burn.

For treatment of a mild sunburn, apply the aloe vera gel frequently. This should reduce the pain and any subsequent peeling. Apply the gel often also for the treatment of itching caused by insect bites, poison ivy, dry skin, and athlete's foot. If any condition persists, see a doctor.

Should you only use a small portion of the leaf, you can keep the rest of it fresh by wrapping it in plastic and storing it in the refrigerator. However, because the aloe leaf's healing powers are affected by the length of time it has been removed from the plant, ideally it's best to cut a fresh leaf for every application—depending on the size of your plant.

The aloe vera plant is available at most nurseries, even five-and-dime stores and supermarkets, and can cost as little as a dollar. The aloe vera plant is hearty and survives with very little attention. It requires good drainage, lots of sun, and only occasional watering. There have been some reports of allergy to aloe vera, so at any sign of rash or irritation, discontinue its use.

Does any child need a smallpox vaccination?

Not a one. It's too dangerous.

Smallpox is a disease of the past—and so are smallpox vaccinations. Although smallpox was once the major cause of death throughout the world, there has not been a case reported in the United States since 1953. And in 1979, for the first time, there were no cases of smallpox reported anywhere in the world. As a result, in May, 1980, the World Health Organization officially declared smallpox totally eradicated.

Nevertheless, many persons still have not got the message, including some doctors. Last year, about 40,000 of their patients, mostly children, received smallpox vaccinations. Not only were they unnecessary, and an unnecessary expense, but smallpox vaccinations can also be quite risky, causing various kinds of rashes and, in rare cases, encephalitis.

The risks were worth it when smallpox was a major, world-wide killer, but now they're not. Neither children nor travelers should be vaccinated—unless going to a remote area. In which case, check with the World Health Organization, Room 2427, United Nations, New York, N.Y. 10017.

Isn't it time you fellas finally took that shot?

For mumps, that is. It's long been known that coming down with the mumps can have serious repercussions for teenage males as well as men. But new studies show that previous warnings about mumps and the danger of other childhood diseases have not been sufficiently heeded by the public.

One survey on mumps indicates that as many as forty percent of potentially susceptible teenage boys—those who didn't have mumps in childhood and, thus, didn't develop an immunity—have not been vaccinated against the disease.

For young children, mumps is a rather mild, nonthreatening illness marked by swollen glands that cause puffy cheeks. If contracted after the age of twelve, however, it can cause malfunctions in the male reproductive system and, in rare cases, result in sterility. Vaccination is safe, assures immunity, and is readily available at low cost through doctors or at health centers. It's a protection no male should be without, too, if he's never been vaccinated.

The continuing threat of mumps symbolizes a broader problem. A 1977 survey found that two out of every five youngsters had not been vaccinated against one or more childhood diseases such as whooping cough, incidences of which have risen significantly in recent years.

Public-health experts say that because of the success of mass-vaccination programs in the 1960s, many persons—women as well as men—erroneously believe that the diseases have been eliminated. This misconception leads them to ignore the precautions necessary to safeguard their children. All youngsters, they say, should be immunized against the seven major childhood diseases—mumps, whooping cough, measles, rubella (German measles), polio, diphtheria, and tetanus.

As for measles, experts in communicable diseases now believe that no child, girl or boy, should be vaccinated until about fifteen months old, unless the youngster has been exposed to the disease. Children who are vaccinated before then seem to be too young for measles antibodies in their body to develop permanent protection against the disease.

Attention was called to the age factor when there was a measles outbreak in the Erie County, New York, school system in 1978. Of the 203 cases of measles, 75 percent occurred in children who had been vaccinated against the disease. Seventy cases broke out in two schools where 99 percent of the students had been vaccinated. Baffled, health officials analyzed the records of the children, most of whom were between five and nine years old, and discovered that the highest contraction rates occurred in those who were vaccinated when ten months old or younger. Students vaccinated at twelve months of age seemed twice as likely to contract measles as those vaccinated at fifteen months.

Any child who was exposed to measles and vaccinated before the age of one should be revaccinated when fifteen months old. There is no danger in revaccination, according to epidemiologists at the Centers for Disease Control in Atlanta.

To avoid mistakes or overlooking a vaccination requirement, parents should keep an accurate record of their child's vaccination history—day, month, and year.

Do you get the most out of an antibiotic?

Probably not. Two out of three persons misuse them, and as a result what should have been a quickly cured infection lingers or may get worse.

Antibiotics such as penicillin, streptomycin, and tetracycline are superb drugs, able to wipe out many infections. But they must be taken properly to work.

It's important to follow the *full course* of antibiotic treatment ordered by your physician. Even if you start to feel better, don't stop taking the medicine. Cutting off the antibiotic too soon can bring an unnecessary risk of reinfection because all the disease-causing bacteria may not have been destroyed.

If your doctor prescribes an antibiotic dose every four hours, follow those instructions to the letter. Antibiotics have to be taken around the clock. Their effectiveness depends on keeping a certain amount of the drug in your system at all times, so missing a dose can reduce your chances for a speedy recovery.

The food you eat and when you eat it can have a major effect on a drug's ability to do its job. If you're taking a tetracycline, you should stay away from foods containing calcium. Milk and cheese can bind the drug in such a way that its ability to be absorbed by the body is inhibited and its effectiveness greatly reduced. Many antibiotics should be taken on an empty stomach, usually two hours after a meal. Otherwise they'll probably be destroyed by gastric acid in the stomach. Tetracycline, which appears in nearly fifty drugs, should never be taken with an antacid.

Storage directions should also be followed exactly. Some antibiotics have to be refrigerated or they'll lose their strength. Liquids should be kept in tightly closed bottles and shaken well before using.

Make sure you check the expiration date on your prescription and discard the drug once it is out-dated. Some antibiotics—tetracyclines in particular—can cause adverse reactions if they're taken after they've become too old. (And tetracycline can stain children's teeth.)

Finally, antibiotics can cure many illnesses, but the common cold isn't one of them. So don't use these drugs for colds or simple upper-respiratory infections. They don't work against viruses and their use in these cases may even cause you problems. Anyway, you should never use a prescription medication without your doctor's knowledge. And if the doctor prescribes one, ask what foods you should avoid.

What's the drug all kids are high on?

Caffeine—from colas, cocoa, and chocolate bars.

Caffeine is a stimulant. Taken in the form of a beverage, it is rapidly absorbed from the gastrointestinal tract and distributed in the various tissues of the body, passing quickly into the central nervous system. Such jolts of caffeine produce almost-instant energy—and a great deal of nervousness. Which is the reason that many parents don't want their children to drink coffee or tea regularly. But perhaps they don't realize how much caffeine also lurks in a soda can.

A study of cola drinks, coffees, and teas shows that the caffeine intake of children and teenagers may be excessive. For example, the intake of a youngster who drinks a twelve-ounce bottle of cola is comparable to that of an adult who drinks four cups of instant coffee. And the intake of a very young child who drinks a cup of chocolate milk or devours a candy bar has the same effect.

It's ten o'clock. Do you know why your child is irritable, restless, and unable to fall asleep?

Is it more important to stretch before or after exercising?

Both times are important, but after is more important because strenuous exercises such as jogging and tennis cause muscles to tighten up from stress, and tight muscles tear easily. Limbering them up immediately afterward reduces that risk—as well as the stiffness, soreness, strains, and sprains that athletes commonly suffer. Stretching improves your circulation, reduces tension in your muscles, relaxes your mind and body, and makes future exercise easier.

When you stretch, the blood vessels in your muscles fill with blood, and the muscles become longer, more pliable, and resilient. In fact, a stretched-out muscle is springy like a rubberband, while a tight, unstretched muscle—like a taut length of rope—has no give.

If you're over twenty-five, stretching is especially important because the muscles become shorter and less flexible with age.

What's the best way to stretch your muscles? The answer is the opposite of what you might think. Don't touch your toes and bounce up and down. Bouncing, bobbing, or jerking the body can cause damage. Quick movements stretch the muscles too far, too quickly, so your muscles then contract further. The key is to go slow and easy. Stretch out one group of muscles at a time—calves, hamstring and lower back, and shoulders. Hold each in an extended position, without moving. Specifically:

Calves—Stand three feet from a wall. Without bending your knees, lean toward the wall placing your palms flat against the wall at the same height as your head. Hold this position for ten to fifteen counts.

Hamstring and lower back—Lie on your back, hands at your

side. Pull your legs to your chest and lock your arms around them. Hold this position for twenty to forty counts. Repeat seven to ten times. If you have trouble with your knees, lock your arms *under* instead of over them.

Shoulders—Stand with your feet apart, shoulder width. Stretch your arms above your head, keeping your heels on the ground. Hold this position for fifteen to thirty counts.

Above all, don't skimp on time for stretching. Take a full fifteen minutes to get the maximum benefits—before and after exercising.

Can what you eat affect what you hear?

Definitely, in the case of tinnitus, or "ringing in the ears." The ringing can actually sound like bells ringing, or like a kettle whistling, an ocean roaring, or a steady clicking or buzzing. And the way to quiet the annoying racket may be as simple as changing what you eat.

An astonishing 36 million Americans complain of ringing in the ears, but for some of them the problem may be caused by low blood sugar or hypoglycemia—and readily solvable.

The inner ear has a high energy requirement and glucose (sugar) is the number-one element of energy metabolism. A significant imbalance in the glucose level may have an adverse effect on hearing ability.

A drop in blood sugar will cause adrenaline to be released; the blood vessels in the ear then constrict, and the ringing begins.

Some individuals have persistent hypoglycemia, or a regular pattern of "reactive" hypoglycemia after meals. Blood-glucose tests will detect whether hypoglycemia is the underlying problem responsible for your hearing disorder. Your doctor may then put you on a special diet. You may be eating a lot more fish, meat, cheese, brown rice, beans, chicken, and soybeans. But you'll also have to cut down on sugar, including processed foods and condiments that may contain hidden sugar. Starchy foods such as potatoes will also be avoided because they can cause the same reaction as white rice and plain pastas (made with white flour) do. You'll eat more frequent but smaller meals.

Tinnitus may also be caused by a wide variety of conditions, such as an obstruction in the auditory canal, an infection, syphilis, meningitis, cardiovascular disease, anemia, or a noise-induced hearing loss. Tinnitus can also be a side effect of certain diuretics and other drugs.

If the underlying problem is properly identified and treated successfully, tinnitus should disappear. The key is identifying the cause, whether it be hypoglycemia, an illness, or a reaction to medication.

Whoever heard of a peanut headache, much less a chocolate one?

Experts now tell us that the cause of some headaches may be what we eat. But how can you find out what food in particular is the cause? The best tactic is to be your own headache detective.

Start by keeping a diary. Jot down when headaches begin, when they stop, and exactly what you're doing and how you're feeling at the time. Also note everything you eat and when you eat it.

Food allergies frequently bring on headaches. Seven foods are the chief villains: milk, peanuts, chocolate, citrus fruits, pork, eggs, and wheat. Your headache diary may point to one particular suspect—let's say it's chocolate. Try eating a lot of chocolate to see if your head begins to pound. Then, go cold turkey for a while. If your headaches disappear, you may have solved the case.

Headaches may also have multiple causes. Here are some other offenders to investigate:

☐ Airborne substances to which you're allergic. An allergist may have to assist you here.

☐ Vitamins. You may be taking too many, or too few. Discuss this possibility with your doctor.

☐ Food additives. Monosodium glutamate (MSG), found in Chinese food as well as in some canned and packaged goods, causes headaches in many people. Check food labels for it and other suspicious additives.

☐ Caffeine. Coffee, tea, chocolate, colas, and aspirin all contain caffeine. (Paradoxically, caffeine relieves the headaches of some sufferers. Also, eliminating caffeine cold-turkey often causes caffeine withdrawal headaches.)

☐ Muscle stiffness. Certain muscles in the neck and upper back contain trigger points for headaches. Do you tend to thrust your chin forward when driving, or in order to see out of your bifocals? Do you sleep on your stomach with your head always turned to the same side? Do you prop the telephone against a raised shoulder for long periods of time? Think about other things you do that might strain these key muscles.

☐ Hormones. If a woman's headaches invariably correspond with her monthly periods, she should consult her gynecologist.

☐ Low blood sugar. If this condition seems a possible culprit, try eating frequent small meals that are high in protein.

Finally, consider the role of stress. Stress usually is a contributing factor in headaches, even when it is not a primary cause. If your life is stressful, notice when you feel particularly tense and make a conscious attempt to relax.

Ever note how you get blue after eating a candy bar?

You have a sudden burst of energy at first, right? But twenty minutes later you feel fatigued and a little sad? If so, you may have trouble metabolizing sugar, and you should probably stay away from any candy, especially on an empty stomach.

If you're on the go and hungry, grab a protein snack such as cheese or yogurt. Pass up sweets until you've had a good-sized meal. If you're particularly sensitive to sugar but you're out to dinner and it's time for dessert, ask for a fruit cup, or order some ice cream. They're better choices than chocolate cream pie or chocolate mousse. There's also a high sugar level in alcohol, so drink moderately, and only on a full stomach.

Persons who get the "sugar blues" have difficulty maintaining a steady sugar level in their body. While they're satisfying their sweet tooth, their blood-sugar level is peaking. They experience immediate exhilaration, but then a rapid decline in the blood-sugar level follows, energy availability virtually goes on hold, and after a while they get a little depressed.

That's why it may not be a coincidence that many individuals feel down in the dumps during the holiday season. For those who don't metabolize sugar well, yuletide cheer filled with cakes, candies, and alcohol may trigger depression.

If you have this problem, hold off on all sweets and keep your blood-sugar level on a steady course.

Is a big lunch the answer to a skipped breakfast?

Of all possible ways to eat, this one is the worst. You're probably aware that going without breakfast is bad for you, but you probably don't know that a big midday meal doesn't even the score. Lunch is not a pick-me-up; it actually pulls your energy down.

A recent study found that a group of people who ate a large lunch lost as much efficiency when they returned to work as if they'd gone without a whole night's sleep. On the other hand, a separate ten-year study found that eating breakfast increases efficiency. Another study, of adolescents, found that kids do better in school when they eat breakfast.

Even so, more than half of all Americans in their twenties skip breakfast. If you're part of the no-breakfast generation, change your eating habits first thing tomorrow morning. Start off the day with a good breakfast, and, at midday, have a light lunch or, if possible, wait until you finish your important chores before you take a break to eat. In some jobs, maintaining your efficiency can be important to your safety.

Why is breakfast so important? When you wake up in the morning, you haven't eaten for eight to twelve hours. Your blood sugar and stored carbohydrates are low, and you may be short of other nutrients as well. Your morning meal "breaks" the "fast" and replaces the calories and nutrients you need to help keep you going all day. The calories are burned up quickly, faster than at any other time of the day.

The U.S. Department of Agriculture says that breakfast is so important that anything you have is better than nothing—even if you only drink a glass of juice. But you'll do yourself the biggest favor of all if you have a good breakfast. Why not try chicken livers, or a bowl of onion soup with cheese? The point is to eat foods that are rich in protein, such as leftover chicken, turkey, or meatloaf; sandwiches made with tuna or peanut butter; cheese and crackers, and raw vegetables.

Of course, the old standards—such as cereal and fruit—are still a good bet.

Can a lemon a day keep the doctor away?

It'll sure help to. Sometimes the old folk remedies are just as good as those you buy at the corner drugstore. Lemons, which are rich in vitamins C, B_1, and other necessary chemicals, are good for coughs and, because they also contain synephrin, act as decongestants, too.

A concoction of lemon juice may give you some of the same relief as do most of the 800-odd over-the-counter cough medications on the market. Just squeeze one lemon into four ounces of water. Add honey until it's sweet. Then chill with ice or in the freezer. When it's cold, sip the lemon juice through a straw.

As for the synephrin in lemons, if the compound sounds familiar it's because synephrin and a number of related compounds are the chemicals contained in commercial nasal sprays. But for *decongestant* power, drink your lemon juice *hot*.

Coughing is an involuntary reflex action caused by irritation in the bronchial tubes or the throat. It serves a protective function by loosening secretions. Although they're annoying, most coughs last no more than a week. For relief, if you don't have a lemon handy, you can also try a hot beverage, a hard candy, or a teaspoon of honey all by itself.

If your cough lasts longer than a week, call your doctor.

Is there hope for the chocolate freak?

There is a way to kick the habit: Chuck the chocolate and choose its taste-alike lookalike, carob, instead.

109

The best thing about carob is that it's actually good for you. It's rich in B vitamins and minerals. When you compare it to chocolate it really takes the cake:

CAROB VS. CHOCOLATE
1 Cup = 8 Ounces

CAROB		CHOCOLATE
252	Calories	1144
2 grams	Fat	120 grams
493	Calcium	103
1.13	Carbohydrates	120

(Statistics supplied by the American Health Foundation)

And carob has twice as much fiber, gram for gram, as chocolate and neither of chocolate's more serious drawbacks—caffeine and high calories.

Carob is dark brown like chocolate. But it's not a fruit, a vegetable, or an artificial conglomeration. Carob is a seed pod that grows on evergreen trees native to Mediterranean countries. Straight from the tree, carob has a leathery skin that's dry, brown, and flat. After the pod is picked, it's broken up into tiny pieces called kipple, and the seeds are removed. The kipple is then roasted and ground into powder.

The pod has a long and noble history. Roman legions thrived on it and John the Baptist took it into the desert. Carob even kept Wellington's cavalry going during the Peninsula Campaign.

You can find carob in health-food stores. It's available in several forms: bar, tablet, powder, wafer, and syrup. And it usually costs less than chocolate.

What's the most effective exercise of all?

Climbing stairs. In fact, the latest research shows that climbing stairs may be the most efficient way of all to burn up calories and strengthen the heart—no matter how much time you may have for jogging, cycling, swimming, racquetball, or just about any-

110

thing else Americans seem to be taking up to shape up. And a British study, for one, found that regularly climbing stairs was directly associated with a reduced risk of heart disease.

According to Dr. Kelly D. Brownell at the University of Pennsylvania School of Medicine, climbing stairs burns up 250 percent more calories than swimming for the same amount of time, 150 percent more than tennis, 150 percent more than bowling, 94 percent more than racquetball, 63 percent more than cycling, 23 percent more than running, and 400 percent more than walking at two miles per hour. That means, for example, a 175-pound man walking up stairs for ten minutes will burn 202 calories, while the same man running at a speed of seven miles an hour for ten minutes will burn up only 164 calories.

Dr. Brownell found that an overweight person can lose up to twelve pounds by climbing two flights of stairs a day for a year—provided, of course, that the climber doesn't eat more when he or she gets upstairs. Only strenuous activities such as dragging logs and sprinting seem to burn up more energy per minute than climbing stairs. And most importantly, regular stair climbing is also a beneficial augmentative exercise in a vigorous cardiovascular workout—but don't overdo it.

The real beauty of climbing stairs for exercise is that most persons can do it as part of their normal, daily routine. All they have to do is skip rides on elevators and escalators. There is no need to buy special shoes or clothes, or join a club. You can do your climbing in your home or office building or a department store. And, unlike joggers, you don't have to worry about traffic and snappish dogs.

Are you ever too old to swim or jog?

All other things considered, no. It used to be that older persons were advised to give up certain strenuous sports and begin to take it easy. But according to recent studies, physical activity is just as important for seniors as it is for juniors. Exercise actually helps prevent heart disease in individuals aged fifty through eighty. It also improves their overall vitality.

At the Andrus Gerontology Center of the University of Southern California, a group of retired men and women ranging in age from fifty-two to eighty-eight were recruited for a study of the effects of vigorous exercise. After thorough physical examinations, they plunged into a three-hour-a-week program that included walking, jogging, swimming, calisthenics, and stretching routines. Six weeks later, the seventy-year-olds, for one, reported that they felt twenty or thirty years younger.

Interest and participation in active recreation currently is blooming among older Americans. A survey of the leisure-time pursuits of retired business managers, for example, discloses that three-fourths of them enjoy sports regularly. The nonprofit National Senior Sports Association, recently founded in Washington, D.C., sponsors golf, tennis, bowling, and fishing tournaments specifically for persons aged fifty or older.

So, if you're a senior citizen, isn't it time for you to put your sneakers back on and join in the fun? The studies show clearly that exercise not only can add years to your life, but also life to those years.

If you're a rookie athlete, begin your exercise program on a moderate scale. Continuity is as important as the length and intensity of exercise, so don't let your enthusiasm flag. If you've never exercised at all, check with your doctor first before lifting a foot.

_____

When is exercise dangerous for you?

When it becomes an addiction. We've all heard about the benefits of keeping physically fit, but an increasing number of individuals push themselves to keep going long after they should stop. They continue an activity despite pain or nausea—to the point of utter exhaustion—are unable to maintain a normal weight, and become so fanatical that they will sacrifice time with their family or miss business appointments in order to follow a rigid exercise schedule.

Experts warn that such compulsive exercising can be just as bad for you as no exercise at all.

Particularly harmful is the reluctance of such exercisers to permit themselves an occasional day off. The body needs twenty-four hours without exercise about once a week in order to cleanse itself of lactic acid and other waste products of strenuous activity. Even hard-driving coaches and trainers advise professional athletes to loaf and take it easy one day a week.

Persons who engage in solitary endurance sports are the ones most likely to be afflicted—for example, joggers, long-distance swimmers, weight-lifters, and cross-country skiers. Occasionally, devotees of these activities set unreasonably ambitious goals and then drive themselves mercilessly to reach them. Like the woman who once was delighted to be able to run a mile several times a week, but now feels she must do ten miles daily in all kinds of weather. She is harming her health and hurting her family, too. A study of New York marathoners a few years ago found that their divorce rate—male and female—was twice the national average.

Except for some aches and pains when you first start to stretch flabby muscles, you should feel good after a work-out. Pain is your body's way of saying stop and relax for a while. One leading physical-education professor—Dr. Howard F. Hunt, chairman of the Department of Physical Education of the University of California at San Diego—even recommends that no one should exercise *strenuously* for more than an hour a day five or six times a week.

What does a female jock need that a male jock doesn't?

Iron. As a rule, a young woman ordinarily needs much more iron in her diet than a man—in fact, almost twice as much. But if she leads an active sports life, that need multiplies in an incredibly short amount of time.

After studying a group of co-eds who participated in an intensive nine-week athletic training program, researchers at the University of Iowa discovered that after two weeks of training, every one of the women suffered from iron deficiency. What's particularly significant about this study is that all the women were moderately fit, with no evidence of anemia, when they began the exercise program.

The risk for a less physically fit woman who suddenly decides she wants to whip herself into shape by exercising is obvious.

So, before you begin a regular exercise program—or if

you've already started one and are feeling unusually weary—see your doctor for a physical, including a blood test. (If you're over thirty-five, an electrocardiogram is a good idea, too.) Iron-deficiency anemia can usually be easily corrected by a proper diet. Beef, pork, fish, and poultry are all rich in iron; so are dark green vegetables such as spinach and broccoli, whole-grain cereals and bread products, dried beans, and dried fruits. Iron supplements in pill form are, of course, readily available. Avoid "fast foods"; they are generally low in iron.

Once your iron level is back to normal, you'll be able to swim, run, play tennis, even pump iron, safely.

Can calcium—and a chair—strengthen old bones?

Absolutely, even for the elderly whose bones have become so fragile that they fracture easily.

Until recently, bone weakening caused by osteoporosis was assumed to be (1) irreversible, (2) a part of the aging process, and (3) a condition that only affected very old persons. But all three assumptions are false:

☐ Bone fragility can be reversed. In a remarkable study, women in their eighties actually increased bone-mineral content significantly by sitting in chairs and doing simple exercises thirty minutes a day, three times a week. The exercises increased the flow of blood and filled the bones with fresh supplies of calcium.
☐ Bone weakening is not inevitable but rather the consequence of improper diet and lack of exercise.
☐ Bone weakening can begin in your twenties.

Although bones seem to be a part of our body that doesn't change, they are in reality constantly changing. The bones are a storehouse for minerals, expecially calcium. When other parts of the body use up their supply of minerals, a fresh supply is automatically sent from the bones. So it's important to replenish the bones by eating foods with enough calcium and by exercising to insure that the calcium reaches bones throughout the body.

The choice of exercise is up to you: swim, jog, play tennis, walk, or, like those women in their eighties, do chair exercises. The point is to stimulate circulation to bones throughout your body.

The exercises used in the study of the octogenarians entailed movement of the head, arms, knees, or legs. But you don't have to be in your eighties to benefit from them. The following four are a sampling of some ninety exercises possible. Start slowly. Do each exercise for fifteen seconds. As your endurance builds, work up to forty-five seconds. Sit in a straightback chair:

☐ Cross your arms in front of you; then swing them open as if to embrace someone; cross them in front again. Repeat the motion.

☐ Clasp your right knee with both hands, bring it to your chest. Repeat using your left knee.

☐ Extend both legs and rotate the feet clockwise, then counterclockwise.

☐ Walk in place as you sit in the chair. Move your legs one second at a time.

Exercise is only part of the story. We've all known that calcium builds strong bones in children, but now experts have discovered that large amounts of calcium are essential for maintaining strong bones throughout life. They recommend 1200 milligrams of calcium a day—the equivalent of a quart of milk. Calcium-rich foods that should be part of your regular diet are milk, yogurt, hard cheese, sardines, canned salmon (with bones), and leafy green vegetables.

And don't wait until you're fifty to start exercising and watching your calcium intake. A recent study shows that by the age of twenty-five, between 10 and 15 percent of the population has already suffered some bone weakening. Another shows that athletes, who of course are constantly exercising, not only have stronger muscles than nonathletes but also have stronger bones.

Women are especially susceptible to bone weakening. To begin with, their bones are less dense than those of men. Childbearing and breast-feeding deplete calcium. Later on, bone weakening accelerates during menopause because low estrogen levels mean that the body absorbs less calcium than it did earlier.

So if you're a woman, pay particular attention to enriching your regular diet with calcium. And be sure your diet is rich in calcium if you go on a diet to lose weight.

Are vitamins the be-alls?

The question is still being disputed by medical authorities, and the last word on the benefits or hazards of vitamins has not been written. But one thing they all agree on: An overdose of vitamins can be harmful. In extreme cases, it can be fatal. And so it's generally better to get the vitamins you need by eating a properly balanced diet rather than by taking vitamin supplements.

If a dose is large enough, vitamins stop acting like foods and start acting like drugs. The level at which a vitamin becomes dangerous varies from person to person. Certain vitamins, however, are known to be toxic when taken in large quantities. The vitamins to especially look out for are A, D, and E. They are not water soluble, and so are not excreted daily in urine. Instead, being fat soluble they build up in the body. An overdose can cause headaches, blurred vision, an impaired nervous system, and affect hormonal action and blood circulation.

Americans are vitamin happy. We spend well over $1 billion on them every year. A third of us take them regularly. But do we know what we're doing?

The Food and Drug Administration has established vitamin and mineral levels to meet our nutritional needs. They're referred to on the nutritional labels of food packages as the Recommended Daily Allowance (RDA). Some vitamin enthusiasts take ten or more times the RDA. That can be dangerous.

What nutrients help to reduce blood pressure?

Potassium for one—invisible, tasteless, but vital. Fortunately, a number of tasty foods contain potassium—bananas, unsalted peanuts, wheat bran, asparagus, lima beans, chicken, avocados, potatoes, spinach, tomatoes, lamb, cod, cantaloupes, salmon, oranges, tuna, and peaches.

Scientists have discovered a delicate balance between potassium, sodium, and blood pressure. With too much sodium, our bodies retain water, and our blood pressure increases. But when we lower our sodium intake while increasing potassium, blood pressure can be substantially reduced because potassium discourages the body from retaining water. For this reason, potassium is now recommended for women who suffer premenstrual swelling.

When hypertensive patients at the London Medical College were put on a low-sodium/high-potassium diet, their blood pressure dropped significantly within six weeks.

It's especially important to pay attention to potassium intake because canning and other processing eliminate almost all the potassium from foods. Stomach viruses and diuretics also deplete our body's supply.

Calcium is also a nutrient that may help to reduce blood pressure. According to a survey conducted by the University of Oregon Health Sciences Center, hypertensives ate 39 percent less dairy calcium and 22 percent less total calcium than normal individuals. The Oregon research team also found that increasing calcium from 0.5 percent to 4 percent in the diet of hypertensive rats dramatically curtailed their blood-pressure rise. The scientists observed that high-salt diets cause less hypertension when calcium intake is also high.

Good dairy calcium sources are ice cream, cheese, skim milk, and yogurt.

Because too little or too much calcium can have a detrimental effect, it's best to check with your doctor if you're contemplating a drastic change in your diet.

What can the Eskimos teach us about cholesterol?

Arteriosclerosis—hardening of the arteries—is not associated with the total amount of cholesterol in our blood, but rather with the kind. For example, Eskimos have a high fat intake but a low incidence of coronary heart disease. One reason is that they eat a lot of cold-water fish. Although their diet is high in cholesterol, it also contains a fatty acid, eicosapentaenoic acid (EPA), that may help prevent the build-up of fatty deposits in artery walls and prevent blood platelets from clumping. Cold-water fish obtain EPA by eating the one-cell marine animals that swarm in northern waters.

A team of doctors at the University of Oregon substituted fish oil for saturated vegetable oil in the diets of healthy volunteers. The results were impressive. Cholesterol levels dropped, triglycerides were lowered, and there was reduced clotting in the subjects' blood. And they were only on the fish-oil diet for four weeks.

Cold-water fish not only supply us with essential minerals, zinc, selenium, iron, and iodine, but may help lower blood cholesterol, too. They're also high in protein (a four-ounce serving normally provides about half the protein required each day). Three ounces of scallops, for example, contain only 80 mg. of cholesterol. On the other hand, one egg has 263 mg.

Cold-water fish include salmon, mackerel, flounder, halibut, sardines, shad, bluefish, pollock, haddock, perch, as well as scallops.

What's in a smell?

If you can't distinguish the fragrance of a flower from cigar smoke, or the freshness of a lemon from a cut onion, you don't need to be told how disturbing it is. But for some of the 15 million Americans who have lost their sense of smell, there is now good news.

One of the contributing factors to an impaired sense of smell in some people has been identified, and it is easily treatable. It's zinc deficiency. By adding large doses of that mineral to the diet, the deficiency can be quickly and easily corrected. Natural sources of zinc include whole grains, brewer's yeast, liver, and nuts.

One of the leading research centers in scent loss is at The Center for Molecular Nutrition and Sensory Disorders at the Georgetown University Medical Center in Washington, D.C. Individuals from across the country come to the center for help. Many have suffered for years from the loss of the sense of smell. Compounding their difficulty is the fact that this sensory loss often drastically reduces the capacity to taste foods. Furthermore, about a quarter of the patients also report decreased sexual pleasure since losing their sense of smell.

Such patients are first instructed to sniff from bottles presented in groups of three, then asked to identify the one bottle in

118

each group that contains a substance different from the other two. In this way, the extent of the scent loss of each individual can be measured. The keenness of a person's sense of taste is then tested by placing drops of sweet, sour, salty, and bitter liquids on their tongues.

In one out of three cases, the cause of the patient's difficulty was found to be a zinc deficiency. Another third of the patients were found to have abnormalities in the transmission of smell and taste sensations to the brain. Treatment with medication may gradually improve the problem.

In the last third, other reasons for the loss were discovered, such as a head injury, flu, or side effects of allergies or radiation treatment.

Because the loss of smell may be an indication of some larger health problem, your doctor should be consulted.

Do those old ladies in sneakers know something we don't?

Could be. They're walking, and the President's Council on Physical Fitness and Sports points out that three miles of *brisk* walking three or four days a week can have almost the same cardiovascular effect as three miles of jogging. That's especially good news for men and women over sixty, most of whom might be taking a big risk trying to begin any more strenuous form of exercise at that age. Walking is also a perfect way to exercise for younger persons with a long history of inactivity, problems with obesity, or a general aversion to strenuous activity of any kind. And, of course, there are no special body movements to learn. During a normal lifetime, each of us will log an estimated 70,000-plus miles on foot—the equivalent of about three round-the-world trips.

A regular regimen of brisk walking can achieve the same results that more demanding forms of exercise, such as jogging and swimming, do by strengthening the cardiovascular system and muscles, building tone and endurance, controlling weight, aiding digestion and elimination, and relieving tension.

In a study at Wake Forest University in North Carolina, sedentary men aged from forty to fifty-seven were put on a twenty-week walking program in order to test the effects of walking on body composition and the heart, which are considered the two key factors in physical fitness. Each man walked about forty minutes four times a week. The distance was gradually increased from about 2.5 miles to 3.2 miles. By the end of the program, all the participants had lost between two and three pounds (all fat), and their resting heart rates had dropped several points, a sure sign of a stronger ticker. The results equaled the fitness gains of a thirty-minute, three-day-a-week jogging program.

For the older exerciser, Dr. Michael Pollack, who directed the study, suggests a slower start; the same is true for anyone, no matter the age, who has been inactive for a long time. One other important requirement for any senior walker: a physical examination before starting the program.

Once your doctor declares you fit enough to begin the walking program, take it slow and easy. Walk two or three blocks and then rest. In fact, always rest when you feel tired. After a few weeks, build up your speed gradually until you are able to cover a mile in fifteen to twenty minutes. The key to success in any exercise program is keeping to it. Set realistic goals so that you won't become discouraged by your progress.

A tip: Your feet will be pounding the pavement more than 400 times a mile, so comfortable, cushioned footwear is crucial. Your best bet is a jogging shoe. Forget tennis shoes, which are made for side-to-side movement and flexibility. In jogging, and walking, your feet are moving heel to toe in one direction. The key is a stable shoe with a cushioned heel, such as a jogging shoe.

Should a diabetic exercise?

If you're a diabetic and you bicycle after breakfast, you might be able to cut down on your insulin intake. The same holds true for other similarly strenuous exercises such as running, swimming, and tennis.

There are more than 5 million diabetics in this country who cannot metabolize the sugar and starch in foods because their bodies are unable to manufacture enough insulin. When insulin is insufficient, or totally lacking, sugar accumulates in the blood.

Many diabetics need to have at least daily injections of artificial insulin.

However, according to several studies, diabetics who exercise regularly have lower insulin requirements than those who don't. In one study, diabetics who bicycled after breakfast required significantly less amounts of insulin. The doctors who conducted the study suggest that the reason cycling works is because exercise alters muscle cells so that sugar levels in the blood decrease, and thus less insulin is needed.

Based on their research, the doctors believe that postmeal exercise "is a valuable adjunct to the treatment of diabetes."

Regular exercise is also important for diabetics because it helps prevent obesity—a common side effect of diabetes—and maintains muscle tone.

Because insulin dosages vary among patients, it's crucial that diabetics consult their doctor before beginning any exercise routine.

Do children need milk?

Not at all after they're twelve months old. Contrary to popular opinion, it is really not necessary for a child over that age to drink milk. In fact, shunning milk may even make the child healthier.

Milk is exceptionally filling and can decrease appetite. Parents often think it's all right if their children don't eat a meal, as long as they finish their milk. But if milk is the staple of the diet, a host of nutrients will be missing. The American Medical Association warns that those who drink too much milk—more than three cups a day—may neglect other necessary foods. It suggests an increase in vegetables, especially dark green and yellow ones such as spinach and turnips, and whole grains or enriched cereals.

And if you're worried about calcium, 1½ ounces of Cheddar cheese, a cup of yogurt, 3 ounces of salmon, or a cup of those dark green vegetables have the same amount of calcium as a cup of milk.

The fact is that growing children who drink an excess of milk and, as a result, neglect their meals are more likely to be anemic. Anemic children have twice as many respiratory problems as normal children. It's a vicious cycle. An anemic child often dislikes the very foods that would cure the anemia—and instead chooses to drink milk. Unfortunately, milk lacks iron, and the anemia gets worse.

Milk is also a common allergen. About 15 percent of all babies are sensitive to milk and dairy products and require a substitute. Milk can be responsible not only for respiratory ailments but also for intestinal, skin, and urinary difficulties. And milk is constipating.

After that first birthday, introduce the youngster to new foods, one at a time, and in small amounts. Milk should be your toddler's sideshow, not the main event, at mealtime.

What bean takes the cake?

The humble soybean. It's as nutritionally complete as a food can be, as well as inexpensive. Best of all, it may also help to reduce harmfully high cholesterol levels.

As part of an experiment, adults who ordinarily ate foods high in fat content were put on a soybean diet. Within only a few weeks, their cholesterol levels dropped an average of twenty percent.

Scientists say that what the soybean accomplished in only a few weeks would have taken an ordinary low-fat dieter months to achieve. The soybean acts as a double-fisted fat fighter. It contains lecithin, a natural fat emulsifier. In addition, it contains a high amount of fiber.

The soybean is a rich source of protein, B complex vitamins, calcium, phosphorus, potassium, magnesium, and iron. It has ten times the calcium of meat and twice that of eggs. Soybean oil contains large amounts of linoleic acid, an unsaturated fatty acid that's essential to the human body, as well as vitamins E and K. Soy milk is often recommended for those who are allergic to cow's milk. It's low in fat and carbohydrates but rich in iron, thiamine, and niacin.

For vegetarians, the soybean holds a special place of honor. Its exceptionally high level of protein often puts it center stage on the dinner menu. There's soybean sweet potato pie, soyburgers, soy grits, soybean patés. Use soy oil for frying. Soy flour and granules may be added to all kinds of food and baked goods, boosting their nutritional value. For a healthy fast-food snack, roast the beans.

Who knows better what a one-year-old should eat— the child or the parent?

Definitely the child. All children seem to have an uncanny ability to eat the foods they actually need.

Between the ages of one and two, children tend to get finicky about food. A terrific little eater suddenly won't eat anything, or only meat today and carrots tomorrow. It drives parents crazy; they think their youngster will starve to death. But such mealtime behavior, pediatricians say, is quite normal. As Dr. Benjamin Spock puts it, "If he kept eating and gaining the way he did when he was a little baby, he'd turn into a mountain."

In a landmark study that has been confirmed many times, Dr. Clara Davis picked three babies, eight to ten months old, who had never had anything but their mother's milk. She proceeded to feed the babies up to eight varieties of food: eggs, cereals, vegetables, fruits, meats, milk, water, fruit juices, and whole-grain bread. The babies had to signal their interest in a particular food before anyone would feed them. If, for example, a baby stuck a finger in some carrots, a nurse would give the infant a spoonful of carrots. If the child's fist went into the cereal, that was dinner.

After studying the children over a period of time, Dr. Davis found that babies who chose their own diet from a variety of natural foods developed quite normally, neither getting too fat nor too thin. The children's appetites varied from meal to meal, day to day. Binges on particular foods were quite common. One day a baby ate six hard-boiled eggs on top of a full meal; another child downed a quart of milk at one meal. Eventually, every baby managed to choose what any expert would agree was a well-balanced diet. Dr. Davis carried out similar experiments with many older children and achieved the same general results.

So let your child eat whatever is wanted. If the youngster cleans the plate, offer praise. But never coax the child into eating anything. Don't bribe with desserts. And don't play games such as choo-chooing the spoon into the baby's mouth. The child will interpret that as a reward for not eating.

One other tip: If you are a smoker, forget the cigarettes at baby's mealtime. A recent study found that infants are so sensitive to the smell of nicotine that it can inhibit them from eating.

Remember to review your child's diet with the pediatrician. Too much juice or milk regularly can be harmful, and the lack of foods containing iron may lead to anemia.

Wanna bet milk is good for ulcers?

You lose. Your best bet, if you're one of the 30 million Americans with ulcers, is to drop milk entirely but eat frequent, small meals of starchy foods such as bread, baked potatoes, rice, pasta, and eggs. And when your ulcer is acting up, avoid aspirin, foods with caffeine, and alcohol.

The medical community used to think milk could act as a neutralizer of the stomach's acid secretion. (Oversecretion of acid in the stomach's gastric juices is associated with some ulcers.) But a study—done at the Veterans Administration Hospital in Los Angeles in conjunction with the University of California at Los Angeles School of Medicine—turned up some surprising results. It showed that milk produces a considerable increase in acid secretion and discomfort in ulcer patients.

The researchers discovered that the protein in milk stimulates stomach-acid secretion. Medical experts also hypothesized that the calcium in milk might also contribute to the stomach's irritation.

The symptoms of an ulcer include pain—usually in the upper abdomen or just under the breastbone—that starts between meals or on an empty stomach. There's usually no sense of discomfort in the morning before breakfast, but the pain is most frequently felt late at night, between 1 and 3 A.M. It has been described as a "sharp burning or boring pain," rather than a dull, aching cramp. Because stomach acid peaks about ninety minutes after eating, frequent eating fights its effect—and the smallness of the meal helps to control weight.

While many mild ulcers respond to dietary therapy alone, there are good drugs available if medicine is necessary. One of the newer ones, called Cimetidine, inhibits the secretion of gastric acid and has proved so effective that the frequency of surgical operations for intractable ulcers has dropped dramatically in the United States since its introduction a few years ago.

What one food is weight, health, and budget wise?

Tofu. If you want to cut down on calories, lower cholesterol, eat less meat, save a fortune on grocery bills, and fill up on something that's as versatile as a food can be, try it.

Tofu is soybean curd. When it's plain it looks like a white, opaque cube. The soft variety has the texture of egg custard, and the firm kind is more like cheese.

There's nothing new about tofu. It's been around Asia for centuries. It's a Japanese food staple. And now tofu is appearing in markets throughout the United States.

There's good reason for tofu's success. Tofu contains 50 percent protein, while lean prime beef contains only 20 percent. Soy has all eight essential amino acids, required B vitamins, fat-soluble E vitamins, and 23 percent more calcium than whole milk. It's also rich in iron, phosphorus, potassium, and sodium, but contains virtually no saturated fats. It is also low in calories. One 200-gram patty of tofu has only 147 calories, while a comparable 200-gram sirloin steak has 760.

Tofu is also incredibly versatile. In fact, it is known as "the food of 10,000 flavors" because it absorbs the flavor of whatever you cook it with. You can blend tofu in a salad dressing; mash it so it resembles cottage cheese or cream cheese and use it to make a low-calorie cheesecake; slice and fry it with spices; scramble it like eggs with some onion, browned turmeric, cumin, and ground coriander.

Tofu even makes an excellent replacement for cheese or meat in pizza, lasagna, tacos, or hamburger. If you have a sweet tooth, it can be used to make frosting, ice cream, puddings, and cookies.

Whet your appetite? You can buy tofu at most health food stores and greengrocers. And it's probably well within your food budget—less than 50 cents a patty.

How can you lower cholesterol, lose weight, and get vitamins from a lamb chop?

By cooking with steam. Steaming renders the fat from meat, leaving it in the water to be discarded. The conventional cooking methods—broiling, baking, and frying—cook the fat back into the meat. Because steaming gets rid of fat, the meat is lower in calories and cholesterol. And you can steam any kind of meat—steak, pork, chicken, or lamb.

Steaming vegetables has been a popular way to cook for some time. It preserves the fiber, color, and flavor of vegetables as well as the B vitamins—riboflavin, thiamine, niacin, biotin, B_{12}, pantothenic acid—vitamin C, and the minerals—calcium, iron, phosphorus, potassium, and zinc.

All you need to steam meat or vegetables is an inexpensive steaming basket, colander, or strainer and a large pot.

Prop the steaming basket in the pot. Cut up the vegetables or meat into bite-sized pieces just before cooking. Rinse and dry them quickly. Then add about an inch of water to the pot. You can flavor the water with salt, lemon juice, garlic, fresh herbs, peppercorns, or bouillon. Or substitute wine for water to make a sauce from the reduced broth. Bring the pot to a boil before adding the vegetables. Then cover the pot. Reduce the heat and cook over a medium flame for a few minutes.

What's the one food that helps you diet, "cures" a cold, and keeps you healthy?

It's soup. The healthiest individuals—those without any nutritional deficiencies—have one thing in common: According to two large-scale government surveys of the dietary habits of more than 100,000 persons across the country, they all eat a lot of soup.

Soups are healthy because they retain fat-soluble vitamins A, D, and E, which are often lost in cooking other foods. They also may contain a variety of foods, especially beans, meat, poultry, or fish, and thus they usually have a substantial amount of protein.

Soups can also help you keep your weight down. In a separate study of one thousand women conducted by the Institute of Behavior Education in Pennsylvania, it was found that those who included soup with lunch consumed fewer calories not only during lunchtime, but throughout the rest of the day as well.

Behavior scientists say soup helps you to lose weight by forcing you to practice better eating habits. You can't eat soup on the run, as you can a sandwich. Generally, you have to sit down and eat it slowly, paying attention to how you spoon it. According to their theory, you eat less and lose weight when you slow down the rate of eating and increase your involvement with food.

And that's not all soups can do for you. Chicken soup *can* help you get over a cold or bronchitis.

Dr. Maurice Sackner, chief of medicine at the Mount Sinai Medical Center, Miami, Fla., reports that mucus cleared from the nasal passages of a number of his patients at the rate of 9.2 millimeters a minute just five minutes after they ate chicken soup. Hot water clears passages at a rate of 8.4, cold water at 5.3.

The Medical Center of the University of California at Los Angeles recommends chicken soup for both a cold or bronchitis, especially if the soup contains plenty of pepper, garlic, even curry powder. The spices affect the body like an expectorant. A bowl of hot, spicy chicken soup can break up the congestion you feel in your throat and chest. The center suggests a dose every thirty minutes for maximum benefit.

Can a pinch of oregano bring back youth?

It can't bring back youth, but it can certainly perk up old age. A major problem among the elderly is poor nutrition. And the solution may be no farther away than the kitchen spice rack.

Proper nutrition is just as important as we get older, yet studies have shown that one out of every three older Americans may not be getting the calories and nutrients, including vitamins and minerals, they need. This includes protein, calcium, iron, several B vitamins, vitamins C and D, and fiber.

The problem, according to a Duke University study, is that our senses of smell and taste may weaken or distort with age. Elderly persons in the study often complained of a bitter flavor in foods. But when the same fare was given to students, the

127

young persons thought the food tasted fine. Even foods such as chocolate, which once tasted sweet, appeared bitter to some of the elderly.

Other times, foods may taste bland or have no taste at all. For example, only 55 percent of the elderly subjects could identify the taste of an apple.

The result: The elderly may lose their appetite and stop eating the foods they need to stay healthy.

To perk up tastebuds and increase appetites, researchers suggest senior citizens take to sprinkling foods with digestible seasonings such as oregano, ginger, dill, cinnamon, paprika, allspice, vinegar, minced onion, and lemon. All help to make flavors distinguishable and food more appealing.

But stay away from salt; it may be associated with blood pressure and cardiac problems. Also avoid seasonings such as red pepper, curry powder, and any mustard, all of which can irritate the stomach.

Adding a little spice to a senior citizen's diet can add spice to life, too.

Can cauliflower and cabbage reduce the need for medication?

Yes, if they're eaten raw.

Researchers have found that some diabetic patients can significantly reduce their need for insulin when their diet is mostly raw foods. Scientists suggest one reason may be that raw foods contain useful enzymes that are destroyed when the foods are cooked. Another factor may be that raw food has more undigestible fiber and therefore less digestible carbohydrates per serving. Because there's less carbohydrate in the meal, the pancreas may not be required to supply as much insulin.

What's more, there's been a negative correlation found between the intake of raw foods in the diet and the incidence of stomach cancer. Doctors attribute this to the high fiber content and quick "transit time" of uncooked foods through the digestive tract. A diet of mostly raw foods passes through the tract in eighteen to twenty-four hours, while a diet of mostly cooked foods can take up to three times longer.

Nutritionally speaking, eating cauliflower raw rather than cooked will supply your body, ounce for ounce, with more potassium, calcium, iron, thiamine, niacin, and vitamin C. A 3½-ounce serving of uncooked spinach provides 20 percent more vitamin C than the same amount boiled. Raw peanuts contain more than three times the thiamine that the roasted variety has. And these examples are the rule, not the exception.

Raw foods include carrots, celery, cabbage, sprouts, broccoli, endive, spinach, cauliflower, lettuce, cucumber, peas, and stringbeans, as well as all fruits, including berries. Honey, nuts, and seeds—poppy, pumpkin, sesame, and sunflower, for example—are also nutritional raw.

If you're diabetic, ask your doctor about adding raw foods to your diet. And do not make any changes without your doctor's approval.

Is decaffeinated coffee the answer?

According to studies done at the Center for Ulcer Research and Education in California, the answer is an emphatic No! If you have an ulcer and you're trying to limit your intake of caffeine, decaffeinated coffee could be your worst enemy.

In the California study, certain foods and beverages were compared as to their effect on the output of harmful gastric acids. The effects of decaffeinated coffee were compared to those of peptone, a product of protein digestion until then considered the strongest stimulant of acid secretion in the stomach. The subsequent analysis of stomach contents disclosed that drinking decaffeinated coffee produced more gastric acids than peptone did.

Earlier studies had already shown that the stomach acids produced by drinking decaffeinated coffee aren't much lower than those produced by regular coffee.

Ulcer sufferers are advised to avoid caffeinated beverages whenever possible. If you're one and can't get started in the morning without a cup of coffee, there's an alternative. Eat something first, then drink a cup of weak tea instead. It has less caffeine than coffee.

If you're trying to cut down on caffeine, it's better to taper off gradually than to go cold turkey. Rapid or sudden withdrawal from caffeine can result in symptoms that include anxiety, muscle tension, irritability, headache, and lethargy.

Should sex be all work and no play?

If you're having sex more and enjoying it less, it could be because you're trying too hard. The current emphasis on the how-to's of sex has prompted many couples to concentrate on technique. They read about averages of frequency of intercourse and orgasm in magazine surveys and sex manuals—and then worry how they themselves rate.

As sex researchers Virginia Masters and Dr. William H. Johnson have pointed out, any time you begin to evaluate your or your partner's performance you inhibit your ability to respond, emotionally and physically. You become, in effect, a spectator of your own sexual behavior. And the more observing and worrying you do, the greater the risk of creating something to really worry about. Thus, the man with periodic problems of erection becomes consistently impotent. Or the woman who feels she must reach orgasm every time she has sex tries so hard that she finds even her ability to be aroused disrupted.

For too many people, sex has become work—or a competitive sport. They are too concerned with producing arousal or orgasm. Sex, however, is supposed to be spontaneous and caring. We all work hard enough. Why make sex just another job?

Shouldn't a heart-attack victim abandon sex?

Absolutely not. The notion that one's sex life is over after a heart attack is a myth. Medical experts agree that there are no physiological reasons why the majority of heart-attack victims, male and female, cannot resume a satisfactory sexual relationship.

Unfortunately, many doctors still help perpetuate the myth by not properly counseling patients about the do's and don't's of sex following release from the hospital. "Take it easy" is hardly the sort of comment that will make heart-attack victims, or their

130

spouses, confident about their sexual future. Studies have shown that most sexual problems experienced by heart-attack victims—and many have difficulties, including lack of sexual response or impotence—are because of the lack of information and the fear of another heart attack, rather than any organic medical complication. Sexual intercourse is no more strenuous than ordinary household activities such as climbing a few flights of stairs.

But one warning: Don't resume sex after a heart attack without consulting your cardiologist. What the doctor will recommend will vary with the severity of the heart attack. On request, most cardiologists will give sexual advice to both partners the day the patient leaves the hospital. It is important that both spouse and patient know it is not dangerous to resume sex.

Most cardiologists suggest starting slowly, by holding hands or caressing. Within two or three months—and after a checkup—you can usually resume sexual relations.

Is there a way to say "no" to sex?

Yes. Tell the truth. For starters, forget the line, "Not tonight, I have a headache." By now it's a tired joke and likely to cause resentment. Still, too many men and women have considered illness the only legitimate reason for passing up sex. But there are other reasons—*good* reasons—for sometimes saying "No."

Sexual appetites are bound to vary, even between the most happy and intimate couples. All sorts of things can stifle sexual desire: a fight with the boss, fatigue, too much tension, hormonal changes, even real headaches. In fact, sometimes a headache can be the symptom of sexual problems between a couple—anxiety about sex, say, or even chronic resentment toward a partner. Such psychological states, doctors point out, can often induce physiological reactions, such as contraction of scalp and neck muscles, that may bring on a headache.

If you find that the prospect of sex inevitably does bring on a headache, you are going to need more than aspirin to set things right. Seriously consider seeking professional help from a therapist or marriage counselor.

For those whose relationships are fine but who still don't always feel like making love when their partner does, therapists advise that you should never be afraid to say no. But be honest. If you've had a rough day with the children or at the office or are just plain tired, tell your partner. The more candid you are about a sensitive matter like sex, the less likely your partner will get the wrong impression or feel slighted. Communication is crucial to any relationship, and you may discover that talking problems over and leveling with your partner just might work wonders for your sex life.

What does your medicine chest have to do with sudden sexual problems?

An entire array of medications—both prescription and over-the-counter—can cause temporary impotence and loss of sexual desire in both men and women. The medications can be those used to control high blood pressure, drugs to promote weight loss, tranquilizers, antidepressants, and drugs for lowering cholesterol. Even decongestants and antihistamines have been reported to produce sexual problems because of their drying effects.

What can you do if you develop a sexual problem and it is coincidental with beginning a new medication? First, discuss it with your doctor. Few people do. They're embarrassed by their sexual problems, believing that somehow it's their fault. They suffer in silence, assuming the worst—they're getting too old, they have a serious illness, or they're subconsciously troubled by a deep-seated psychological problem.

Just knowing it's not you but rather the medication can be enormously reassuring. But there are also some concrete recommendations your doctor can make. He or she may be able to lower the dosage or prescribe another drug that may not have the same effect on you. Some drugs cause sexual dysfunction in half the persons who use them; others cause the reaction only in rare cases. It's difficult to predict, so be patient. It may take some trial and error before the doctor and you find the drug with the least side effects.

Sexual problems caused by medications are completely reversible once you stop taking the drug. Also, if you are required to take a drug for a long period of time, your body may adjust to the medication, reducing the side effects. The key point to remember is that the medication is probably the cause, not some hidden problem, and that in many cases your doctor will be able to help you.

Male sexuality after sixty: To bed or not to bed?

There are things people may have to give up with age—fancy food, strong drink—but sex is not one of them. Doctors agree that people can lead an active sex life as long as they're healthy. The notion that the elderly—male or female—are sexually inactive is a myth.

Studies have found that 70 percent of healthy married couples over sixty years old are sexually active, some even into the late eighties. Because sexual arousal is slower in older men, their sexual activity tends to be more leisurely—and, hence, more satisfying. Together with experience and sophistication, this means that sex can even get better with age.

What about the so-called "male menopause" that's been talked about? Recent findings from the National Institute of Aging demonstrate that, as far as hormones are concerned, the idea of male menopause is largely exaggerated. Male hormone levels drop somewhat during the late twenties, but they level off at about the age of thirty and may stay at that level for the rest of a man's life.

The frequency of sexual activity does tend to go down with age, but that is more than offset by the greater closeness that many couples report when they get older and after their children have left home.

Is there sex after arthritis?

Not only can rheumatoid arthritis sufferers have sex—surprising as that may seem to those in constant pain—but also the very act of sex, doctors have discovered, seems to provide relief from pain in severe cases.

There are about 20 million people with arthritis in the Unit-

133

ed States, and the majority of them are women. As anyone with severe arthritis knows, the disease attacks, and sometimes destroys, the body's joints, particularly in the knee, hip, and lower back. The joints stiffen, and the pain can become almost intolerable. A sufferer usually shuns sexual intercourse because it's extremely painful for the hips, legs, and back.

Unfortunately, doctors have not generally been very helpful to the victims of arthritis when it comes to the topic of sex. But arthritis experts and the Arthritis Foundation are increasingly getting the word out: Sex is good for it.

After interviewing hundreds of rheumatoid arthritis sufferers, Dr. John Erlich, an arthritis specialist in Philadelphia, found that 70 percent of the victims reported they experienced less arthritis pain after sex. It's suspected that the reason the pain abates is that sexual arousal stimulates the adrenal glands to produce more cortisone in the body, and cortisone reduces inflammation—the cause of pain in the affected joints.

Because sexual arousal is the key, actual intercourse is not necessary to get relief from arthritic pain. Sexual stimulation of any kind seems to lead to the production of cortisone.

For more information on sex and arthritis, including advice on various body positions, write to:

The Arthritis Foundation,
Lenox P.O. Box 18888,
Atlanta, Ga. 30326.

What is every man's secret fear?

Few things are more upsetting to a normal, healthy man who enjoys a good sex life than to find that he is becoming impotent, unable to achieve or sustain an erection. It's a dilemma faced by an estimated 10 million American men.

Can anything be done for them, and if so, what? Until very recently, most doctors estimated that 90 to 95 percent of all cases of impotence were psychological in origin, that is, the problem was emotional. And treatment often began on a psychiatrist's couch.

But more and more, doctors are finding that many cases of impotence, perhaps half, have physical causes. And these prob-

134

lems can be treated. For example, a recent study of 105 impotent men found that 37 of them had disorders of the endocrine system, a network of glands that govern sexual potency, among other things. When the disorder was treated, 33 of the 37 regained potency.

Disorders of the endocrine system include thyroid dysfunction, testicular failure, and pituitary tumors. Illnesses such as prostate-gland infection and blood-vessel disease can also play a role. So can surgery or spinal injury.

And then there's the influence of drugs and medication. Alcohol can bring on impotence and so can tranquilizers, antidepressants, and drugs used to fight high blood pressure. Impotence may also be a sign of diabetes.

The message is clear. Impotence can certainly be brought on by tension, stress, or anxiety, but the ailment is not necessarily all in a man's head. It may be embarrassing to talk about, but a visit to the family doctor or a urologist could disclose that the problem is physical—and treatable.

Is infertility reversible?

Yes, in some cases. New treatments—including such widely publicized advances as microsurgery and frozen sperm banks—are making parenthood possible for more couples than ever before.

Statistical studies show that infertility is increasing. Fifteen years ago, approximately one couple in ten was unable to procreate. Today the percentage is one in six. Part of the increase is attributable to the rising number of men and women who have venereal diseases. A few women develop ovulation difficulties after they have used an oral contraceptive. And a few who use an IUD may have suffered pelvic infections or scarring. And both men and women who have postponed parenthood suffer slight fertility decreases with age.

Some couples panic when, after trying to conceive for a few months, nothing happens. But, actually, nearly 40 percent of all couples fail to conceive in the first six months of trying to do so. Doctors advise would-be parents to wait a year before they conclude that they have a problem and seek professional help from a fertility specialist. However, if either partner is older than thirty, they shouldn't wait longer than six months before visiting a specialist. Human fertility gradually declines after that age, and time, therefore, is a factor.

It's important that both husband as well as wife see the physician, because each is about equally likely to have some problem that contributes to infertility. Interestingly, a substantial number of patients conceive within two months after the first consultation, before any treatment is started. Because the emotions affect the reproductive system greatly, couples troubled about infertility often are anxious, guilty, and angry. Such feelings can upset delicate hormonal balances, hamper sperm production and potency, and disrupt the peristalsis, or movements, of the fallopian tubes. With the support and encouragement of a doctor, such couples often relax—and succeed.

After a battery of tests that may take months to complete, fertility specialists are able to make a definite diagnosis of the cause of infertility in nine out of ten cases. Diagnosis usually begins with an evaluation of each partner's emotional, physical, and nutritional status. In addition, instruction in the proper timing of sex and in intercourse positions that promote impregnation is provided. The woman is ordinarily advised not to use a douche.

Some of the abnormalities that interfere with female fertility—such as vaginal infections, venereal disease, and polyps—are relatively simple to treat. New hormonal drugs that stimulate ovulation are highly effective. In addition, microsurgery to open a blocked fallopian tube is also often successful. (The amazing fertilization of egg by sperm in a test tube—which is then transplanted into the woman's uterus—is useful when both the ovaries and the uterus are functioning normally though the fallopian tubes are blocked.)

There are also some therapies available for men. Doctors will often advise a man to build up his general health and to avoid wearing tight-fitting clothes or taking hot baths, both of which may discourage sperm development. Artificial insemination with a husband's sperm or that of a donor (when the husband is impotent or has a low sperm count) is another option today.

The progress of modern science has now made it possible for more than half of those couples whose infertility is diagnosed to become parents. For many of them, a baby is truly an impossible dream come true.

Does menopause mean no sex?

For the majority of women, menopause causes no disruption in sexual relations. The hormonal and other changes taking place in her body need not affect a woman's desire for sex or her capacity to experience pleasure.

In fact, many women report increased desire for sexual activity during this time of their lives. The Kinsey study of female sexuality showed that 20 percent experienced heightened interest in sex *after* menopause. Several practical matters may be responsible for this upsurge. For one, a couple may find more opportunity for relaxed private times together once their children have grown up and left home. Then, too, sex relations may be freer and more spontaneous than ever before because fear of pregnancy is a thing of the past.

A word about birth control. Menopause is not a single event but a process that takes place over about fifteen years—from about the ages of forty-five to sixty. Nearly half of all women are still fertile at the age of fifty. The first missed period is definitely not a signal to abandon birth-control measures. Experts advise that if a woman is under fifty, she and her partner should continue to use contraception for two years after her last period. Over fifty, one year without menstruation is long enough. (Incidentally, women past the age of forty should not take the pill, especially if they are heavy smokers, because oral contraceptives increase the risk of heart disease and stroke.)

So, forget whatever myths you may have heard about negative effects of "the change" on sexual relations. More likely than not, the only change you will notice is one for the better.

For the single parent only: How do you manage a sex life?

By keeping your sex life private. Being a single parent is never easy, but sex is one of the most thorny problems of living on your own with a child. How do you manage a normal social and sex life? How much should the child know about it? When should you introduce the new man (or woman) in your life?

The first thing to keep in mind is that no matter how much you sense that your child would prefer you to remain unattached, you do have a right to live your own life. After all, your happiness is important to the child's happiness, and it won't hurt to point that out.

Family therapists advise all single parents to keep their sex lives private. A child who sees you going casually from one sexual, intimate relationship to another may become anxious and confused—and believe that there is no such thing as a serious commitment between two adults. There's also the risk that the more partners your child sees you with, the less likely the youngster is going to take any one of them seriously. Why bother getting close to a person if chances are next week there will be someone else in mom or dad's life?

Research has shown that children of single parents are inclined to be quite anxious about separation. Every child needs a stable, constant person—a sense of security. You, the single parent, are it.

When you think you've finally developed a steady and good relationship, then by all means involve your child in it, too. But don't expect too much too fast. Children who have lost a parent through death or divorce may not be too quick to accept a new member to the household.

Be patient. It has probably taken you a while to get to know your new partner. Give your child a chance to get to know that person, too.

Will talk about sex put ideas in a teenager's head?

Some parents worry that discussing sex with their teenage children will lead to promiscuity, but research shows that the opposite is true.

The Institute for Family Research and Education at Syracuse University in New York reports that teenagers who are better informed about sexual matters have lower incidences of unwanted pregnancy and venereal disease. Furthermore, adolescents whose parents discussed sex freely and easily with them were less likely to have intercourse at an early age.

138

Family studies show that when a young person's sexual questions are met with parental silence, an air of mystery may follow that makes sexual behavior all the more enticing. Teenagers sometimes interpret parental silence as a form of rejection and use their own sexual behavior in retaliation.

Children begin to ask questions about sex and reproduction almost as soon as they notice the difference between girls and boys. They should be answered clearly and simply. Discussing sex doesn't necessarily mean that you're encouraging sexuality, but a refusal to answer questions may have results that last a lifetime.

By the age of puberty, youngsters are ready for specific answers. And a parent is more often than not the best person to provide them.

However, if you feel awkward or uncomfortable about discussing sex with your children, you're not alone. Here's what child psychologists suggest to help you through those sticky moments:

☐ Don't wait to be asked. Bring up the subject yourself. Be alert to special occasions when sex can be talked about comfortably.

☐ Be serious about your children's requests for information. Don't laugh if a lot of what they believe is wrong.

☐ Don't preach. Be conversational.

☐ Don't assume a child's questions are personal. (If your daughter wants to know how a woman becomes pregnant, it doesn't mean she thinks she is.)

☐ Don't expect your children to accept your opinions automatically. Respect their views and discuss them.

☐ Take sexual subjects one at a time. Your youngster may not be able to digest more than that.

☐ Be truthful. Intentional misinformation can destroy your credibility later.

☐ Don't pretend to know everything. If you can't answer a question, admit it. But suggest someone who does know the answers. Usually that'll be the family doctor.

Parental attitudes about sex are more important than you may realize. Adolescents may never say so, but they want to know what their parents think, especially about sex. So, don't hesitate to express your opinion and explain your own values.

139

Can a baby get depressed?

Definitely, yes. But unlike an older child, or an adult, the infant cannot express it. Instead, as experts are finding, psychological problems in babies can show up as colic, rashes, respiratory or bowel problems, listlessness, or simply "failure to thrive." A good baby is not necessarily a quiet baby. And though we all are aware that a baby cries when it wants something, we're now learning that the infant's silence can also be a cry for attention.

To help troubled babies, special Infant Psychiatric Clinics in major hospitals across the country are now diagnosing and treating infants as young as two weeks old. The earlier the diagnosis and treatment, the greater the chance the baby will grow to be a healthy and happy youngster.

During the first two months of life, a healthy baby will develop a deep attachment to one parent, normally the mother, and establish regular eating and sleeping patterns. In addition, the infant will begin to interact with the environment. By the third month, the normal baby will smile. The stages of infant development, of course, vary a great deal. But if an infant does not pass through any of these normal stages, psychiatrists will suspect that the infant is disturbed. The next step is to discover the cause.

First, the possibility of a physical illness is checked through a series of tests, usually administered by the baby's pediatrician, and these are followed by comprehensive muscle coordination and responsiveness tests. Once a physical difficulty is eliminated as the source of the problem, the psychiatrists will observe the interaction between the mother and the child. Is it warm and trusting? Does she feel comfortable with her baby? Does she cuddle her child? Can she rock or play with her infant?

Once the problem is pinpointed, a program is designed for both baby and mother. It very often includes special exercises or games, lessons in emotional support—such as eye contact, holding, and rocking—as well as counseling for the entire family. If the infant is underweight, the doctor may prescribe a special diet with increased calories and nutrients.

Psychiatric problems that are not corrected in the early stages of life may be difficult to resolve later on. But if a troubled baby gets the special attention needed early in life, there's an excellent chance the child's future can be bright and happy.

Is it safe for children to baby-sit for themselves?

In many cases, yes, if the parents set up firm rules and guidelines.

More and more mothers have been joining the work force these days. While it does help the family's finances, it creates other problems. A major one is, who minds the children?

Finding adequate care can pose a serious economic dilemma; many parents can't shoulder the financial burden. As a result, what often happens is that the children end up watching themselves. It's not an ideal arrangement, but for many youngsters too old for day care, it's the only alternative. An estimated 2 million children are now baby-sitting for themselves.

Recently, a child-development expert decided to see how these children are doing and what their mothers and fathers did to make self-care work. The survey covered children up to the age of fourteen, but most were between seven and twelve—children older than those in day-care centers.

What the study disclosed was that self-care works best when parents set up a list of rules and make the children stick to them. For example, the children are not allowed to let anyone in the house without prior permission. They are specifically forbidden to open the door no matter what, and they are warned against telling a phone caller that they're home alone. The children are also barred from using risky appliances such as the stove.

The expert found that most parents in the study make valuable use of the telephone. They call home several times a day and have the children call them. They leave a number where they can be reached and also provide the numbers of the police and a doctor. The parents also arrange to have a special neighbor for the children to call in an emergency.

Two words of caution: A child who is home with a much older brother or sister—a responsible teenager, for example—can receive excellent care. But anytime two or more children are home alone, there's always the risk of sibling rivalry. A parent should leave clear instructions about responsibilities—who washes the dishes, who walks the dog—and other activities—who gets to watch TV and when, who can play outside, and where, and until when.

Second, self-care is probably not appropriate for younger

141

children—that is, those less than eight years old. It's difficult to state a hard-and-fast age when children are old enough to stay home alone. Some mature earlier than others. But parents can usually tell, and their instincts are usually correct.

Can color affect your baby's IQ?

Colors play a large role in a child's intellectual and emotional development. Some colors produce a positive reaction, others a negative one.

In a three-year study, researchers exploring the impact of the environment on mental growth found that selecting certain colors for a child's room could raise average IQ's by as much as twelve points. Taking a random sample of almost 500 children, a group of researchers tested them in rooms that were painted light blue, yellow, yellow-green or orange—colors the children described as "beautiful." All the children scored higher on IQ tests.

On the other hand, rooms painted in what the youngsters called "ugly" colors—black, brown, and, surprisingly, all white— had a negative effect. Among the children who played in these rooms, IQ's dropped an average of fourteen points.

The popular colors, according to the researchers, also stimulated alertness and creativity. The boys and girls playing in the brightly colored rooms tended to be more sociable and friendlier than those in the darker room.

Other studies confirm the effects of colors on children, including infants. Babies can discriminate almost a full range of colors when they are as young as fifteen days old, and some experts feel that the right colors will help the infant feel comfortable in its new, strange environment. You might, for example, avoid wearing a red apron while bathing your baby. As one expert on the psychological effects of color warns, "You then become a flashing red thing with a voice." And that's enough to scare an infant.

Moreover, color experts agree that certain shades of green and blue are likely to have a relaxing effect, while red and other warmer colors can be so stimulating as to increase blood pressure, pulse, and breathing. That's worth keeping in mind if your child is already quite excitable. Softer colors—pastels, yellows,

142

or rose—may help calm down the antsy toddler, but for a quiet child, brighter colors—oranges for example—might add a little stimulation.

When you're decorating, keep in mind that your favorite color may not necessarily be the best for your child.

Don't parental spats set a bad example?

Not if they're put into the proper perspective. If your youngster overhears you and your spouse quarreling heatedly, follow a few simple ground rules so that the child can learn to take such fights in stride. Then he or she may actually benefit from the experience.

First of all, children shouldn't be allowed to believe that they caused the argument. Youngsters often assume that some minor misbehavior on their part—such as being late for dinner—provoked the anger of their parents. If you can possibly manage to do it, it is well worth pausing for a moment in your fight to tell your youngster, "This has nothing to do with you. It's just between me and your mother (or father)." Relieved of guilt, children find parental disputes far less painful and disturbing.

Next, never ask your child to serve as a go-between, to choose sides, or to otherwise enter the boxing ring with the two of you. To try to draw a child into one parent's corner in this way is clearly unfair to the youngster and may be emotionally harmful.

Finally, let the child know when the battle is over and the dust has settled. If the disputed issue remains unresolved, you can explain with a statement such as, "We still don't agree, but we're thinking about it and we're not angry any more." Reassure the youngster that you and your spouse still love one another—and the child.

But if your marital squabbles tend to be frequent and involve belittling one another or intimidation, try to keep the kids well out of earshot and eyesight. In such instances, professional counseling is probably necessary. Also useful may be several recent books that provide guidelines for arguing constructively: *Creative Aggression: The Art of Assertive Living* by George Bach and Herb Goldberg; *Intimate Enemy: How to Fight Fair in Love and*

Marriage by George Bach and Peter Wyden; and *Stop! You're Driving Me Crazy* by George Bach and Ronald M. Deutsch.

Parental fights that are not excessively bitter clear away tensions and can even be instructive. Children can learn from them how to maintain a point skillfully and forcefully. They can see both sexes engage in verbal struggle on an equal footing. And they can overcome the exaggerated fear of expressing anger that afflicts so many people.

Arguing is a natural part of a healthy relationship, and it won't harm your child to find that out.

What do you do when the kid tells a whopper?

Don't be alarmed. If the child is under five years old, she or he is really not lying. Telling tall tales is a normal part of growing up.

Few things tend to distress parents more than their child's lies. But recent studies have cast new light on why children lie, and an appreciation of those reasons can help parents formulate appropriate responses to this very common and always troublesome situation.

Up to the age of four or five, children rarely distinguish between fact and fancy. Their inner lives are filled with fantasies and sometimes those dreams spill over into real life. During this period a child's lies aren't usually meant to be deceptive. Young children tend to believe that events can be controlled by wishes, so unpleasant situations, for example, can be wished out of existence.

When your four-year-old daughter tells you that "the Road Runner knocked over the coffee table," she wishes that that's what happened. Don't scream at her. Instead let her know that you understand the reasons for her fib, and, firmly but calmly, point out where fantasy stops and reality begins. Because you've refrained from scolding her, you'll be taking a big step toward teaching her not to fear telling the truth.

The child's conscience begins to form about the age of six. During this process, which continues until ten or eleven, children have strong urges to deny doing anything bad because they're trying so hard to be good. Children at this stage see issues in stark black and white and conceive of harsh punishments for their misdeeds. When an accident occurs their impulse is to deny responsibility at all costs.

Discipline should be logical and easily understood by the youngster. Parents shouldn't reinforce fears of extreme penalties. If parents treat a child fairly, the habit of telling lies is less likely to form.

Can getting angry with your child backfire?

No, the exact opposite is true. There's a time to get angry, and it's best for your child if you do.

Let's say your preschooler hits a playmate with a toy—hard enough to make the other child cry. How can you teach yours to feel sorry so he or she won't do it again? Researchers at the National Institute of Mental Health (NIMH) say the best way for parents to react is to show their anger and to let the child know exactly why they are mad.

Many parents believe that it is best to control their emotions, to wait until they're calm and collected before reprimanding their youngsters. But the mother or father who explains reasonably to a youngster, "Peter was crying because you hit him," is not likely to make much of an impression. Young children need to be told off swiftly, and strongly, before they'll take criticism to heart.

When your youngster misbehaves, scold him or her vigorously at once. At the same time be sure to tell the child clearly what he or she has done wrong. *An angry response without an accompanying explanation does little good.* Physically restraining a child or taking away television privileges as a punishment can also be effective—but only when combined with explanation. Make certain your child understands that although his or her behavior has upset you, you still love him or her. Use simple, direct words such as, "You hurt Peter. How would you feel if he hit you? You must never, never hurt people." If your tone of voice communicates intense feeling, your message will carry conviction.

Theories of child development have long stressed that preschoolers are just naturally self-centered and unconcerned about the feelings or needs of others. But a government-sponsored

145

NIMH study found that children as young as eighteen months old were capable of showing sympathy. By expressing your disapproval strongly and without ambiguity and explaining to your child what it means to hurt someone else, you're teaching him or her sympathy, caring, and acceptable behavior toward one's peers.

What's the most fragile item in your moving van?

If you're preparing to move, you may be surprised to learn that the most delicate item in your household is your son. A series of important studies have disclosed that boys who move between the ages of six and eleven tend to have problems adjusting to their new environment, particularly school. The research showed that moving during those ages could be so traumatic for boys (the effects on girls were far less conclusive) as to cause a drop in academic achievement or even IQ.

The issue first came to light when Israeli researchers Michael Inbar and Chaim Adler analyzed how immigration affected children who had moved to France and Israel with their families. They expected to find younger children adapting best. Instead, they were surprised to discover what Inbar called the "Vulnerable Age": Children who immigrated between the ages of six to eleven did not do as well at school and fewer attended college than those who moved before age six or after age eleven.

Inbar, a professor of psychology and sociology at the University of Haifa, confirmed this finding in studying the 1971 Canadian Census. In checking on two different groups of men who had immigrated to Canada at various ages, he found that in both groups, fewer of those who moved between six and eleven attended college than those who immigrated before or after.

Inbar tested his theory for a third time with information on 400,000 California high-school students compiled by the American Institutes for Research in Palo Alto. Comparing the educational success of persons who moved during various ages, the Israeli psychologist again found that boys who moved during the vulnerable age of six to eleven tended not to go on to college.

What is especially interesting about these studies is that the conventional wisdom had always been that younger children are

146

more flexible and adaptable; after all, because they seem to learn new languages and customs quicker, it seemed to follow that youngsters would fit into a new environment easily. But just the opposite is the case for young boys. Why this is so isn't known, but Inbar speculates that disruption may occur in some as yet unidentified language or cognitive development stage, or that the problem is linked to the "juvenile era," when a boy is learning to become "social."

What can you as a parent do to reduce the psychological risks of moving for your son? Psychologists suggest you talk to him before you move, explaining carefully why the family must make this change. Get him to express his own feelings about this major crisis in his life. Don't let him hide his anger and depression.

Once you have arrived in your new neighborhood, talk to your son's teacher about how to help the child adjust socially and academically. Ask what classmates he may like best and how to get in touch with their parents. Join the PTA, whether it's your cup of tea or not; this is an easy way to get to know the people in your community with children your son's age. You might also invite your son's best friend from the old neighborhood for a visit.

Above all, don't treat any move as a casual event. When moving with a young boy, the rule is: Handle with care.

Can criticism actually bolster your daughter's self-image?

Yes. How you criticize her may make all the difference between a negative outlook and an achieving one.

Although little girls today can aspire to be or to do anything, recent studies show that many of them do not aim high because of self-defeating attitudes that make them prone to failure rather than to success.

Compare these three reactions to a daughter who has failed a third-grade arithmetic test: (1) The teacher made the test too hard; (2) The girl didn't pass because she didn't do her homework every night; (3) She just isn't any good with numbers. The parent who responds with (1) or (2) allows the child to believe that, with different outside circumstances or with more studying, a better result might be obtained in the future. But response (3) is

147

a complete dead end. It makes the child feel helpless to ever alter the situation, while responses (1) and (2) leave room for improvement and ways to correct the situation. Basically, it's the difference between constructive and destructive criticism.

The average girl is a better-behaved student than her brother. So parents tend to take a more sympathetic approach to her failures, using such reassuring phrases as, "Well, you tried your best. Don't worry about it." Ironically, the end result is that the child blames herself for her lack of ability and feels that she can do nothing to change things.

Psychologists warn that when your daughter tries to do new things on her own it is important not to discourage her or to put down her attempts. If she encounters problems, don't jump in to assist. Let her muddle through by herself and finish whatever she is doing no matter how imperfectly. Afterwards, praise her efforts while teaching her how to correct her mistakes. That way, she can build self-esteem and strengthen her will to try harder next time.

And see that your daughter pats herself on the back when she achieves a goal. It'll help her to believe in herself and to gain the confidence to work harder for what she wants.

Should you play to lose in games with your child?

You should, even though most of your friends may advise that it is wrong and a disservice to the child to lose deliberately. Psychologists say it may be helpful to let children win, at least until they reach the age of seven. The important thing during early childhood is learning how to play, not how to lose.

Parents, of course, want children to realize that in the adult world no one can always win. But small children attach so much importance to winning that losing in a game may seem like a real disaster to them. One four-year-old was out maneuvered in three consecutive checkers games with her father. By the end of the third game, she was crying. "I hate checkers, anyway," she shouted angrily. Another youngster's mother challenged him to a round of badminton and then proceeded to trounce him. The child finally accused his mother of cheating and quit the game.

It's clear that neither of these children gained any useful

knowledge through these experiences of defeat. The games were serious blows to their self-esteem. The sense of comradeship that successful game-playing helps to foster never developed. Both children went away mad, missing out on the sense of comradeship that successful game-playing helps to foster.

Young children try out new skills while playing a game. The success that victory brings makes them feel secure about their abilities. When they're happy with themselves, they feel friendly toward others.

Moreover, some children worry too much about being "best." For these children, it may be important to plan activities in which nobody wins and nobody loses. Games that can end in tie scores—races, for example—may be helpful in taking the edge off competition that becomes too extreme. Some psychologists also suggest playing games that are based on luck, not skill, so the parent does not have any advantage over the child.

At about age seven, children become sharper about realizing that you are letting them win. They question you as to whether you really tried your hardest in a contest. They don't like it if you win all the time, but they don't want their victories to come too easily either. They are concerned about fairness and are interested in measuring their skills against those of others. This is the proper time—not before—to teach children to accept defeat gracefully. But children must be good winners before they can be good losers.

Can playing peek-a-boo get you a night out on the town?

If your baby cries so hard you feel guilty about leaving the infant with a baby-sitter, you'll be happy to know that by following a few simple steps, you can teach your youngster to accept short separations cheerfully.

At some point during their first year babies begin to wail in protest when their parents leave the house without them. It's a sign that they're starting to realize how dependent they are. After all, they don't know for sure when, or even if, their mother and father will return.

This is the perfect time to introduce your baby to peek-a-boo.

149

Babies love this game, which helps them master the fear they feel about being left alone. When you pretend to hide from your youngster, and then suddenly reappear, the child gradually comes to understand that while you may be gone for a moment, you will be back. Peek-a-boo is one of a baby's first tiny steps toward independence.

To avoid heart-rending scenes of farewell, many parents tiptoe quietly out of the house while a child is playing with the baby-sitter or is asleep. It is, however, essential to resist the temptation to do this. If you repeatedly sneak off without telling a child that you are going, the toddler eventually will be anxious all the time that you might suddenly disappear. Children who fear abandonment cling nervously to their parents all day and suffer nightmares and insomnia.

What the experts advise is that you establish a fixed routine for saying goodbye. First, say you're going out and assure your youngster that you'll be back shortly. Then, allow some extra time for the child to get acquainted with the baby-sitter. When you're ready to leave, kiss—and *go*. Even if the child cries piteously, don't hesitate and don't apologize. If you seem uncertain, the child may conclude that there really is something to worry about.

Stick to this routine each time you leave your child with a baby-sitter. The youngster will know that you always tell when you're going, and that you always return. You'll have established trust.

How do bells on the toes make learning a breeze?

Child prodigies in the music world don't come along every day, but one thing a baby comes with at birth is a natural response to rhythm. And why not? A baby's been listening to the sound of the mother's heartbeat for the last nine months.

Many expectant mothers report they can feel their babies respond to music during the later months of pregnancy. It doesn't seem to matter if the music is live, recorded, classical, or rock. Baby responds regardless.

Child-development studies show that music provides an important stimulus to a baby's learning development because the same rhythmic patterns exist in both music and speech. Babies all babble before they speak, and they sing their first efforts at communication. So introducing music helps to foster their speech development.

"One two, buckle my shoe/Three, four, shut the door." As baby repeats this simple rhyme he or she is introduced to counting and building a vocabulary.

"Twinkle, twinkle little star/How I wonder what you are." Now baby is learning to master new concepts and follow a sequence of ideas.

When the child gets a little older, playing musical games such as "London Bridge" and "Farmer in the Dell" provides an opportunity to interact with other children and help develop physical coordination.

Researchers say it's never too soon to introduce your baby to a musical environment. You can encourage the child to make musical sounds by hanging toys or mobiles over the crib that play little tunes when pushed or kicked. Bells on booties make nice sounds, too.

By the time your toddler is ready to create rhythms independently, kitchen pots, pans, and wooden spoons make good percussion instruments.

Dance with your toddler, too, and encourage the tike to move around and make up dances. You'll be helping to build motor skills while both of you are having fun.

Can you get that underachiever achieving?

Definitely. Researchers using simple goal-setting techniques raised the expectations of underachieving students—and their grades as well. You can use the same method. It often works like magic to improve motivation.

A day or two before your child takes a school test, casually ask the youngster: "What grade do you expect to get?" It's important to use the word "expect" rather than "hope," because it's been found that students set more realistic goals with "expect." Also, see if you can get a specific response. A vague comment such as, "Oh, I guess I'll do all right," is not what you're after.

When you inquire beforehand about expectations, you force

the child to think about goals for that task. The mere act of setting a goal, it's been discovered in most cases, will cause the youngster to try harder in order to meet it. Many usually feel that they are working only to satisfy the expectations of parents, teachers, or other authority figures. Taking responsibility for their own goals can be a big step forward. Moreover, a successful outcome usually makes students more confident about their abilities and they aim a little higher next time.

The idea behind this technique is based on sound educational theory. And it works equally well with tasks in nonacademic areas, such as typing or shop. You may be pleasantly surprised to find that your youngster does better than any previous time.

Your child, a new toy—show how, or learn alone?

Preschoolers sometimes need help from an adult to discover the creative possibilities of modeling clay, building blocks, and other playthings. There's nothing wrong with intruding and helping to launch a child's own explorations.

Some early-childhood specialists advise a strict hands-off policy. They insist that if a child and a toy are brought together, something worthwhile will automatically happen. But a recent study conducted among youngsters in a nursery school—which is essentially a playtime setting—indicates that this isn't always true. The study showed that the presence of a responsive adult can stimulate and enrich a child's skills and creativity with play equipment.

In this particular nursery school, the children had very little curiosity about blocks and rarely used them. One day, a researcher entered the block area and began building. She looked as if she was enjoying herself. Immediately, children gathered around her and joined in the play. She was friendly to the youngsters and welcomed their participation. At the same time, she encouraged them to develop their own play ideas. The researcher then left. In the following days the children continued to take a lively interest in block-building, but on their own. They expanded their games, carrying dolls into the block area to live in the houses they had constructed. Their imaginations were fully engaged.

152

So go ahead and join in the fun. Certain games and materials—such as paints, clay, blocks, model kits, puzzles, and math-concept equipment, for example—seem to naturally invite adult participation. Just be sure that you are receptive to your youngster's suggestions and do not try to direct things.

Are creative children born or made?

Until recently, it was assumed and accepted that creative children are born that way. But now evidence is accumulating that creativity can be nurtured and developed.

In 1979, two family development researchers, Brent C. Miller and Diana Gerard, reviewed some seventy-five scholarly articles concerning "family influences on the development of creativity in children" and found that creative children have parents and family environments with certain consistent characteristics:

☐ Parents of creative children tend to be more secure in their own lives and ambitions. They are generally less concerned than most persons about social status and demands.

☐ Both the mothers and fathers of creative children are likely to have diverse interests and be highly competent, intellectually and interpersonally.

☐ Such parents treat their children with respect, giving them plenty of responsibility and encouragement.

☐ The relationships between parents and the children are not, as Miller and Gerard put it, "overly close." There even seems to be a sense of distance between the parents and the children—a certain coolness.

☐ But if parents show hostility toward their children, reject them, or seem detached, the creativity of the children seems to be adversely affected.

☐ Authoritarian parents—those who are overly restrictive, dominating, and too vigilant—tend to stifle their children's imagination and creativity.

The key to encouraging creativity seems to be treating children as individuals deserving respect and the opportunities to flourish. If your child, for example, wants to produce a carnival in the backyard, help with the preparations instead of complaining how the lawn is sure to be ruined. The more imagination and flexibility you show about your children's activities, the more creative they are likely to be.

Which parent in a broken home is the more important?

Perhaps *more* important is misleading. But in a traditional divorce situation, with mothers having custody of the child, it is the father who holds the key to how well a youngster will cope with divorce. According to a recently completed five-year study, the continued involvement of a father with his child can make the crucial difference in the youngster's feelings about himself and about life in general.

When parents announce that they are separating, most children react in shock and fear. A difficult period of readjustment of a year or longer is the rule. However, what the long-term study of the children of divorce found was that, five years after the break-up of a marriage, one out of three children had recovered completely. These youngsters were happy, doing well in school, and loving and optimistic. The key was a continuing relationship with their father. On the other hand, the children who had fared worst had seen their fathers infrequently since the break-up.

It helps if divorced fathers and mothers both understand that the participation of the out-of-home parent is essential to the child's successful readjustment. The wise mother will do nothing to block the visits of the father or to make them difficult or uncomfortable. For his part, the father will be reliable and prompt in getting together with his child.

The frequency of a father's visits is far less critical than the regularity. Children who can count on regular contact with dad— be it once a month, once a week, or more often—feel secure about his love and concern. If the father's schedule is flexible enough to permit an occasional unscheduled trip to a baseball game or a school play, so much the better.

But the father who disappoints his youngster frequently, stays away for long periods of time without explanation, or visits only at his own whim or convenience, may hurt the child more than he realizes. If father and child were close to one another before the divorce, the child's feelings of loss and rejection may be particularly intense. Such children also suffer from greatly diminished self-esteem.

The above remarks also apply, of course, in cases where the father has custody, and the mother visits.

It is important for children to know that while parents may stop loving one another, they never stop loving their children. The best way for a youngster to learn this is through an on-going relationship with *both* mother and father.

Can you spoil a baby?

Nope. Try as you might, all you'll accomplish is to give your newborn heir a great sense of love, comfort, and security.

Forget about that friend or relative who's always warning you to be careful not to spoil the baby. If you pick your infant up when crying or rock the child when fretful, you're bound to hear disapproving remarks about being an overindulgent parent who gives in to the child's every whim. Ignore them. Child psychologists confirm what some parents have suspected: It's impossible to spoil a baby who is less than a year old. In fact, what is harmful is if the parents fail to respond to and fulfill the baby's needs. Of course, once the baby turns into a toddler and becomes more sophisticated at making demands, parents must learn how to say no.

The newborn human being is a pretty helpless creature, entirely dependent on others for literally everything. The baby's only means of communication is crying. If that signal fails to gain the desired response, the infant's development may be slowed. This is what sometimes happens to babies raised in institutions with insufficient personnel to look after them.

Some persons also claim that providing a baby with a frequent supply of new toys and talking and playing with the child will produce an ever-lasting dependency on adults for entertainment. But there is no evidence for this. Babies need variety and challenge in their environment in order to learn. If they don't get enough attention, their mental growth may be blocked.

Years ago, parents were instructed to let their babies cry for at least fifteen minutes before going to them. Nowadays, parents can give their infant everything the child needs without being concerned about giving too much. The only way you can "spoil" your baby is by not loving the child enough.

―――――――――――――

What is this thing called huggermuggering?

It's love. More specifically, it's affection, it's touching, it's a hug—and it does wonders for everybody.

Studies show that the first few hours after birth are crucial in establishing strong emotional connections between a child and parents. Touching is, in fact, one way babies know they are alive. And, new findings indicate that affection is even more important than nurture: A child can survive on a minimum of food, but total deprivation of affection is often fatal.

There is evidence, too, that lack of maternal affection may create schizophrenic children. The therapy that most often works for these children is touch. On the other hand, children raised with affection usually have higher self-esteem.

In the early months of life an infant needs continued hugging, stroking, and caressing for both emotional and physiological reasons. Affection communicated through touch helps the baby's immunological systems, providing life-long resistance to certain diseases. Conversely, asthma, for example, is common among children deprived of affection.

Sometime about the age of eight, a child will want to withdraw from the kind of exchange of affection sought at an early age. This rejection is important for the child's growing sense of identity and independence, and it is important that parents respect the "touch" and "hold" boundaries a growing child establishes. It is a time to ask yourself whether, as a parent, you are hugging your child for your own needs or for the child's.

The need for affection reverses in adolescence, but adolescents are ambivalent and are often affection-starved as a result. On the one hand they withdraw by choice from their family; on the other they feel hostile to their parents, who in turn respond by being less affectionate. Teens are afraid to hug mom or dad, or a best friend of the same sex, for fear of being thought strange.

And unless sex is involved, they avoid hugging someone of the opposite sex. Research suggests that teenagers turn to alcohol or drugs because they are hungry for affection, though afraid to admit it. The best thing a parent can do for a self-conscious teenager is to provide as much touching and affection as possible.

By the time young adults emerge from adolescence they have probably received confusing messages about the meaning of touch. For a young man, acknowledging the need for affection may be unmanly. For a young woman, acknowledging the need for affection can be misinterpreted. It is important for the maturing child to realize that affection is loving touch whose purpose is to acknowledge someone else's feelings. Sexual touch, in contrast, is designed to arouse sexual feelings in both the other person and oneself.

However, this does not mean that affection has no part in sex. On the contrary, in a recent survey of successful marriages, touching and hugging were cited as key factors in maintaining a long-lasting relationship.

Dr. Virginia Satir, a therapist and social worker, recommends four hugs a day for survival, eight for maintenance, and twelve for growth. Whatever the number—lesser or greater—the essential point is to make contact.

What's the most difficult age for a girl?

Twelve. A recent study of eight hundred adolescents made the unexpected discovery that girls are particularly vulnerable to emotional problems at the age of twelve, much more so than boys. They need special attention.

One surprising statistic of the study was the large number of twelve-year-old girls who reported a generally poor opinion of themselves—twice as many girls as boys of the same age did. Low self-esteem was especially voiced by girls whose bodies were undergoing the changes of puberty and who had begun dating. If at the same time they were moving from the protected world of elementary school to the larger, more impersonal environment of junior high school, their situation was even more stressful.

Parental understanding can make a big difference for these

preteenagers. If you have a choice, your daughter might prefer to stay in the same school for another year. That might help relieve a good deal of the insecurity she feels.

It may be puzzling that girls are more likely to react negatively to the physical and social changes of early adolescence than boys. But psychologists believe that this is because girls are more concerned about personal attractiveness and popularity.

Anything parents can do to tone down these concerns is helpful. So let your daughter know that it is all right to delay going out with boys. Help her to get involved in sports or other activities where she can have friends of both sexes without playing the dating game just yet. And a compliment from dad about her appearance can work wonders to elevate her confidence.

Taking the time to explain to your twelve-year-old that she is facing new pressures in her life that she will adjust to in time can make her feel better about herself. Just knowing that she is not the only preteen having these problems can be tremendously reassuring.

What happens to a child when a parent is out of work?

Child psychologists report that children, young ones in particular, are likely to develop colds, stomachaches, asthma, and eczema when a mother or father loses a job. The cause: family stress. School absenteeism also is often a by-product of parental unemployment.

The situation has taken on added concern because of recently rising unemployment rates. Family counselors suggest that out-of-work parents do their job hunting while their child is at school, then take advantage of their free time to engage in activities with the youngster that couldn't be done when they were at work. One psychologist recommends developing a hobby or starting an after-school play group, scout troop, or athletic team—any activity that can be shared together.

Many adolescents confess they find unemployed parents hard to deal with. After an initial flurry of activity and optimism, the jobless parent may begin to suffer severe depression. Fathers, especially, frequently lose their sense of self-worth and become withdrawn when they feel they can no longer fill the role of breadwinner for the family.

Very often this is just the time some teenagers choose to get in trouble, perhaps subconsciously hoping to jolt a withdrawn parent into some kind of active behavior. Other adolescents refuse to accept the reality of their new financial circumstances and may increase their spending in an effort to prove to themselves that nothing has really changed.

This is a good time, instead, for a teenager to take stock and to take steps to help ease the tensions at home. The following are suggestions to improve the family picture:

☐ Be aware that your parent's frustration may lead to an overreaction to your behavior.

☐ But also be aware that how you act may mean you're acting out your own frustrations.

☐ Be honest with your parent. It's best to discuss the job loss openly.

☐ Ask how you can help out in lean financial times. (For example, forget about that new bike and try repairing the old one.)

☐ Find time to spend with your parent to express your feelings of love and respect. (It's important to let your parent know he or she means more than just a paycheck.)

☐ Find yourself another family member, a good friend, or someone at school to talk to whenever you feel you have to "let off a little steam."

On the positive side, many families report that a period of unemployment has brought them closer together.

How guilty should a working mother feel?

Not guilty at all if the time spent with her child is filled with care and love.

Too many working mothers feel guilty because they think that, if they're not home most of the day, they're neglecting their youngsters. Well, recent time studies of how mothers interact with children yielded some surprising results. Working mothers

159

spend the same amount of time directly involved with their children as mothers without jobs. It seems that too many at-home mothers tend to romanticize the time they spend with their youngsters. In another study, for example, doctors found that mothers and children interacted only one third of the time that the mothers claimed they were attending to their children.

Clearly, the number of hours at home is not the criterion. That old adage that it's the quality of time, not the quantity, that matters really holds true. And it holds true whether you're a working mother or one who stays at home. Children need a mother's affection and encouragement, but they also need time to play on their own and to play with peers. Again, it's the balance that's important.

At what age is it "safe" for a mother to go to work? Unfortunately, there are no hard-and-fast rules. And for many American women, there is also no choice; they need the income. But it's useful to know that most nurseries prefer the child to be two years nine months old or toilet-trained.

One interesting footnote: Many working mothers worry that their children will forget them and identify with the professional care-giver. According to a study by Jerome Kagan, the well-known Harvard child-development expert, when children get bored or tired or upset, they turn to their biological mothers for comfort rather than to the surrogates who spend more time with them day to day. Kagan calls this special tie between mother and child "mysterious"—but it is definitely a mystery working to the advantage of the mother who wants to or has to work.

Why does your teenager suddenly turn loner?

Your fourteen-year-old son is in his room, door closed, radio blaring—again. Would he like to come along on a family picnic? "No thanks. Not today," he responds. Is this the same youngster, you wonder, who loved to join eagerly in family outings? What's gone wrong?

Probably nothing. Researchers tell us that many normal teenagers, like film star Greta Garbo, simply "want to be alone."

A recent study found that both boys and girls of high-school age need a good deal of solitude. These are the years when youngsters are going through the difficult process of separating emotionally from their parents. They want to become more independent and more sure of who they are and what they want. But first, there's a lot of important sorting out they have to do.

Parents of young teens who suddenly become loners usually worry that something is seriously amiss. The youngsters not only isolate themselves, but they often also complain of being terribly lonely. Talk to your youngster and make sure there's nothing serious troubling him. If everything seems okay, be relaxed, but sympathetic. Explain that it's all a part of growing up. Becoming an adult means that we must give up the security and certainty of being dependent children. That isn't easy or comfortable at first for anyone.

Don't try to force your teenager to participate in social activities. It'll happen as soon as the youth is ready. Meanwhile, the stretches of solitary time often are creative interludes for writing in journals, drawing, listening to music, or just thinking. Chances are, before you know it, your lonely teenager will be a busy ball of fire again.

Hey, baby, who's the new face in town?

Yours, Funny Face—and what a clever way to get your baby used to strangers!

About half of all infants between six months and a year old experience some form of "stranger anxiety," as psychologists call it, when they see a new face. They'll howl and hide their faces the minute a stranger walks into the room. Some children even get upset by the face on a toy, if it's weird enough.

It may be embarrassing, but such reactions are actually a normal stage in development as the youngsters begin to tell the difference between immediate family members and strangers. So don't take it personally. Your baby's response has nothing to do with any failure on your part. Explain what's happening to friends and relatives who might be wounded when the child responds to their affection with a piercing scream.

And, yes, an easy way to help the baby overcome a fear of strangers is to play Funny Face. If you make a variety of faces at your child, the youngster will get used to seeing new expressions on a face already trusted. The more faces you can conjure up, the less worried the child will be when a stranger appears.

Children also like looking at their own faces—and yours—in a mirror. This also helps them to get used to a variety of expressions and eventually a variety of new faces.

Is daydreaming really a waste of time?

Psychologists, who used to think it was pure escapism, have changed their minds: Daydreaming, it seems, can actually be both healthy and therapeutic. Some now believe that daydreaming for only ten minutes a day will not only help you relax by diverting your mind from your problems, but it also might help you solve them.

Daydreaming is a kind of meditation technique that focuses a troubled mind on more pleasant activities or thoughts. It's a good way to rehearse things we might want to do in the future as well as analyze what we have done in the past. Our brains store millions of scenes, events, and conversations. By running a little documentary of our past or scenario of our future, we can learn a lot about who we are and what we may become.

Instead of sitting in the doctor's office or standing in line at the bank tapping your foot in frustration or boredom, let your mind go. Who knows? You may come up with a great idea that will help you in your work or family life.

And if you catch your child off in another world, let the youngster dream on. It's not such a bad habit to develop.

What is the first thing your baby should see?

Your eyes. For your baby, it's the most important part of you. According to a recent study, eye contact is more important for a baby than hearing your voice or seeing your smile.

Until recently, it was believed that newborn infants could perceive only light and dark. But scientists have now discovered that in the first days of life babies are already able to focus their eyes and follow bright, moving objects. And what this means is that newborns only two or three days old can benefit from eye contact with the person who's caring for them, an essential element in their social and emotional development.

Despite the fact that newborns probably have little or no depth perception or color vision—they cannot see detail, and tend to look at the borders of objects rather than the centers—they do have visual preferences. In simple tests, researchers found that babies seemed to prefer looking at people's faces rather than at inanimate objects. And nature has arranged things so that a baby cradled in your arms is just the right distance away from your face—seven to ten inches—to be able to see you with maximum clarity.

When you look into your baby's eyes, it makes for a closer emotional tie between the two of you. It also helps baby to learn to recognize your face and increases alertness. By the age of four or five months most babies can distinguish the faces of persons whom they see every day from those of strangers. At this stage of development, the need to maintain eye contact, particularly during feeding, is especially pronounced.

What's best as a birthday present: an empty milk carton, an old tire, or a set of blocks?

Any or all of them. The best toys cost practically nothing. The costliest, most elaborate toys and games are often of little value for a youngster's development. Child-development experts and psychologists agree that you, and the child, will be just as well off if you save your money and use your imagination.

Play is important. Any parent can tell you that children take play very seriously, indeed. Psychologists point out that play enables children to master their environment and teaches them problem-solving skills they will use later in life.

Free, imaginative play also promotes psychological development. Studies have shown that children who are given ample time to play and have fun eventually have more highly developed intellectual skills.

Psychologists advise that the best toys are those that encourage a child to play "Let's pretend." And such toys do not have to cost money. For example, a set of empty milk cartons and jars becomes a play supermarket. A bunch of round clothespins standing on their heads can become a football team. Or a large empty box magically becomes a car, a boat, or a house.

If you are buying a gift for your child, a recent study that compared different kinds of toys showed that the best choice would be a set of blocks. The youngster will turn them into houses, airports, castles, space stations—whatever fantasy can invent.

The same principle applies to outdoor play, too. Cast-off equipment—railroad ties, drainage pipes, ropes, old tires, pieces of chain, or telephone cable spools—can be put together to make a playground that's ideal for growing imaginations. Tires become swings; pipes become caves and hideouts. And materials like these are often available free or at little cost from lumber and building companies, gas stations, groceries, marinas, even the phone company.

It's easy to spend a lot of money on toys and playground equipment, and your child will certainly not discourage you if you do. But there's no evidence that children who go without fancy toys, or so-called "educational" toys, are in any way deprived. On the contrary, they may be just as happy when they are provided with those inexpensive simple things like old pots and pans, grocery cartons, or cast-off clothes. Give them the chance to let their imaginations run free. They'll certainly have just as much fun.

Can you bribe a kid?

Sure, but it won't work. Trying to motivate a child to do anything by promising a reward tends to backfire: The child may accomplish a task, but probably because there's more interest in the reward than the task.

In a study directed by John Condry, a psychologist at Cornell University, researchers found that, though an occasional reward may spur on accomplishment, promising rewards too often tended to result in lackluster performances and dampened enthusiasm.

To learn more about how rewards affected children's behavior, Dr. Condry and his associates gave a group of nursery-school youngsters colored markers and paper and then asked the children to draw pictures. A third of the children were promised gold stars and certificates for good work; the rest were not promised anything, although some were surprised with gold stars when they finished.

The researchers discovered that the group promised gold stars turned out more drawings than the rest of the class—but the drawings were less creative, less complex, and less inspired than those drawn by the children who were not promised anything for their efforts.

The same class was again given markers and paper and asked to draw more pictures—but no rewards were promised to anyone. This time the researchers discovered that the children who had been rewarded after the fact in the first test along with those who received nothing were happy to draw their little hearts out. But the group that originally had been promised gold stars were now quite disinterested in the task.

"The carrot and the stick approach works fine for animals," says Condry. "Kids, however, are more complicated. They can think. And they start thinking more about how to please than the work at hand."

Condry and other educators point out that children have a natural desire to learn that can be undermined by enticing them with gold stars, ice-cream cones, or trips to the movies. The key is to find something that holds your child's interest and gives the child encouragement and support. That is the way children learn and enjoy doing so.

_____

Is your child's best friend an imaginary rabbit?

If so, don't fret. Remember how, in the movie *Harvey*, Jimmy Stewart talked to his make-believe confidant? Well, perhaps it wasn't normal for him, but the opposite is true for preschoolers. Recent research shows that children who dream up imaginary playmates are exceptionally bright and well-adjusted youngsters who use language with unusual skill for their age.

In the past, child-development specialists regarded the youngster who invented a fantasy friend as emotionally troubled or possibly even out of touch with reality. Now, however, they know that flights of imagination are a normal part of growing up.

Imaginary playmates often take the form of another child who eats, sleeps, plays, and even climbs into the bathtub with its inventor. Or they can be animals that act like people, such as one little girl's friendly and cooperative pal, "Laughing Tiger." Occasionally, they are television characters with superhuman capabilities. Some youngsters invent a virtual parade of fanciful friends, while others are loyal to just one, who may remain an invisible member of the family for many months.

The creation of an imaginary companion generally represents a child's attempt to solve problems, overcome fears, or dispel boredom. An only child livens her solitary tea party by inviting a pretend playmate and chatting happily with it. A small boy who is afraid of dogs imagines a strong, brave bear to protect him out-of-doors until he masters his fright. A three-year-old is ashamed of having scratched the dining room table, so "Sam"—a naughty child who exists only in the imagination—is severely scolded for the deed.

You need not worry that, like Harvey, your child's imaginary playmate will be a permanent tenant in your home. As children grow older, these miraculous guests disappear. Until then, parents who know how helpful and comforting they can be to youngsters should welcome and enjoy them.

Is all that headbanging normal for a baby?

It's probably normal, common, and temporary. If you're a new parent, you may have noticed your baby rocking back and forth on hands and knees in the crib or playpen. Sometimes babies rock quite violently and bang their heads as well. The sight can be frightening, but don't be alarmed. An exhaustive twelve-year study of the rhythmic movements of babies brings reassuring news.

What the researchers found was that such behavior—despite its rather bizarre appearance—usually does not signify any mental or emotional disorder. Rocking occurs in approximately one baby out of ten and is seen in boys twice as frequently as in girls. Headbanging typically begins after the rocking stage and lasts for a shorter time. When parents hear baby's head thud repeatedly against a wall or crib, they often become extremely upset. They worry that the youngster may be permanently harmed as a result. But rest assured—no injury will occur. The child seems to know when enough is enough.

Doctors speculate that rocking is one way youngsters express tension. Perhaps that's why babies who rock usually don't suck their thumbs, and vice versa. Rocking generally appears after the age of six months and often coincides with major developmental stages such as learning to stand, starting to say words, and trying to walk.

Parents who are bothered by this harmless behavior may on occasion be able to distract the baby from rocking by setting a metronome nearby. Tapping on the crib in time to the youngster's rocking, dancing with, or swinging the baby may also satisfy the wish for rhythmic movement.

But if none of these techniques work, remember that rocking usually disappears on its own by the age of two. Just keep your pediatrician informed about the behavior and then proceed to ignore it. After all, rhythmic motion has comforted infants for a long time. That's why we have cradles and why *Rock-a-by-Baby* is a favorite lullaby.

Are fingers the key to the fourth-grade blues?

Some schoolchildren breeze through the early years of elementary school in fine style, learning to read well and to memorize their multiplication tables. Then, in the fourth grades, something happens. Their grades start to fall, they lose interest, and they don't keep up with their classmates.

What's happened is that the fourth grade marks an important transition in early education. Before then, a student has mostly to *take in* information, to learn to figure out numbers and letters, to become able to read. But by the fourth grade, it becomes increasingly more important to *give back* information. Writing long reports becomes more important and for many children gets to be the most challenging and problematic part of school work. This is where otherwise successful students start to have trouble.

Recently, researchers have begun to realize that the problem with these children is not intelligence or motivation. Instead, one out of six children, especially boys, has certain motor problems that make writing unusually hard. The boy may find it difficult to manipulate a pencil, or he may have poor hand–eye coordination, so his written work suffers. Grades fall, and the youngster becomes discouraged and ready to give up. Parents and teachers may conclude that the child is lazy or just not trying. But the problem may be just in the fingertips.

What can be done? Teachers may find that otherwise unproductive children do very well if they deliver reports orally, or even learn to type, albeit slowly. And parents can ask about special (and easy) exercises that can help improve finger coordination. Nearly all school districts have specialists who deal with these problems.

Finger coordination is not, of course, the only cause of problems in school. But it is one that is easily overlooked. Once the problem is recognized, the solution may be a lot simpler than you think.

Can children with dyslexia be helped?

Yes, and for free. Thanks to a federal law, which many parents may not know about, all handicapped children are guaranteed an education no matter what their difficulty is. Special diagnostic testing must be made in schools. And every state must set up programs for children who suffer dyslexia and other learning disabilities.

Dyslexia is a learning disorder that makes reading difficult. Parents, and teachers, of many of the affected children are unaware of the problem. They assume that the children are slow learners or lazy, when in fact the youngsters have a specific disability. They want to read, but simple words get mixed up, letters get reversed, and short sentences become incomprehensible.

Dyslexic children often have difficulty in telling the difference between squares, circles, and triangles, or they reverse letters when reading or writing. For example, they confuse the letters "b" and "d," or the words "saw" and "was." They might see the word "dog" as "bog."

Another sign of dyslexia may be alternating right- and left-handedness. Children usually demonstrate a preference for one hand or the other by the age of six; dyslexics do not, and are confused by left-or-right options.

Dyslexic children—about seven boys to every one girl who suffers the disorder—feel that they are stupid. But dyslexia has nothing to do with intelligence. Some eminent individuals have been dyslexic—Albert Einstein, for one.

The cause is uncertain. Researchers generally agree that dyslexia probably has a physical or organic origin. Heredity may be a factor. But whatever the cause, dyslexics can be helped.

State health departments and departments of education can offer information about testing and educational programs. Reading can be taught by sight, sound, even touch. Eye-training techniques have helped some children. It's also been found that exercises that develop coordination skills, such as tumbling, can help dyslexics overcome their disability.

What's important to remember is that children having difficulty in school may be neither slow nor lazy. They may be the victims of a treatable disability. Although there is no quick cure, they can learn to correct it.

If you have problems finding the right program in your community, write to:

Learning Disabilities Program,
Office of Special Education and Rehabilitation Services,
U.S. Department of Education,
Washington, D.C. 20202.

Is the only child a lonely child?

The opposite is likely—and three can make a perfectly happy family. Several recent studies have dispelled the myth that an only child is necessarily doomed to be miserable and spoiled as well as lonely. And deciding to have more than one child because you're afraid you'll be somehow depriving that child is foolish. You'll only be depriving yourself of the joys of parenthood.

Reviewing the literature on only children and then conducting their own study, Sharryl Hawke of the Social Science Education Consortium and David Knox of East Carolina University in

Greenville, N.C., found that only children tend to be more self-confident, more verbal, more resourceful, and as smart or smarter than peers from larger families.

In an article in *The Family Coordinator*, Hawke and Knox report that single-child families often seem to be closer, more democratic, and more affluent. "While money does not buy happiness," they write, "it does provide recognized benefits." The costs of education, recreation, and entertainment are less, and parents definitely end up with more time for themselves and each other, which increases the odds for a happy marriage. A child, lone or not, is bound to benefit from that.

The main risk of stopping at one child is that the parents tend to be overindulgent. Some parents are also inclined to put too much pressure on an only child to succeed—or on themselves to make good at their one and only chance at parenting. Hawke and Knox also note that many parents fear the possibility of death of an only child, or ending up themselves in old age as a financial burden for a single offspring.

Nevertheless, they conclude that having additional children that the couple neither wants nor can afford is not the solution to these potential problems. Nor is having no child at all. "Disadvantages of the one-child family," they emphasize, "can be overcome by positive attitudes and actions."

Can your child dance his or her way to better grades?

Probably. New studies show that elementary-school children with a wide range of problems—including poor coordination, short attention span, and hyperactivity—can often improve their learning ability greatly through dance therapy, a technique that makes use of simple, repetitive movements.

Dance therapy is offered both in group or individual sessions conducted by trained therapists, who develop a warm, supportive relationship with the children. Participants stretch, run, bounce, roll, skip, and creep. They also play movement games, pretending to be a machine or to walk as if on peanut butter. Or they focus on a specific body part, a shoulder for example, and see how many ways it can be moved.

The key to the success of dance therapy is rhythm. Children

respond on a deep level when they move their bodies in time to music, drum beats, counting aloud, tapping feet, or clapping. They experience the joy of self-expression and release tensions caused by emotional conflicts. The relaxed, accepting atmosphere of the sessions, where there is no such thing as a "wrong" motion, makes the youngsters feel better about themselves. Their coordination usually improves markedly—including the eye–hand coordination so essential to mastering writing skills. Many children also increase their ability to concentrate for a sustained period of time, and some find it easier to sit through a class without jumping out of their seats every moment.

For the youngster with problems that impede learning, dance therapy is worth a whirl.

How do you get a kid to remember anything?

Does your child continually forget the lunch bag on the kitchen counter? Ignore instructions to pick up a quart of milk? Come home with an empty schoolbag? A new study has discovered that children's memories respond better to what they *see* than to what they *hear*. Using visual clues sparks children as young as six years old to remember better.

The principle is the same as the old custom of tying a string to a finger, but the clues are special and specific. For example, children are always forgetting their mittens. So, have a picture of a smiling clown taped to your youngster's school locker and say: "This clown will help remind you about your mittens." To make sure the connection is understood, ask the youngster "What will you think of when you see the clown?" That's all there is to it. The chances that the mittens will be left behind are greatly reduced.

Notice that there are two parts to this simple technique. The first is to provide an attractive memory cue and to place it in a location where it will catch the child's eye. The second is to tell the child that the object is there for a specific purpose, as a reminder of something that must be done.

When they are very young, children have their schedules set for them by adults; they don't have to remember things. But as they grow, their lives become more complex and self-directed, and remembering becomes important. Children who have a lot of trouble mastering this skill often view themselves as disorganized and are regarded as unreliable by others. So if your youngster has this difficulty, provide an attention-grabbing memory aid.

Is it possible for both parents to have custody?

Yes. When each spouse in a divorce wants custody of the children, it is possible to arrange a joint-custody agreement in half of the states.

In a joint-custody agreement, the divorced parents have equal rights and responsibilities in raising the children. Crucial decisions about health care and education are arrived at jointly. Financial burdens are shared. And both parents have a hand in the youngster's day-to-day care.

Joint custody may involve having the divorced parents live in the same neighborhood. The children then divide their time between the two homes without interrupting their schooling. Some children move back and forth every few days, some every week, and some spend alternate months or a full six months with each parent. There are even cases where the children remain in the original family home and the parents take turns living with them there.

The principal benefit to children of this double-housing arrangement is that they can continue to have close relationships with both parents. Although it is too soon to be sure, psychiatrists note that such youngsters seem to suffer less from a sense of loss than other children of divorce. They appear less depressed and have fewer behavior problems and sleep disturbances.

However, there also are risks. Shuttling between households can be a nuisance at best—at worst, it may cause feelings of instability. There are bound to be inconsistencies in rules, discipline, and overall life-style. Finally, if one parent moves or remarries, the entire arrangement may be jeopardized and the child forced to readjust again.

Not all couples are good candidates for joint custody. A strong desire to make it work and a commitment to the interests of the child is needed. Also necessary is the ability to cooperate

172

with and trust the former spouse. To some parents, joint custody offers the opportunity to share in the rewards and intimacies of parenthood that weekend dads or moms rarely can enjoy.

The states of California, Idaho, Kansas, and Nevada have the most advanced joint-custody programs. Twenty-one other states have such programs but with varying stipulations. A clearinghouse for information is currently being organized. For help, contact James A. Cook, 10606 Wilkins Ave., Los Angeles, Calif. 90024.

Can hating school really make you sick?

If your child complains of a headache or stomach pains on school mornings, and the doctor finds nothing wrong, chances are the youngster nevertheless *is* sick—of school. The child is likely to have a compelling reason for avoiding school, and it's up to you to find out what it is and to help overcome it.

Does the youngster's illness mysteriously disappear on weekends? Is getting out of bed, dawdling over breakfast, or playing hooky a chronic problem? Child psychologists warn that it is critical to recognize a symptom and to discover and deal with the underlying cause immediately, so that staying away from school does not become a pattern.

One reason for hating school is that the academic work is too hard—or too easy. Then, too, a child may fall behind during an absence and need special help to catch up. Or there may be an unrecognized physical disability, such as poor vision or hearing, that impedes learning.

Perhaps the youngster is picked on by other children, has no friends, is ridiculed, bullied, or is excessively shy or insecure. Maybe the child does not get along with the teacher. Sometimes a serious problem at home—such as a financial crisis, severe sibling rivalry, divorce, or a death in the family—claims too much of the child's emotional energy.

How can you find out what is behind your child's resistance to attending school? Of course, listen carefully to complaints, but often children cannot explain what's bothering them. In that case, consult the youngster's teacher and guidance counselor. Ask to review school papers and aptitude-test scores. Perhaps

173

you can visit class to observe the child's performance and social interaction with classmates. Try to figure out if there have been any important changes in the child's life that you are unaware of.

Above all, let your child know that you are supportive and want to help. Just knowing that you are sympathetic can make the youngster feel better. Before long those symptoms should vanish. Pinning down the problem as soon as possible, and then correcting it, is important because you can help to prevent the problem from becoming a fixed pattern.

Who's a boy's best buddy?

More often than not, dear old mom. Most boys, studies show, like to talk to her about dating and sex.

Say you're the mother of a teenage son whose deep voice, muscular frame, and stubbly cheeks still are new to you. Suddenly his mind is on girls and dating. Perhaps he puts up a cool front about it all. But don't be fooled. Despite bravado, he's probably just as awkward, shy, and scared as many girls are about the whole complex, unfamiliar world of relationships with the opposite sex. He wishes he could talk with someone about it all. As researchers unexpectedly found, don't be surprised if you're the one person he'd be most comfortable talking with.

Adolescent boys worry about what teenage girls are like, how to talk to them, and how to act toward them—and mother seems the likeliest person to be an expert on the subject. You might make a start with your son by telling him about your own nervousness when you first began dating. Knowing that his problems are not unique can help him to open up more about them.

A mother can assist by reassuring her son that feelings such as tenderness, uncertainty, or self-consciousness are neither womanly nor manly—just human. That girls look for the same qualities in friends as boys do: sincerity, thoughtfulness, honesty. Above all, you can reinforce his wish to follow his own needs and standards and to resist pressures from his classmates to become involved in more dating and sexual activity than he is ready for.

If you think your teenage boy is confused and anxious about girls and sex, be alert to signs that he wants to talk. Respect the

174

privacy of his personal life, but let him know that you're willing to lend a friendly ear. And don't hesitate to offer advice—if it's asked for. After all, who can serve as an expert on the subject better than a former teenage girl?

Are hypochondriacs born or made?

According to the latest study, they may definitely be a parental creation—and develop into adults who chronically overreact to minor symptoms of ill health.

A sixteen-year study of 350 mothers and their children found that youngsters who are kept home from school frequently because of inconsequential ailments such as stomachaches or sniffles may well grow up to be chronic complainers. And if parents make too much of their own symptoms, their children are likely to follow a similar pattern when they become adults.

The study also shows that adults who reported such psychological problems as loneliness and depression were found to have been often kept home from school as children. Yet researchers found that few of the adult complainers had really suffered chronic illnesses when young.

Psychologists believe that parents can help forestall the development of hypochondriac tendencies in their children by encouraging the youngsters not to surrender to minor ailments. If Susie wakes up in the morning with a light stomachache, or a little sniffle but no fever, let her know that it will soon go away and that there's no cause to miss a day of school over it.

Is there hope for poor spellers?

If you're game, yes.

A recent study of twelve-year-olds has found that one way to help children become aware of how letters go together to make words is to play games in which they are called upon to guess at letter patterns.

Educational researchers have learned that there is a direct

relationship between a child's ability to spell and later development of reading skills and vocabulary. About 10 percent of all elementary-school children are considered poor spellers. They frequently have difficulty reading and building a vocabulary—and getting good grades as a result.

How do games help? Educators have discovered that good spellers have a good sense of how letters form patterns and how our language is structured. They know, for example, that "q" nearly always has a "u" after it, or that few words end in "k" unless the "k" has a "c" before it. The idea is to get poor spellers to play games that highlight such patterns.

Remember "Hangman," the game where you fill in the blanks and guess your opponent's word before he or she strings you up on the gallows? For example, you may get to the point where your opponent's word reads C-H-A-I-. You know that the last letter would be an "N" or an "R." A poor speller might not guess the last letter so easily, but after playing the game for a while the guesses would become easier and more accurate. There are similarly popular games. "Word Mastermind," like "Hangman," involves guessing an opponent's word, but it is a bit more challenging. Or just correctly arranging the letters of a word that are mixed up can help a child master spelling.

While the study found that such games helped develop a child's spelling ability, it also discovered that, just as importantly, the children had fun while they were learning. Even the poor spellers—those who might otherwise be discouraged—got to love the game and eagerly joined in.

━━━━━━━━━━━━━━

What do boys, noise, and good grades have in common?

If your son insists on doing his homework while the radio is on, let him. It may help his grades. According to a recent study, loud background noise may actually help boys to perform better academically. On the other hand, girls need a quiet environment.

Researchers at Ohio State University tested the effects of noise on students in the first, third, and fifth grades. Each student was given a problem to solve. Half the students were tested in a room with a decibel level of 70. That's equal to the sound of a radio at normal to midhigh volume or to the noise level in a class-room in which all the students are talking loudly at once. The other students were placed in a quiet room.

The boys solved the problems more frequently, and more accurately, in the noisy room. Girls did worse with noise, but improved with quiet.

Researchers aren't exactly sure why boys need noise and girls require quiet, but they hypothesize it has to do with early conditioning. Stereotypically, boys are expected to be loud and rowdy while they play, while girls are often encouraged to play quietly.

Whatever the reason, the results are clear. So, if your son wants to play the stereo while he's doing his homework, and your daughter wants peace and quiet while she's doing hers—let the boy use headphones.

What's better for teenagers, Shakespeare or sci-fi?

The important thing is that children read and love to read, so science fiction is as good a beginning as any. In fact, the fascina-tion most children have for sci-fi—both books and movies—is normal. A recent study at the University of Iowa shows that most boys and girls between the ages of fifteen and nineteen seem to prefer reading science fiction to all other kinds of books.

Educators are now encouraging that interest. Adolescents, they and we know, tend to reject what bores them, and any book that looks like a school book or a homework assignment is un-likely to turn a teenager on, despite its literary worth. So if your child prefers Ray Bradbury to Charles Dickens, don't worry about it. You're not raising an illiterate.

Quite the opposite is true. Science fiction is a perfect way to introduce a child to philosophical speculation about the role of change in the world and the possibilities of the future. Reading should be mind-expanding; books should give the child the op-portunity to use the imagination, to reflect on society and the child's role in it, now and in the future. Science fiction can en-courage that. Children should read the great sci-fi writers like Bradbury, Arthur C. Clarke, and Robert Heinlein, "not because these writers can tell them about rocket ships and time machines," as the futurist Alvin Toffler has written, "but, more important, because they can lead young minds through an imaginative exploration of the jungle of political, social, psychological and ethical issues that will confront these children as adults."

And who knows, after all that reading about the future, your child might even get interested in the past—and pull Dickens, Jane Austen, and Shakespeare off the shelf.

How do you tell if your child is an Einstein or a Picasso?

First, forget the stereotypes. Gifted or talented children do not necessarily have to be frail, pale creatures squinting through soda-bottle lenses, nor are they always star pupils. Indeed, especially bright children often have problems in school, mainly because they are bored or frustrated by the class or the pace, which is geared to slower learners.

By and large, parents appear to be the best talent scouts. Of course, every parent is inclined to think his or her baby's a genius, but it is extraordinary how many parents are right. The best guess is that about 2 million children in elementary and high schools in this country are especially gifted or talented. But, according to the U.S. Office of the Gifted and Talented, 86 percent of these children are not getting the kind of training and education they need to develop their talents. Unless such children are identified and given special attention, their gifts may be wasted.

The old rule of thumb to tell whether a child was gifted used to be an IQ of 130 or higher (average children range between 90 and 110). But lately the definition has been broadened to account for children who demonstrate superior talents not only in intellectual and academic matters, but also in leadership and in the performing and visual arts.

The U.S. Council for Exceptional Children points out that the gifted or talented child does things a little earlier, a little better, a little more quickly, and a little differently than other children do. Keep an eye out if your child:

☐ Learns to read early and loves reading. Many gifted children teach themselves to read.

☐ Asks probing questions and shows insatiable curiosity.
☐ Has a variety of interests and explores them independently.
☐ Displays unusually long attention spans.
☐ Learns basic skills more quickly than others of the same age.
☐ Enjoys working or playing alone.
☐ Has an unusually sharp memory.
☐ Is highly imaginative.
☐ Sees subtle relationships between things.
☐ Is popular and often chosen to lead activities.
☐ Has an advanced sense of humor.
☐ Enjoys and displays unusual abilities in literature, art, music, dance, or theater.

It will take time to evaluate your child, but keep in mind that, as a parent, you play an important role in the child's development because the youngster needs your support and encouragement right from the start.

If you would like more information on how to cultivate your child's talents to their fullest, write:

Gifted Education Specialist,
Office of Elementary & Secondary Education,
Room 1725-A,
Donohoe Building,
400 Maryland Avenue SW,
Washington, D.C. 20202.

What's the best way to study for an exam?

For some people, the best way to study is with classmates. According to a University of Washington study, students who got together before an exam to review their notes got much higher grades on the test than students who studied alone. Scientists say that's because social support from peers helps to reduce the stress of an exam. Studying with others makes you less worried about your individual problems and more concerned with the group's contributions. As a result, you're less nervous and do better on the test.

It's also not a good idea to stay up too late the night before an exam, and you should think twice about drinking coffee to keep awake. Researchers found that for some people there is a strong correlation between high coffee intake and low grades, both for semester averages and individual class marks.

A few more tips: On the day of the exam, try to keep things as normal as possible. Eat what you usually eat—stuffing yourself or skimping on meals can cause a headache or upset stomach. Wear comfortable clothes, so that your apparel doesn't distract you during the test.

Finally, when the exam paper is handed out in class, take a deep breath or two and relax. Concentrate on only one question at a time and read it carefully. Skip hard questions and return to them later. And keep telling yourself you have enough time to finish.

Can you get a kid to like homework?

Probably not, but at least you can get a child to do it. Home-workitis is a common but often curable affliction that is a symptom of immaturity and an attempt to avoid the aches and pains of growing up.

Curing homework avoidance takes work on the part of the parents. A systematic approach seems to work best. The idea is to foster academic discipline in a delinquent school child.

Dr. Thomas P. Millar, a Canadian child psychiatrist, has come up with a simple system that has had good results. Here's what he advises parents to do to encourage reluctant learners to do their homework:

☐ Ask your child's teachers to keep you up-to-date on what the class's assignments are and to let you know at the end of each week what homework the child has failed to do or complete.

☐ The teacher's report can be sent home in a sealed envelope via the child every Friday. A precaution may have to be taken because many children tend to "lose" such envelopes—and parents assume that no envelope means the child has done his or her work that week. If an envelope doesn't arrive, take your child back to school to get it. Most children tend to "remember" along the way where they lost the envelope.

☐ Over the weekend, send your child to his or her room with the envelope for a three-hour stretch of work. When the time is up, let the child quit without any comment on your part, even if he or she has not done a stroke of work.

☐ Send the homework back to the teacher with the child on Monday.

☐ Repeat the process for several weeks or until the youngster is doing the homework as it's assigned.

☐ Don't worry if the child's work is a little sloppy at first. The initial goal is completion, not quality. Once he or she learns to finish the homework, the quality should improve. If not, the child may have to spend some extra time working on neatness.

Regardless of what gets done, progress is made the very first week. The child knows that there is a responsibility to finish homework—and that not completing it is going to cost him or her part of the weekend.

Dr. Millar found that, within a month, children usually get the message: There is no way around it, homework has to get done.

What's one reason many children don't learn?

They don't know how to listen. Listening is a far more complex skill than is generally realized, and it requires a good deal of practice before children develop their powers of concentration adequately.

To be a good listener, a child must be able to "tune out" the unimportant random noises that bombard the ears. Even in school, there are many distracting sounds—the ringing of bells, the squeaking of chalk on the blackboard, the whispers of classmates. A child has to know how to focus attention on what really matters.

To learn to read, the first-grader must be able to distinguish

181

sounds and to repeat them. To take tests, it's often necessary to follow verbal directions. Then, too, when teacher explains addition at the blackboard, the beginning arithmetic student had better be able to pay close attention.

You can work with your toddler to begin developing essential learning skills by playing "listening games" together. Here are a few activities suggested by educational experts to get you started:

☐ Describe an object and tell the child to find it and bring it to you.

☐ Give a series of verbal directions for your youngster to carry out, such as "Go to the closet, get your green hat, and put it on the hall table."

☐ Collect things that make interesting sounds—a watch, a harmonica, sandpaper, and some wooden beads, for example. Then, blindfold the child and see how many can be identified by sound alone.

☐ Clap out a rhythm and ask the child to repeat it.

☐ Most important of all, read aloud to your child, regularly and frequently, from babyhood on. Discuss details of the story to make sure the youngster is listening carefully. A good listener makes a good learner.

How can a child find self-esteem?

By running—not from problems, mind you. Just running. A recent study of fifth and sixth graders shows that children troubled by a sense of failure felt markedly better about themselves after participating in a supervised running program.

To measure the children's own opinions of themselves, researchers used a standardized Inventory of Self-Esteem form. On it, the children were asked to indicate whether each of a list of fifty-eight statements described "how you usually feel." The statements included: "I often wish I were someone else"; "I find it very hard to talk in front of the class"; "I can usually take care of myself"; "I'm popular with kids my own age"; "Kids usually follow my ideas," and "I'm a failure."

After filling in the form, the children were instructed to jog a distance of at least one mile three times a week for seven weeks. Those who did not have the stamina to complete the entire mile were allowed to stop and rest, then continue. Records were kept of each runner's speed and distance, so they could see the improvement.

Upon completing the seven-week running program, the youngsters again answered the questions on the form. The results showed a remarkable boost in children's estimations of their own capability, successfulness, and overall worthiness.

We've always known that running keeps one physically fit, and now this study indicates that it aids emotional fitness as well. Jogging, it seems, can get an out-of-joint child back on the right track.

Can sorting socks teach a young child to be a math wizard?

Maybe. Sorting socks by color and size teaches the child about classifying objects, about discriminating between larger and smaller articles, and about separating by pairs. These are basic lessons in mathematics, which is concerned with bringing order to things.

If your three-year-old learns to recite from one to fifty you may think the child is a budding Einstein. But experts say that such feats of memory do not really provide a child with any understanding of the relationships between numbers.

Another way for a preschooler to learn math at home is by helping to set the table. This involves figuring out how many places will be necessary. It also requires rearranging objects from one pattern (how the flatware is laid out in the drawer) to another (how it's placed around each dinner plate). And before filling the water glasses from a pitcher, the child must estimate approximately how much water will be needed.

Once you get started you'll find math concepts hidden in all sorts of everyday household tasks.

To further enrich these early math experiences, make a point of using the appropriate words. For example, say to the child, "Let's cut these tomatoes in *half*," or, "Put the *largest* socks in daddy's drawer," or, "Your doll is *behind* the chair." Words referring to size, quantity, measurement, location, or geometric shapes are all useful additions to a youngster's vocabulary.

Can a baby be bored?

Sure. Like adults, infants get bored if they don't have a variety of interesting things to gaze at. And when they're bored, they don't learn as well.

Infants even have strong preferences. According to new research, they enjoy simple, bold patterns more than solid colors. Special favorites are checkerboards, bull's eyes, large geometric shapes, and animal silhouettes.

A changing display of these patterns placed within eight to twelve inches of their eyes fascinates babies. In one study, newborns seemed to get bored when they looked at the same thing too long. But when a new pattern was shown to them, their attention picked up immediately and their looking time increased.

Infants can move their eyes to follow objects. This is called tracking, and it encourages youngsters to focus, turn their heads, and eventually reach for and grasp things. Brightly colored mobiles hanging above crib or playpen and swinging gently can absorb a baby for quite some time. And just talking to your baby while you move around the room gives the child a target to follow and also experience in associating sight and sound.

Change the location of the crib, or the child's position in the crib, occasionally. Most carriages and car beds offer a limited range of vision, so try raising the child's head into a better viewing position from time to time. If necessary, hold the youngster over your shoulder (not of course in a moving car). A change of scenery is as good for babies as it is for grown-ups.

Can soccer pay your daughter's way through college?

If your daughter has a dynamite pitch, kick, or hook shot, it could mean a free shot at a college education.

The chance for a sports scholarship for your son may not surprise you, but your daughter can now win one, too. In fact, it may be as easy for your daughter to win a sports scholarship as it is for your son. Each year, 10,000 partial and full-time scholarships are available to outstanding female athletes.

The scholarships are available to young women in sports that were at one time chiefly the domain of men: basketball, soccer, field hockey, and softball. They are offered by major colleges and universities such as the University of California at Los Angeles and Notre Dame. All your daughter needs are good skills, grades, and the desire to compete.

If your daughter comes from a small town or attends a high school that's not big on sports, sending her to a summer sports camp may be a good idea. Sports camps for girls are growing in popularity and in number across the country. They can help your daughter to improve her skills and give her the opportunity to play with some of the best athletes around. Another plus is that they're a good place to make contacts. Often, sports camps are the first place where coaches go to scout new talent, evaluate campers' skills, and forward recommendations to colleges.

If you want more information about sports scholarships and camps, write or call the universities your daughter wants to attend to find out if scholarships are available for a particular sport, and what she can do to qualify. Or contact a sports camp and ask for details about its program and scholarship-preparation activities.

When is college a vacation?

If you are sixty or older, with a yen for adventure, you can go away to college for your next vacation. Last year more than 20,000 men and women combined traveling and learning by taking part in Elderhostel, a nonprofit network of more than 300 colleges in the United States and Canada that offers year-round vacation-study programs for older citizens.

Elderhostel is based on the belief that retirement does not mean spending the rest of your life on a park bench. Inspired by the youth hostels and folk schools of Europe, Elderhostel gives older persons the opportunity to study just about anything that interests them—from macramé or Shakespeare to computer science. You'll attend classes taught by the regular members of the college faculty. Better still, you'll learn at your own speed without the pressure of tests and grades. And it doesn't matter whether you are a Ph.D. or a high-school dropout.

"Senior" students generally take up to three courses a week. Classes are small—thirty to forty persons in all. Elderhostelers live in college dormitories and take their meals in the school cafeterias. The cost for room, board, tuition, and extracurricular activities is about $130 a week. Couples are welcome.

Many Elderhostelers get so addicted to the program that they spend their vacations traveling from one campus to another, taking new courses and making new friends. As one satisfied couple put it: "We're going next year and the year after that, and the year after that . . . as long as they'll accept us."

You can register for any program or series of programs through the organization's national office, 100 Boylston Street, Suite 200, Boston, Mass. 02166. Elderhostel will send a free catalogue describing all the colleges in its network, as well as their course offerings.

Do coeds over thirty-five shape up?

They often do even better in school than their youthful counterparts, and many excel. And the years they may have spent working or at home rearing children are paying off tangibly. A number of colleges give course credit for work experience and such life experiences as mothering, volunteer work, and nutrition.

More than a million women over thirty-five years old are now back in school—in high schools, colleges, and graduate and professional schools—either to finish their education or to prepare for a new career. Since 1972, the number in college has doubled. And they're doing quite well, thank you.

The increase of community colleges around the country, which are located close to home and work, has made it easy for many women, and men, to fit an academic schedule into their lives. But some worry whether they're too old to learn or to compete with all those smart young adults. The answer is: They are not too old, and they can compete.

In a study done almost twenty years ago at DePaul University in Chicago, researchers found that older women (in this case, over the age of forty) who matriculated in four-year degree programs at both DePaul and Roosevelt University, also in Chicago, gave "a better than average total performance" in their college work. The women also proved successful in every field of study, and when researchers analyzed performance in terms of grades, they found the older women gave "a superior total performance and a superior performance in each of the fields of study." They got more As than their younger classmates, about the same percentage of Bs and Cs, and fewer Ds and Fs.

Recently, Fordham University in New York City did a special study for *FYI* and confirmed the earlier DePaul findings: Older women do as well in Fordham as the traditional student.

College scholarships for a lefty? A rodeo rider? A caddy?

Like most parents, you've probably wondered how you're going to pay for your child's college education. Your teenager may not qualify for a sports or academic scholarship. But did you know that there are thousands of other grants awarded each year—many based on very unusual special conditions?

The Rochester Institute of Technology in New York has promised $1,500 in future tuition assistance to each of 150 youngsters who were born in the United States on June 12, 1979, the 150th anniversary of the school's founding. The waiting list is still open.

Your last name may be the key to scholarship funds. Harvard has grants for freshmen named Anderson, Baxendale, Borden, Bright, Downer, Have, Murphy, and Pennoyer. Yale offers $1,000 a year to incoming students named Leavenworth or De-Forest. If you are a descendant of one of New York's founding Dutch families, your daughter may be eligible for special Barnard College scholarships.

Certain offbeat occupations or skills can qualify a student for financial aid. The University of Arizona will provide $500 to any applicant with a grade average of at least 2.5 who has roped calves in a rodeo. The children of fishermen are eligible for a grant at Tufts University. A youngster who has worked as a caddy

187

may apply for one of the nearly 3,000 scholarships endowed by golfing enthusiasts. Work on an Indian reservation for at least six weeks qualifies students for $600 from the federal government.

Other unusual qualifications include: the country or state of a student's birth, ethnic background or intended course of study, or a parent's union affiliation or the business or industry in which he or she works. For example, Cornell University gives $1,000 a year to American Indians from New York State who enroll in their agricultural program. An American citizen of Austrian–Jewish extraction who will major in genetics can receive $10,000 from a private foundation in Switzerland.

Even being left-handed may entitle one to a scholarship. Juniata College in Pennsylvania awards $10,000 each year to a southpaw.

Take the time to investigate your child's eligibility by getting in touch with the financial-aid office of the university or college he or she is considering. Or you can contact a commercial company, Scholarship Search, 800 Huyller Street, Peterboro, N.J. 07608, which stores this information on a computer.

What's the easiest way to save for college?

For starters, forget about putting money toward your child's education in your ordinary savings account. Savings accounts earn a minimum of interest, and, with inflation, each dollar in such an account is almost certainly going to be worth less by the time the child is ready for college. And you'll be paying income taxes on the interest, too.

On top of that, the cost of a college education is definitely getting more and more expensive. Currently, the average cost of a four-year college education—room, board, and tuition—comes to about $13,000 at state universities, and upwards of $48,000 at Ivy League schools. Projected costs for a college education for a child born this year, accounting for inflation over the next eighteen years, are about $50,000 at a state university and $80,000 at a private college.

Fortunately, there is a way to soften the financial blow: a trust or custodial fund in your child's name. If, for example, you were to set aside $500 a year for eighteen years at, say, an average 10 percent per annum, you would end up with a college fund of nearly $23,000—even more if interest rates are as high as they have been in the recent past.

The key is to put that money in your child's name. If you were to save the same amount of money in your own name, you would end up with only about $17,000 after eighteen years, assuming you were in a 30 percent tax bracket, because of the taxes you would have to pay. Your child does not have to pay taxes on the interest earned until the youngster's total annual earnings exceed $3,300. Because it's likely your child will be earning less than you, the taxes will be minimal. Before setting up a custodial or trust account you'll need to get a Social Security number for the child, but that's no problem whatsoever. Pay heed, though, that once you set aside money in the youngster's behalf, the decision is irrevocable. The money belongs to the child, and, while you may serve as a custodian of the account, managing the money for the child, you must do so in the youngster's best interests. You cannot use any of it for paying family bills, buying a new house, or a financial emergency.

Another thing to keep in mind: Depending on the state you live in, when your child reaches the age of eighteen, nineteen, or twenty-one, all the money accumulated in the trust or custodial account legally belongs to the child, not the parent. That means your son or daughter can choose whether to use the money for college or for something else, for example, a sports car. There may be no legal way to prevent that.

Check with your bank. All things considered, if you want to plan early for your child's higher education, a trust or custodial account makes sense.

When is meditation called for?

Meditation is a proven stress reducer. In every research study so far, it has dramatically reduced anxiety in the majority of subjects.

Meditation also helps insomnia. In one study, persons who had difficulty falling asleep, tossing and turning for about one and a half hours, fell asleep within fifteen minutes after lying down in bed once they began to practice meditation.

The New York Telephone Company recently conducted a study to see if meditation could reduce stress among employees. After practicing meditation for twenty-two weeks, the 154 workers involved in the study showed a sharp decrease in symptoms of depression, high blood pressure, and other stress-related illnesses.

Other studies have proved the technique effective in relieving headaches, back pain, and asthma.

To meditate, sit comfortably, quietly, and still in a chair. Pay close attention to a single stimulus, such as your breathing or a word that you repeat silently. If your mind wanders, which it will, gently bring it back to the stimulus.

Begin by meditating five minutes a day, and increase gradually until you can comfortably meditate for twenty minutes.

While meditating, your mind will remain alert, but your heart and respiration rate will drop to what it would be after seven hours of sleep.

When you complete your daily meditation, you'll feel more alert, refreshed, and able to cope.

Who's the most important person to talk to before buying a new car?

For sure, neither a car salesperson nor a banker. Talk to your insurance agent, who could save you quite a lot of cash.

Insurance companies are revising the methods they use for computing the cost of collision and comprehensive policies, and you can profit from the changes.

Traditionally, the cost of car insurance was determined primarily by the price paid for the vehicle coupled with the owner's personal driving record, frequency of use, age, sex, and place of residence. These factors still count, but more and more companies—including many of the nation's largest ones—are taking each particular model's safety-performance record into consideration. The fewer claims, the lower the premium charge. This means that the insurance costs for two cars in the same price range might vary as much as 20 percent. By choosing your new car carefully you could save up to $1,000 over the life of the auto.

A model's safety-performance rating is determined by its collision, fire, and theft records. Less favorable ratings go to cars with complex designs that result in higher labor charges for post-collision body work. Premiums are higher for compacts and sub-compacts because they suffer more serious damage and are involved in more collisions than larger vehicles. Two-door models also have higher collision costs than four-door versions of the same car. And that flashy sports car is more likely to catch a car thief's eye than a more conservatively styled vehicle.

Insurance companies update their safety-performance ratings every year. Your agent can tell you how long the car you're interested in has had a good rating. If the model has a consistent record of lower losses, the odds are that it will stay that way—and the premiums will remain lower, too.

The full nest: How do you cope?

If you want the reunion to succeed, a family summit meeting should be called to discuss all the adjustments that will be necessary for parents and returning children to live together again.

For many parents, the discovery that their adult children do come home is producing what has been dubbed "the full nest syndrome." An increasing number of grown children are returning to reside with mom and dad as a result of inflation, unemployment, deteriorating urban housing, soaring divorce rates, and a tight mortgage market.

If your adult children, married or unmarried, want to move back with you, what can you do to ensure a happy reunion? Accept the fact that, although you love your children, you understandably may harbor mixed feelings about enlarging the household. You and your spouse have been looking ahead to years of less responsibility, more leisure, and lower expenses. Perhaps you've considered moving to smaller living quarters or doing some traveling.

So before you welcome the offspring home again, call a family meeting. First on the agenda ought to be household expenses and how they'll be shared. Asking your grown children to contribute to rent, food, and other essentials is not only fairer to you but will also help to restore their self-esteem, which is probably bruised by the need to move in with you.

Next, discuss the question of guests. Everyone in the house should be notified before visitors are invited. Friends who are accustomed to dropping in can be politely told of the change and the reason for it. One situation that disturbs many parents occurs when unmarried children invite boyfriends or girlfriends to stay overnight. Make sure to voice your feelings about this.

Helping out with household chores should be talked about, too, because there's bound to be more cooking, shopping, laundry, and cleaning. Responsibility for specific tasks should be clear. Guard against falling into a pattern of picking up after your children or running personal errands that they are more than capable of doing themselves.

Privacy is probably the key to success in two-generation households. To the greatest degree possible, live in separate areas of the house with your own telephones. Some families are able to convert a garage or a portion of the house into a complete apartment.

For most young adults, returning home is a temporary measure. They plan to move just as soon as circumstances improve. For both you and them, being together again can be a harmonious interlude that cements your relationship as adults who not only love but thoroughly like one another.

How do you say no to a door-to-door salesperson?

Just because you said yes the first time and bought that vacuum cleaner doesn't mean you can't change your mind. The Federal Trade Commission has established regulations designed to protect the consumer with regard to door-to-door sales.

If your purchase cost more than $25 it's covered by the government's new rules. A salesperson is required to give you two copies of a printed cancellation form as well as the selling company's name and business address and information about your cancellation rights. If you change your mind about the purchase, deliver or mail the forms to the seller within three business days.

The company that sold you the goods must return any down payment, deposits, and signed papers or contracts within ten days after receiving your cancellation order.

If you've already received the merchandise the company has

twenty days from the time it receives your cancellation order to pick up the goods. If it doesn't reclaim them within the allotted period, they belong to you and can be kept or disposed of as you wish.

If you're denied any of these rights, you should file a complaint with the Federal Trade Commission, Correspondence Department, Washington, D.C. 20580, or write to the regional F.T.C. listed in your phone book.

Is there a way to beat inflation?

Don't buy what you need. Swap for it.

A dentist in Denver repairs a patient's bridgework in exchange for a carpentry job in his home. A housewife in Harrisburg, Pa., trades her living-room rug for a neighbor's fur coat. A farmer outside Atlanta tends the vegetable garden of an electrician who's rewired his barn.

The barter system didn't go out with the advent of coinage. Studies show that it's making a strong comeback across the country because of tightening economic conditions. Many persons are turning to trading goods and services as a means of making ends meet or acquiring an otherwise unaffordable item.

Nonprofit neighborhood barter clubs are popping up in communities in every part of the nation. The clubs provide a clearing house for would-be barterers. They can register their available skills and merchandise with the group and specify what they're looking for in return. Other organizations serve the business community by providing a vehicle through which merchants and manufacturers can exchange surplus goods.

In addition to clubs, prospective barter partners can often be found through newspaper advertisements. Many community papers now offer barter columns in their classified sections. Church and community bulletin boards can also be good sources of potential exchanges.

Once a trading partner is located, barter arrangements should be entered into with the same care you would show in any other business deal. Both parties should have a clear understanding of what each is offering the other—and in what condition. Being specific and firmly agreeing on terms in advance can

193

minimize the chances of future disagreement. There should be some give-and-take in negotiations but you should never commit yourself to a deal in which you feel compromised.

Moreover, bartering is not a tax-free proposition. The Internal Revenue Service considers the fair-market value of goods and services taken as payment as taxable income. It must be reported.

For more information on nonprofit barter groups, write Volunteer, The National Center for Citizen Involvement, P.O. Box 4179, Boulder, Col. 80306.

Divorce: Can you avoid a lawyer?

Couples can now resolve property and custody disputes peacefully through low-priced divorce mediation rather than engaging in expensive and often fierce courtroom contests. The procedure has been made possible through the passage of no-fault divorce laws in recent years in all states but Illinois and South Dakota.

Instead of standing off to the side while lawyers argue their fate—often at $100 an hour or more—couples who choose divorce mediation sit down with an impartial professional mediator and work out the critical issues of their own futures: How will they divide their property? What provisions can be made for the individual support of each? What type of child-care arrangement is sensible? A lawyer is not called in to draft the necessary legal papers until the couple reaches an agreement.

Divorce mediation makes use of techniques developed by labor negotiators, social workers, and attorneys. These involve bringing together people with strong opposing views—but with a common interest in working out a solution—in face-to-face meetings. Mediation helps relieve much of the stress of divorce, and helps couples arrive at settlements with greater ease.

At the first session, the couple sign contracts in which they agree to disclose their finances fully. They are given detailed questionnaires to fill out on their monetary assets and needs. A property settlement generally is the first order of business, and clears the way for the discussion of other matters. Mediation is most useful when the property settlement is small and uncomplicated.

If an impasse is reached, the mediator may appoint an arbitrator who hears both sides—with witnesses if desired—and makes a decision that is binding in most states. All but the most complicated cases can usually be completed in five two-hour sessions. A settlement drawn up through mediation can cost thousands of dollars less than one hammered out by lawyers.

California has a mandatory divorce mediation and conciliation system. Low-cost or free divorce mediation is available through the family courts of more than a dozen states as well as through the offices of the American Arbitration Association, a nonprofit organization located at 140 West 51 Street, New York, N.Y. 10020. A growing network of lawyers, psychologists, social workers, and marriage counselors have been trained and certified as divorce mediators.

When's the right time to prove an insurance claim?

Before a serious catastrophe such as a fire occurs. Documentation of all your property is necessary to recoup all your losses.

About eight out of ten homeowners fail to document all their property—furniture, tableware, rugs, paintings, jewelry, whatever is of value. And without proof, no insurance company is going to pay a claim in full.

The best way to establish proof is to have a photographic inventory of everything in every room of your home—pictures of walls, ceilings, chairs, sofas, tables, dressers, rugs, TV, and stereo sets. Your entire collection of chinaware should be photographed—within the cabinet you house it in is acceptable. If that's not possible, spread the dishes out on a table and photograph. Spread out all the silverware, too. Also, take closeups of several pieces of the chinaware and the silverware to show details of their patterns.

Once developed and printed, the photographs should be dated. Include on the back any additional information you deem important. Then store the photographs in a safe place, preferably outside the home—in a bank deposit box, for example. If inside the home, put them in a fireproof and waterproof container.

Although sales receipts seem an obvious proof of worth, they aren't unless the purchases were made within the last three years. Inflation outdates the receipts and the cost of replacing the lost items. Inflation also affects written appraisals of jewelry and art valuables; they must be updated periodically to reflect replacement costs.

Estate inventories can serve as proof of ownership, but don't use them as proof of value for a claim. The appraisals are usually quite low because they were done for inheritance-tax purposes. The figures do not reflect the cost of replacing items but rather what the various goods would bring in a forced sale.

Should disaster strike in the form of fire, earthquake, hurricane, freezings, heavy storms, even an auto accident—as long as you weren't willfully negligent—you can deduct what the insurance doesn't cover from your income-tax returns.

Why should a woman borrow money when she doesn't need it?

Because it's the surest way to establish credit. And if she doesn't borrow and then needs credit, she may not find it so easy to get.

In 1975, Congress passed the Equal Opportunity Credit Act, which made it illegal for a woman to be denied credit because she is a female, no matter whether married, divorced, separated, single, or widowed. The problem is that many women are still unaware of their rights under this law, and, even among those who are, establishing credit can be a slow process. Women are still refused credit because of a "lack of a sufficient credit history," and it may take them as long as three years to develop one.

For this reason, financial experts strongly advise a woman to go about establishing a credit history long before she needs it—especially in these times of tight credit.

First open a savings and checking account in your own name. Second, apply to department stores for a charge account—also in your own name. After using these charge cards for a year, apply for a bank card. Then apply to your bank for a check guarantee or overdraft privilege on your checking account. Finally, ask your bank for a loan. That's right—paying off a small loan promptly is one of the best ways to assure credit. And make sure to pay your bills on time. That will help make your credit history solid.

The procedure may seem lengthy in itself, but if you are suddenly widowed, separated, or divorced, you'll appreciate the trouble you went to. That's why the financial experts believe you should act now rather than wait for a personal crisis to develop.

Do service contracts for household appliances really pay off?

Beware. A recent university study found that service contracts frequently are not good buys.

Major household appliances always seem to break down unexpectedly, just when you need them most. The service contracts offered to consumers by appliance dealers and service companies may appear to protect the family budget from soaring repair costs, but researchers at the Massachusetts Institute of Technology have discovered otherwise. They kept track of repair charges on a number of different types of equipment for six years and then compared the totals with the costs of service contracts on the same items for the same period.

For color television sets, service contracts turned out be ten times more expensive than the actual repairs. Refrigerator contracts were sixteen times more costly than the price of fixing each malfunction as it occurred.

If you have the bad luck to be the owner of an appliance that is a "lemon" and your warranty has run out, a service contract will no doubt save you money because of the number of repairs or parts needed. But if you prepay for a year of service and then don't need any repairs, you obviously have made a bad deal. So you have to play the odds. For a piece of equipment that is old or has a poor performance record, a service contract is more likely to be a worthwhile investment, provided the charge is not outrageous.

A few pointers to remember: New appliances often come with factory warranties; make sure you are not purchasing protection for which you are already entitled. See if parts as well as labor are covered in whatever contracts you consider and whether calls are unlimited. Read the fine print to learn if you can transfer the contract to a new owner (if you sell the appliance) or to a new appliance (if you replace the originally insured piece of equipment). Make certain that the provider of service under your contract guarantees a fast response to your call for help; this can be important when your dishwasher pours a few inches of water on the kitchen floor or the freezer that you've just stocked with food suddenly goes on the blink.

Who's afraid of a big, bad phobia?

There are 20 million victims of phobias in the United States, half a million of whom have phobias so serious that their lives are severely affected. But new ways to conquer the fears have been discovered.

The most common phobia is agoraphobia—the fear of leaving home and mingling in public places, a terrifying experience for anyone who has visions of crushing crowds, threatening strangers, or dangerous animals. Phobias take many other forms—fear of heights, of enclosed places, of animals, of insects—and any one of them can be debilitating.

Until recently, these fears were difficult to treat. Long psychotherapy sessions offered some relief, but the success rate was low. But now psychologists have developed techniques that offer much better results. One of the most successful is a procedure called "desensitization therapy"—a method of gradually exposing a patient to the source of the fear until it is overcome. The success rate with this therapy can run as high as 90 percent. Although some phobias take longer to treat than others, desensitization can sometimes conquer the problem in a matter of weeks.

Another new method of treating phobias is called "contextual analysis and therapy." It is a procedure in which the patient learns to control the onset of a phobic attack by recognizing the irrationality of the fear, and then prevents it from getting out of hand by focusing on the reality of the situation. Some doctors also report excellent results with new forms of medication.

Phobia clinics, specifically designed to help victims of the disease, have been springing up around the country. They offer substantial promise to sufferers. Some will send outreach workers to persons afraid to leave home, and the costs are often covered by health insurance. Other treatment facilities operate on a sliding-fee scale, with fees based on ability to pay.

Persons who are interested in learning more about phobia treatment would do well to begin at the local library. Most have several books explaining the new therapies. Also, state psychological associations will gladly refer phobia sufferers to certified psychologists and treatment centers.

The Seven-Year Itch: Fact or fiction?

"The Seven-Year Itch" has been popular in fiction—as a funny play and then a movie—but for many marriages it is no comedy. Therapists report that the "itch" is a genuine marital phenomenon, a dissatisfaction, usually characterized by sexual restlessness, that occurs about seven years into a marriage. It can lead either to a severe marital crisis or, if worked through, to a stronger and more committed relationship between husband and wife.

Researchers with the Marriage Council of Philadelphia found that the itch seems to be associated with a "period of life review" that many persons go through at the age of about thirty. Census data in the United States shows that couples tend to marry in their early twenties and have been married for about seven years when one or both reach thirty. The Marriage Council, a marriage-counseling organization, reports that their "intakes" included twice as many couples with one partner or both between twenty-eight and thirty-two years old, and that the average length of these marriages was seven years.

Several psychological studies undertaken since the 1930s indicate that at specific ages we tend to move through distinct stages of life. Age thirty seems to be the time when many of us begin evaluating our life-styles and ambitions, with a sense of pressure to change "before it's too late." One result is a tendency to experiment with different life-styles, and that usually includes thoughts of separation, extramarital sex, and general marital dissatisfaction without any identifiable cause.

In one study, two researchers found that the "happiness measure" in marriage shows a steady decline from the early days of the relationship to a low point five to eight years after the marriage. There is a second low point, usually fifteen to seventeen years later.

199

As the research seems to indicate, the Seven-Year Itch is real enough, but it is more of a symptom of a transition—or, as author Gail Sheehey has labeled it, a "passage"—than a genuine marital crisis. Nevertheless, if a couple does not realize what is happening, the episode can easily end their marriage. Counselors at the Marriage Council found that when couples with difficulties were helped to view their marital dissatisfaction in the larger context of the gradual growth most adults must go through, both spouses appeared greatly relieved.

Is going wacky a sane thing to do?

You bet your bananas it is! When periods of stress and symptoms of tension arise, some psychologists believe that it is healthier to stop worrying and to take a completely different tack. Yell at the television set. Make faces in a mirror. Tramp around the house like Groucho Marx. Hold a conversation with yourself.

We've all got a bit of the outrageous lurking beneath our sometimes overly self-controlled exteriors, and it can be healthy and tension-relieving to let a little of it surface. Anything will do, as long as it's unusual and fun but harmless to yourself and others.

Breaking out of your normal routine through a little harmless wackiness isn't difficult. Most importantly, it can help you take the world and yourself less seriously and, by doing so, ease some of those stressful feelings.

Being wacky should help you survive those particular moments of stress when you feel like screaming out loud, but it's also important to try to control stress on a regular daily basis. The simplest way is to relax, although, for most of us, that's apparently not as easy as it sounds. According to the National Institute of Mental Health, few Americans really know how to relax or how to benefit from relaxation. And the benefits may be considerable indeed, because relaxation can help prevent headaches, ulcers, and hypertension.

What exactly is relaxation? According to the experts, it's doing something you really enjoy that is totally absorbing, a complete change of pace from your normal routine, and doing it for at least a half hour each day. Don't be afraid to try something new,

200

completely off your beaten path—like needlepoint, learning how to dance, or taking up painting, sculpting or any of a number of hobbies you always wanted to try. Start an indoor garden. Build a bookcase. Do anything out of the norm you want to—but do it regularly.

Many persons feel guilty when they're relaxing. They feel that it's not productive and they're doing nothing. But the experts reassure us that relaxation is not at all inactivity and it is not self-indulgent. In fact, it could be an important key to safeguarding your mental and physical health.

What's a fast, cheap way to avoid rear-end collisions?

Put a third brake light in the middle atop the trunk, near the rear window.

Rear-end collisions are the second most common type of road accident—some 3.5 million drivers are involved each year. But the latest research confirms that improving the visibility of vehicles can significantly reduce that number.

Recently the National Highway Traffic Safety Administration conducted a major study of the effect of installing a third brake light on the back of cars. The result was a dramatic 50 percent drop in the number of rear-end collisions. The new lamp was found to be most effective when centrally positioned on the trunk, just below the rear window of the auto.

The new brake light has several clear advantages over the traditional style. For one thing, it is not used as a directional signal, or to illuminate the back of the car at night. It remains dark until the driver steps on the brake. Thus, when it does glow, it is an unambiguous signal that the car is slowing or stopping. Also, its higher position puts it directly in the line of vision of the driver of the car behind.

The cost of purchasing a brake light of the recommended type is low: One easily available model costs under $30. The installation is a do-it-yourself project for a reasonably handy person, a snap for an auto mechanic. The wires go directly into the car trunk and are connected to the existing brake lights.

Another important hint for avoiding collisions is to drive a light-colored car. Accidents at night or in bad weather often occur because drivers don't see the other vehicle until it's too late. Recent safety tests disclosed that motorists can see light, bright cars from a distance of up to four times farther away than they can see dark ones. White is best of all.

Is it midsummer madness to turn on the car heater?

Not if the radiator temperature is climbing. Car heaters work by drawing off heat from the engine. So, strange as it may seem, to cool off the engine, turn on the heater.

The heat generated by a car traveling at fifty-five miles an hour is enough to comfortably warm a seven-room house in sub-freezing temperatures. An engine can build up even more heat under sunny skies in the middle of the summer. If you're driving in hot weather or stuck in a midday traffic snarl and the red radiator warning light flashes on, the American Automobile Association advises:

☐ Turn off the air conditioner if your car has one.
☐ Turn on the car heater. It will act like an auxiliary radiator.
☐ Race the motor in neutral for a minute or two. This will speed up the fan and move more air through the coils of the radiator.

The heater solution works for both gasoline-powered and diesel cars. It will not work, however, if the radiator is already boiling over. It's too late by then. So, at regular intervals or before starting out on a lengthy trip:

☐ Check the coolant level in the radiator.
☐ Check fan and drive belts and hoses as well as the air pressure in all the tires, including the spare. Underinflated tires are especially hazardous in hot weather, when they can blow out more readily than at other times.
☐ Remove all shiny objects from the dashboard. They'll reflect sunshine onto the windshield.

Check your own fluid level, too, particularly if you don't

have air conditioning. A person can lose up to a pint of water an hour when driving in hot weather—and a dehydrated, hot, tired driver is a dangerous one. Plan on making stops regularly to get something to drink, preferably water.

Where must landlords put out the welcome mat for children?

In eight states—Arizona, Connecticut, Delaware, Illinois, Massachusetts, Minnesota, New Jersey, New York—and the District of Columbia. All have laws prohibiting housing discrimination against families with children. If you want to live in one of these states and you're refused a rental because of the children, contact the state agency responsible for housing or your state attorney general's office.

If you want to rent elsewhere, check with your local elected official or the community board. Many municipal ordinances have been enacted to prohibit a no-children policy. In addition, check to see if there is any grass-roots group in the area you want to live in. One such group in Santa Monica, Calif., the Fair Housing for Children Coalition, campaigns actively for legislation to protect families and also helps to find housing by offering a list of rental units that allow children. The coalition suggests trying to change the mind of a landlord who is reluctant to rent because children may cause damage, by offering a larger security deposit.

If a "no children" clause prevents you from renting a home or apartment, and you can't get information about a local ordinance, you can contact the U.S. Department of Housing and Urban Development. It'll be able to tell you where such discriminatory clauses are legally in effect.

Is it possible to beat high legal costs?

There is a way. It's called a legal clinic. For individuals with simple legal problems, the clinics offer a money-saving alternative to the traditional law firm.

203

Comparative studies show that the quality of legal services performed by the clinics are generally equal and often superior to those provided by standard practitioners.

The clinics are best for simple cases: uncontested divorces, wills, personal bankruptcies, adoptions, and real-estate closings. Their fees for such services are generally a fraction of those charged by law firms. In more complicated cases and those involving court appearances and negotiations, there's little difference between a clinic's fee and those charged by private attorneys.

The clinics can charge lower fees because they are generally high-volume, highly computerized operations, and, whenever possible, paralegal workers rather than attorneys are used to handle cases.

You can locate clinics in your area through newspaper advertisements or the Yellow Pages. It's a good idea to do a little comparative shopping. Call several clinics and ask about their fees. If they won't quote prices over the phone, determine the cost of a consultation and how long it lasts.

If you visit the office for a consultation, make sure you receive written estimates of all anticipated costs. The advertised prices of the clinics ordinarily cover only the simplest paperwork, so be specific about the type of service you require. Any extra work will probably result in additional charges.

Is there such a thing as a Social Security checkup?

Do you assume, like most Americans, that your Social Security records are kept by the government with flawless accuracy? Well, the truth is that Social Security deductions from your paycheck may *not* always be fully credited to your account. About one in ten of us will have lower benefits than we're entitled to when we retire because of incomplete records. And the miscalculation will affect Medicare benefits, too.

The employment history of nearly everyone who has ever worked for pay is on file with the Social Security Administration. Obviously, a record-keeping effort of mind-boggling enormity is required. Even with the assistance of the most sophisticated computers, errors inevitably slip in.

204

To be absolutely certain that the records on your employment are correct, you should verify them periodically. A preaddressed postcard for this purpose—Form SSA-7004—is available from your local Social Security office, and at some banks, too. Fill in your name and address, date of birth, and Social Security number—and provide your signature. If you prefer, you can send the information on a regular postcard or letter mailed to:

Social Security Administration,
P.O. Box 57,
Baltimore, Md. 21203.

When shouldn't you pay a bill?

When it's incorrect, even if your credit rating is threatened. The federal Fair Credit Billing Act provides relief for the consumer who is involved in a billing dispute.

The law applies to virtually any type of bill, including utility bills, repair charges, or merchandise. You are not required to pay the bill if it lists the wrong purchase price, fails to credit your account for returned merchandise, charges you for goods you didn't buy, or includes some item you simply cannot figure out. Nor do you have to pay for the delivery of a wrong item or anything you ordered but never received. All these protections apply regardless of how many times the store has dunned you.

What should you do if any billing problem arises? You can call the company that sent the bill and try to settle the matter over the phone. However, a phone call will not protect your rights under the law. To do that, you must write to the company. Your notice must reach it within sixty days after receiving the erroneous bill. Your letter should include your name and account number, describe the mistake, and provide an explanation—for example, that you never bought the item. Be as specific as possible. Keep a copy of the letter. If the dispute involves a large sum, send the letter certified mail, "return receipt requested."

The company must let you know that it received your letter. And within ninety days it must inform you of its decision in the matter. The law requires the company either to correct your bill or to conduct an investigation. You are entitled to written notice explaining why the firm believes its bill is correct. You can ask

205

the company to send you sales slips or other proof. If the company fails to reply within the ninety-day period, it may not collect the money in dispute or any finance charges up to a maximum of $50, even if the bill turns out to be correct. The company has no responsibility beyond that under this law. A consumer may sue for charges between $100 and $1,000.

Previously, consumers often spent months or even years trying to straighten out a mistake on a bill. Some finally threw in the towel and charged it up to experience. But with the new law, you can get credit where credit is due.

Who's the biggest bargain salesperson of all?

Uncle Sam. The federal government conducts auctions each year with a wide variety of unclaimed and surplus goods and real estate going on the block. Together with municipal and state sales, more than a thousand auctions take place annually.

Federal real-estate auctions often list numerous white elephants, but there are usually enough good values to make these sales worth checking out. In most cases mortgage terms are based on going market rates. Local city-sponsored auctions sometimes offer even better breaks. The City of New York's real-estate auctions, for example, usually arrange mortgages at bargain rates.

The federal government's chief auctioneers are the General Services Administration and the Department of Defense. A GSA sale may offer data-processing equipment, musical instruments, or mobile homes. A late-model car might be available for as low as $3,000. The GSA also handles all sales of federal land and real estate throughout the country. You can get information on upcoming auctions and be placed on its mailing list by contacting the GSA regional office in your area.

The Defense Department has a similar line of property for sale that includes not only cars and trucks, but also airplanes, furniture, and plumbing and heating equipment. (If you've got your heart set on a Jeep, though, you may be out of luck. It seems Jeeps don't come up for sale very often and, when they do, they're usually in terrible condition.) To get on its mailing list, write to Department of Defense, Surplus Sales, P.O. Box 1370, Battle Creek, Mich. 49016.

206

The customs and postal services also conduct periodic sales of a wide variety of high-quality confiscated or unclaimed merchandise. Your regional office of the Treasury Department has information on customs sales. Check your local post office for news of that service's upcoming auctions.

The federal government uses three different auction methods. In a sealed-bid sale, offers are submitted in advance; you base your bid on information supplied by the selling agency about the type and condition of the merchandise. In spot bidding, written bids are submitted while the sale is in progress. The third method, public auction, follows the normal procedures of commercial auction houses.

City police departments also put a great deal of quality merchandise on the block at periodic auctions of unclaimed stolen property. Anything from Cadillacs and stereos to jewelry may be available at bargain rates.

Information on city or state sales can be obtained from your state or city's general services agency.

Caveat Emptor: Everything in a government sale is sold on an "as is, where is" basis, so complaints about a faulty transmission in a just-purchased truck will get you nowhere. If possible, it's better to personally inspect the merchandise prior to a sale. You should figure out pick-up or shipping costs ahead of time, too, because they're the sole responsibility of the buyer.

What three initials may spell an end to your tax problems?

PRP—which stand for Problem Resolution Procedure, a relatively new agency of the Internal Revenue Service set up to handle problems that taxpayers have dealing with government computers.

If you are having trouble getting an answer from Uncle Sam about that tax refund that's overdue, an incorrect billing, or the status of your IRS audit, try PRP. That may sound a bit like a commercial for a headache remedy, and it is—sort of.

PRP is designed to give special, personal attention to taxpayers when normal IRS channels do not work. The IRS advises that if a person has tried more than twice to get a problem resolved without any response, it's time to apply to PRP. For example, if you are expecting a $150 refund and receive instead a bill for $250 in additional taxes, and you try but fail to sort this out with your local IRS service center, turn to PRP for help. PRP will try to resolve the problem within five days; if a delay is unavoidable, PRP will give the taxpayer a status report along with a projected completion date. Hundreds of thousands of persons tangled in bureaucratic red tape have been helped since the program was instituted in 1977.

The IRS, however, advises that PRP is not a substitute for traditional taxpayer services or the tax-appeals process. Nor will it handle Freedom of Information requests, complaints about IRS hiring practices, and Privacy Act inquiries.

Taxpayers can contact PRP by calling IRS Taxpayer Assistance, which is listed in the telephone book, and asking for the PRP office. Be prepared to describe your problem and provide details of previous IRS contacts, a Social Security or employer identification number, and your current address and telephone number.

How can independent-minded senior citizens live alone safely?

By using, if possible, a recently developed beeper system called Lifeline that has already been established in more than 350 communities across the country. Lifeline provides regular contact with an emergency-response system should accident or illness require prompt attention. The system also offers twenty-four-hour access to health, social, and protective services.

Subscribers to Lifeline are given a small, wireless call unit that they can clip to their clothing, wear around the neck, or carry in a pocket. Whenever help is needed, the subscriber pushes a button on the call unit. This activates a transmitting signal connected to the home telephone. The signal will transmit even when the phone is off the hook or during a power failure.

Trained personnel at the response center where the signal is received will try to reach the subscriber by phone. If the line is busy or if there is no answer, they will dispatch immediate help.

An important feature of the service is a timer attached to the phone that can be set at twelve- or twenty-four-hour intervals. Each time the subscriber makes a phone call, the timer is automatically reset. If the subscriber fails to make a phone call or doesn't reset the timer during the prescribed time period, a signal goes off automatically at the response center. Personnel will then try to contact the subscriber by phone. If unsuccessful, they will attempt to reach the subscriber's personal list of friends or relatives who live within ten minutes' distance of the subscriber's home. If emergency help is necessary, the center will then send a medical team and/or ambulance.

The Lifeline system costs from $10 to $20 per month and in some cases is covered by medical insurance. For further information, write to the National Office of Lifeline Systems, Inc., 400 Main St., Waltham, Mass. 02254.

Interested in making a mansion out of a molehill?

If you've been put off from owning your own home by the high cost of buying and financing, try homesteading. No, don't jump into a covered wagon and take off for the Badlands. Homesteading is now possible in ninety-eight cities across the country.

The federal government's Urban Homesteading Program provides funds to purchase old, abandoned buildings at bargain-basement prices. The buyer must agree to restore the structure within a specified time period—usually three years—and to live in it. There are also minimum income and credit qualifications.

Although rules vary from city to city, some general steps apply to all. The first step should be to check the urban homesteading districts in your town and fill out an application. The houses are usually in the inner city because the program has two basic aims: to attract and keep the middle class and to encourage low-income residents to own their own homes. Sales prices may range from an unbelievable one dollar to several hundred, depending on the city.

If you need a mortgage it can be arranged through a local bank at the rate charged for federally guaranteed loans, usually 10 percent. In addition, some cities in cooperation with local banks may provide low-interest loans.

Most of the homes require major rehabilitation work, and the cost of renovating can be high. Often you'll need the assistance of an architect and contractor. Most cities have lists of approved contractors; the advice of other homesteaders is also useful in locating competent craftspersons. Many cities provide lower than bank-rate loans to cover much of the cost of rehabbing. And you can reduce some of the renovation expenses yourself by doing as much of the work as possible.

For more information write to the Rehabilitation Management Division, Office of Urban Rehabilitation, Community Planning and Development, Department of Housing and Urban Development, Washington, D.C. 20110.

There's also a federal program, the Self-Housing Loan Program, that provides financing to build and mortgage homes in rural areas with populations of less than 20,000. It's available in all states and U.S. territories. A recipient's income must be under $18,000 to qualify. The family does the work with the assistance of professional builders and government inspectors.

Some 12,000 homes have been built under this program. To find out more, contact your local Farmers' Home Administration, under U.S. Department of Agriculture in the phone book.

What's the secret to a good day-care center?

Its staff, its surroundings, and its size.

The federal government reports that the use of day-care centers has doubled over the last decade and will continue to rise as the number of working mothers increases. By 1990 an estimated 10.5 million children will have working mothers. To cope with all the questions working mothers have about day care, the U.S. Department of Health and Human Services has published a pamphlet, *A Parent's Guide to Day Care*, which aims to help parents find a suitable day-care situation. Here are some tips from it and other experts in the field:

☐ Look for personnel who are well-trained, warm, and loving toward children. No matter the age of the child, the "care-giver" should encourage the child's interests and stimulate the child to explore new things.

☐ The setting should be safe and healthy with plenty of air

210

and light and an adequate supply of toys and cots, all in good repair.

☐ The optimal size of a day-care group depends on the age of the child: For three-to-five-year-olds, the group can be as large as eighteen, with one staff member for every nine children; for two-to-three-year-olds, the group should have no more then twelve youngsters, with one staff member for every four.

☐ Check out a particular day-care center carefully. Visit several times to watch how the children relate to the care-giver, and the care-givers to the children. Talk to the director to make sure the program squares with your own attitudes toward childrearing and education.

☐ The costs of day care will vary with the center, the amount of time your child spends there, and transportation, so shop around.

To get a copy of *A Parent's Guide to Day Care* (Stock No. 017-091-00231-2) send $4.75 to:
U.S. Government Printing Office,
Washington, D.C. 20402.

Can you collect those overdue child-support payments?

If you're one of the 4 million women in the United States who aren't receiving the child support you were awarded in court, there's a little-known federal program that can help you collect the money you're entitled to.

The program is administered by the Federal Office of Child Support Enforcement (OCSE) in conjunction with state and local CSE agencies. It requires that states try to locate and collect from the missing parent—usually the father. About half the states have a minimum application fee (usually under $20) for non-welfare custody parents who are seeking back payments.

Services include that of public attorneys whose only responsibility is support-enforcement work. The government also operates a computer that can locate absent parents' addresses from records kept by the Internal Revenue Service, the Social Security Administration, and the military.

211

In case the missing parent is living in another state, the Uniform Reciprocal Enforcement of Support Act requires cooperation between states.

If you fail to receive your child-support payments, follow these steps:

- ☐ Find the local agency that handles child-support enforcement. In all states but Michigan it's either the welfare, human services, or district attorney's office. In Michigan, go to the Friend of the Court office in your county.
- ☐ Go to the specified office in person to open a file on your case.
- ☐ Or write to:
  The Office of Child Support Enforcement,
  6110 Executive Blvd., Room 900,
  Rockville, Md. 20852.
- ☐ Get help as soon as possible. It's not a good idea to wait for the missing payments to accumulate. Agency experts report that it is more difficult to collect larger amounts.

The law is on the side of the custody parent. So take action, be patient but persistent, and you'll probably be able to collect the child support that you're due.

Does moving day have to be a losing day?

Not if your family is one of those tens of thousands of families who will make a major move—from one state to another—sometime this year. Federal laws within recent years now make it possible for moving companies to offer several important services that could save you worry and money.

Many moving companies today are providing clients with *binding estimates* of the final cost of the move. What this means is that you no longer need fear that the cost quoted to you beforehand will have multiplied when it comes time to pay. The fee for this service is moderate, about $25. Not every firm offers binding estimates and you may have to shop around, but it could prove to be well worth the effort.

212

You should also inquire about *guaranteed pick-up and delivery dates*. Without a guarantee, the mover will probably give you a spread of several days during which your goods will be picked up and a second series of dates on which they will be delivered to your new address. If your plans are flexible enough to accommodate to this indefinite arrangement, there's no problem. But most families find it much more convenient to have a specific moving day, even if they have to pay a little extra for it. Then, if the van fails to appear on schedule, the company is liable for any out-of-pocket expenses (such as hotels or restaurant bills) incurred as a result.

What if some of your belongings are damaged or lost in transit? If you've ever had that happen to you, you know that filing a claim can be a time-consuming matter that often ends up in the courts. But now some companies are setting up independent arbitration programs. That way disputes can be settled quickly and without cost to the consumer.

For free pamphlets to learn your moving rights, contact:
American Movers Conference,
P.O. Box 2303,
Arlington, Va. 22202.

Can you have a baby after menstruation stops?

In most cases, once the ovaries stop producing eggs, a woman goes through menopause and pregnancy is impossible. But doctors now find that what appears to be an early instance of menopause in women under forty may actually be a curable medical problem called premature ovarian failure. If, as a result, a woman has ceased menstruating, a diagnostic procedure can pinpoint the problem and new fertility treatments may help her resume ovulating. With menstruation restored, she still has a chance to become pregnant.

Treatments for premature ovarian failure are available at special fertility clinics in most parts of the country. The first step is an ovarian biopsy. A sample of tissue is taken and the cells examined under a microscope to see whether the ovaries still contain a supply of follicles. These are the cells that mature into eggs. If the supply of follicles is depleted, this means that a wom-

213

an has already passed through menopause and cannot conceive. But if there are enough follicles present the doctor can try to stimulate ovulation.

In rare cases a woman may have ceased to ovulate because she has developed an "allergy" to her ovary. If this is the case, a new treatment called glucocorticoid therapy can correct the problem in her immune system. The Mayo Clinic reports that this treatment has succeeded in leading to pregnancy.

What's the logical way to give birth?

In, of all things, a chair. Most women deliver babies lying on their backs, not for their own comfort but because of tradition. The obstetrician can more readily check infant heartbeat or use forceps if needed. But an ancient method of delivery using the birthing chair is being brought back to practice. And, according to a special *FYI* survey of 150 maternity hospitals, 99 percent of the women who have used one are enthusiastic about its advantages.

Up until the eighteenth century, the birthing chair was the customary method of delivery. It wasn't unusual for women to include a decorative birthing chair as part of their trousseau. Then, according to legend, a curious thing happened. Louis XIV decided he wanted to watch the birth of his child and ordered his queen to lie down for childbirth. The nobility imitated the king, and so later did the bourgeoisie. Eventually, the sitting position and the chair went out of style. Coincidentally, doctors also felt they had more and better control of the delivery if the patient was lying down.

The modern-day version of the birthing chair is less ornate but much more functional. It's a specially molded chair set on a pedestal with a motor that makes it possible to raise, lower, or tilt the chair to an almost horizontal position should that prove necessary.

There are several advantages to the birthing-chair method of delivery, according to its supporters. Sitting is the natural position for childbirth because gravity is on the mother's side. The sitting position is also more comfortable, easier, and faster. Research shows that a woman uses 18 percent more pushing power

214

to give birth when flat on her back than when she's sitting up.

In addition, the use of the chair seems to shorten the second stage of labor—the delivery of the baby after the cervix is dilated. In one study at New York City's Lenox Hill Hospital, women using the chair averaged only thirty minutes in second-stage labor, while those on their backs averaged ninety minutes. And according to Dr. Warner Nash at the hospital, there was a much lower incidence of fetal distress because the chair allows greater blood circulation to the fetus.

Because of the chair's unique design, women are able to push against it, thereby relieving the pressure on their backs and reducing the pains that often follow a strenuous childbirth.

The success of the birthing chair in the Ashland District Hospital in Ashland, Kansas, was so overwhelming that the hospital stopped using a standard delivery table altogether.

If you're interested in the sitting method of birth, speak to your obstetrician. More than 250 hospitals across the country have birthing chairs available.

Who can replace the husband?

In the labor room, a good friend. The point is someone should be there.

Ideally, it should be the husband. But recent research has found that having someone else present during labor and delivery may also reduce labor time and the chance of complications. It seems that having a reassuring face in the room helps calm most about-to-be mothers.

Some husbands prefer not to be present during childbirth because they're afraid that just the opposite will take place: Their wives will pick up on their anxiety. Other men are simply squeamish.

In a study published in *The New England Journal of Medicine*, doctors from Case Western Reserve University in Cleveland and the Institute of Nutrition of Central America and Panama in Guatemala City compared the labor experiences of expectant mothers with and without companions. The companions were untrained women whom the mothers-to-be had never met before. The doctors found that expectant mothers with companions averaged nine hours of labor compared to nineteen hours for the lone mothers. Moreover, labor complications or problems in delivery and the neonatal stage dropped by 42 percent when a companion was present. The mothers also seemed to be able to stay awake longer after the birth, giving them an opportunity to hold, smile, and talk more with the new baby, an important bonding procedure ensuring closeness between mother and child from the beginning.

Why does the companion make the difference? Doctors theorize that during labor, anxiety raises the blood levels of chemicals that affect uterine contractions and blood flow to the placenta. This in turn may result in longer labor or even fetal problems. The researchers hypothesized that the companion, by calming the mother-to-be, helps to reduce the biological impact of anxiety.

Can a pregnant woman jog?

Yes, she can—and bowl or swim or play tennis, too. Recent comprehensive studies prove false the conventional wisdom that says exercise is dangerous for pregnant women, possibly damaging the fetus or leading to a miscarriage. The heart rates of both the expectant mother and the child were measured while the women exercised. The mother-to-be's heart rate nearly doubled—but the fetal heart beat increased by less than 1 percent.

You should, of course, discuss your exercise and athletic program with your doctor if you're pregnant. There may be individual aspects to your pregnancy—for example, high blood pressure or a weak cervix—that rule out physical exertion. Your previous medical history may also dictate a more limited athletic schedule, particularly during the first three months when the dangers of disturbing the fetus are greatest.

The odds are, however, that your obstetrician won't raise any barriers to your continuing your favorite sport. But don't expect to break any records in the marathon or play six sets of tennis a day. Your body will tell you when to ease up and you should listen to its signals.

And if you're not athletically inclined, you should follow a system of moderate exercise to cut down on physical problems that sometimes accompany pregnancy. Research shows that such a program can also help prepare your body to cope better with the stress of labor and delivery, and can also contribute to a speedier recovery.

Many Ys and other facilities offer exercise programs specifically tailored to meet the needs of mothers-to-be.

Should a pregnant woman get "fat"?

Yes, within reason. Despite what many advise about keeping weight gain to an absolute minimum, a pregnant woman is indeed, as the saying goes, eating for two.

The most recent finding is that restricting the intake of food can be unhealthy for both mother and baby. If a pregnant woman is undernourished, her baby is also deprived—not only of adequate nutrition but also of a good start in life.

Babies born to women who rigidly control their weight tend to be small at birth. However, these women may not necessarily experience easier deliveries, because a deficient maternal diet also increases the risk of complications such as prematurity, prolonged labor, and stillbirth. Low-birth-weight infants are more susceptible to infection, and are more likely to be mentally retarded or to suffer from epilepsy, cerebral palsy, or other defects. In addition, expectant mothers who eat insufficient nutritious food are subject to high blood pressure.

How much weight should a woman gain during pregnancy? Some doctors now recommend that if your weight is normal at the time of conception, you should gain about twenty-five pounds. If you are underweight, you may have to gain more. Women who wish to reduce should not choose to do so during pregnancy. Not only can dieting rob the developing fetus of protein and other essential food elements, but chemicals called ketone bodies, which are produced by the breakdown of fat, may be harmful to the baby as well.

In the last eight weeks of pregnancy, babies undergo a tremendous growth spurt, and brain development is at its peak. Research done in England over a twenty-year period has demonstrated that an adequate nutritional supply is vital during these

217

weeks in order for the child to have optimal brain function. Even a slight degree of maternal undernutrition may hinder the development of the child's brain. The mother-to-be of average height who engages in moderate activity needs approximately 2,600 calories a day in the final months of her pregnancy. If she is carrying twins, her caloric requirement jumps to 3,100.

What all the recent studies stress is that the emphasis should be on nutrition, not on pounds and ounces. This is the period in your life to forget about the scale and to concentrate on high-quality foods. A diet rich in protein, calcium, iron, and the B-vitamin folic acid is what the doctors are now ordering.

What do pregnant women really crave?

Just what they say they do: pickles. The old cliché, it turns out, makes sense scientifically. Pickles are salty. Craving salt is nature's way of telling an expectant mother she needs more salt than usual in her diet.

For years, obstetricians have recommended low-salt diets for mothers-to-be, but new research has demonstrated the importance of salt during pregnancy for both mother and baby.

Human cells must be continually bathed in salt water if they are to remain healthy. The same applies to the unborn fetus. During its development, the fetus floats in a sac of salty fluid, getting whatever salt it needs from its mother's bloodstream.

In a normal pregnancy, the mother's blood volume increases by 40 percent in order to feed the placenta and keep it functioning efficiently. Salt is the most important factor in maintaining this higher blood volume. Restricting salt during pregnancy will limit the expansion of blood volume. Blood volume is important for the function of the placenta, which sustains the fetus.

While healthy mothers should eat as much salt as they like, those who suffer from heart disease, hypertension, or kidney failure should be encouraged to limit their intake.

One word of caution, however. During pregnancy, be sure that all meats, including beef and lamb, are cooked thoroughly. Undercooked meats can produce a disease called *toxoplasmosis,* which is as dangerous during pregnancy as German measles. At any stage of pregnancy, toxoplasmosis may be transmitted to and

218

harm the fetus. And the results may go undetected until the child is more than a year old, when it's too late to correct complications.

Toxoplasmosis has also been traced to the handling of kitty litter. So:

☐ Put the saltshaker back on the table.
☐ Always cook meats thoroughly.
☐ Let someone else take care of the cat.

---

hat's crucial for the would-be mother-to-be over thirty?

An annual pelvic examination by your gynecologist for a condition called endometriosis. Endometriosis is caused when cells from the lining of the uterus build up, either within the uterus or outside of it. During pregnancy, endometrial cells that may have implanted often shrink and disappear. This might be because ovulation ceases at this time. But when pregnancy does not occur for a long period of time—as with the growing number of women who are delaying pregnancy until their thirties—the chance of endometriosis increases because there has been no rest period from the output of estrogen and progesterone. The symptoms include:

☐ Unusually heavy menstrual bleeding
☐ Increasingly intense menstrual cramps, especially on the second and third day
☐ Dull, aching pain when urinating during menstruation
☐ Discomfort during intercourse
☐ Pain in the lower abdominal region or tenderness on either side of the pelvic area

Endometriosis can be treated if detected early enough. To make a definite diagnosis, your doctor might use an instrument called a laparoscope to view the inside of your abdomen. Treatment for early endometriosis includes drug therapy and continued observation.

Even if you're not experiencing any symptoms but you're

planning to have a baby someday, make sure to have your doctor check for endometriosis during your annual gynecological examination.

What does a stuffy nose have to do with pregnancy?

Obviously the same thing that sore gums do. If you're expecting, your estrogen levels increase and not only promote the growth of the fetus's tissues, but also cause your own body tissues to swell, especially the tissues of the nasal passage.

So if your nose is chronically stuffed, it's probably not a cold. Don't medicate yourself. Ask your doctor for advice.

If, however, major congestion occurs, see an ear-eye-and-throat specialist. With your obstetrician's approval, such a doctor can give you medication to clear up the problem.

Increased estrogen levels also cause gums to become swollen and irritated, and you may have more plaque than usual between your teeth and gums. Brush carefully, according to a dentist's instructions, and use floss every day. Check in with your dentist frequently.

Because estrogen loosens the ligaments between the joints to prepare the pelvis for the baby's delivery, your back may feel out of joint as well. In addition, the growing weight of both the baby and the uterus puts excess stress on your spine. That's why four out of five pregnant women develop back pain.

Instead of grinning and bearing it, you can do daily stomach exercises to strengthen your muscles and reduce the strain on your back. Here are two recommended by doctors:

☐ Lie on your back with knees bent and cross your arms over your chest. As you count to five, raise your head and shoulders off the floor. Then, slowly, lower your head back down. Repeat three to five times, four times a day.
☐ Lie on your back with your knees bent. Place your right hand on your abdomen, your left hand under your back. Gently press the small of your back to the floor. The buttocks will raise slightly from the ground. Squeeze them for three counts. Then relax, lower the buttocks, and let the pelvis tilt forward. Repeat three to five times.

What should every woman have—before she gets pregnant?

Probably vaccination against German measles, even if she's had one before.

Let's say you're twenty-five years old and planning to get pregnant. You're positive there's no need to worry about rubella (German measles) and the birth defects it causes. But current research indicates that even if you had German measles as a child or were vaccinated against the disease before 1977, you may not be immune from rubella. One recent investigation showed that 36 percent of the women studied had lost their immunity within four years after receiving the vaccine.

The results were particularly disturbing because an immunity acquired in childhood must last for three to four decades if it's going to protect a woman throughout her fertile years.

In light of these findings specialists recommend that a woman consult her physician at least three months before she intends to become pregnant. The doctor will give her a simple blood test to determine whether she is immune to the disease.

If the results are positive, the woman need not do anything further. If negative, she can be inoculated with a recently developed, longer-lasting vaccine called rubella RA27-3. This new immunization will enable you to enter pregnancy without fear of contracting German measles.

How can you insure the health of an unborn child?

By counting the child's movements with a new technique called fetal monitoring. It's something a pregnant woman can do herself to check the development of the child and possibly prevent a miscarriage or stillbirth. This is particularly important for the one woman in ten who is considered a high-risk case because of medical problems such as diabetes and hypertension.

In studies of high-risk expectant women, a significant number of babies were saved because of the mother's quick response to the signals of fetal distress. Fetal monitoring has also proved

221

remarkably calming for all mothers-to-be. It helps to ease their worries about how the baby is doing.

At least once a week you'll lie down for two hours after eating in order to monitor the baby's movements. You'll place your hands on your tummy and count the baby's movements over a specified period of time. The number of counting sessions increases as your pregnancy advances. Your obstetrician can provide precise information on the counting technique. Any drop in the frequency of the movements is a warning to call the doctor.

The more a baby kicks and squirms in the womb, the healthier the unborn child is likely to be after birth. Studies show that active fetuses have a lower mortality rate and fewer respiratory problems than those who move less frequently. The last three months of pregnancy are particularly critical for keeping watch on the baby's movements.

Can a hospital be home to a pregnant woman?

Yes, if it has a birthing room or a child-bearing center. Both feature most of the comforts of home and all the safety of a hospital maternity ward.

More than a thousand hospitals around the country offer the option of giving birth to a baby in a birthing room. In it a woman can go through labor, delivery, and recovery without the physical strains of moving from labor room to delivery room to maternity room. Birthing rooms are decorated with all the comforts of home—paintings on the wall, drapes, comfortable chairs—and your husband can be there to lend support. Many hospitals also allow children to join their parents and new sibling right after the birth.

Using a birthing room, as one doctor puts it, "can be very good medicine." And although it may be like having a baby in your own home, the room is still a hospital with all the proper medical equipment and talent nearby in case of emergency.

Another, newer alternative to having a baby in the traditional hospital maternity ward is the child-bearing center, a facility run by trained nurse–midwives usually located minutes away from a maternity hospital. To cut the risks of childbirth, such centers carefully screen and monitor patients to insure that no high-risk

222

pregnancies or difficult deliveries will be encountered. Only women with normal medical histories are accepted and monthly physicals are part of the program. So are prenatal classes for both parents. And indeed, 95 percent of the births, a recent study found, are problem free.

One of the primary attractions of the child-bearing center is that it generally costs much less than a hospital delivery. Its fees are covered by medical insurance. And as in the birthing room, families are welcome at a child-bearing center.

Check with your obstetrician about the availability of birthing rooms and child-bearing centers in your area.

Can premature labor be stopped?

It is now possible to prevent premature birth, the leading cause of infant deaths. A newly released drug, ritrodine hydrochloride, is expected to reduce dramatically the number of babies—300,000 each year in the United States—who are born ahead of schedule.

Babies born prematurely—less than five pounds in weight when their mothers deliver—are highly susceptible to serious lung, heart, and stomach troubles. Some cases of cerebral palsy and mental retardation are also directly linked to premature birth.

Until the development of ritrodine hydrochloride, marketed under the brand name Yutopar, doctors relied on bed rest and dosages of hormones and other medication to delay delivery, but the results were only sometimes successful.

Ritrodine hydrochloride, though only recently licensed for sale in this country, has been used in Europe for the last ten years. It prevents a woman from going into labor by causing the uterine muscle to relax.

Studies show that the drug enables women who are prone to premature delivery to carry their baby for eight months or longer. However, doctors generally rule it out for women with histories of hypertension, heart disease, or certain types of abnormal pregnancies, and it's also not recommended for use before the twentieth week of pregnancy.

Patients being treated with the drug do report some side ef-

223

fects. Increased heart rate, tremors, and nervousness are among those frequently mentioned. Usually, however, the side effects are short-lived and don't interfere with continued treatment.

Doctors recommend ritrodine hydrochloride for use in uncomplicated cases of early delivery. Consult your obstetrician if you think you might benefit from its use.

Maternity leave for fathers?

Yes. Only it's called paternity leave. More and more fathers are taking a growing interest in caring for their children. And more and more men around the country are taking time off from work, often without pay, to be full-time fathers while their wives return to work.

The law now supports this interest in fathering. According to the Pregnancy, Disability Amendments to the 1964 Civil Rights Act, which took effect October 31, 1978, the rules of eligibility for existing and future medical and sick-leave programs must apply equally to men and women. The chief intent of the amendments was to protect female workers who got pregnant and were forced to take time off from work. Congress declared that pregnancy constituted a legitimate disability and that employers could not deny pregnant workers sick leave and disability pay or medical benefits if they gave such benefits to men.

It was a real victory for women employees, but it has also turned into a boon for a small but expanding group of caring fathers. Any company that now offers its women workers a *maternity* leave must extend the choice of a *paternity* leave to male workers, too.

At least thirty companies have now formally established paternity-leave programs for male workers, among them the American Telephone and Telegraph Company, Procter & Gamble, CBS, the Security Pacific Bank in California, and the Ford Foundation.

Some child-care experts are predicting that being a full-time father may become the major trend of the eighties. As one exuberant father put it: "I wouldn't trade it for anything. It's an experience most men miss out on and can never know unless they do it."

224

Is breast-feeding a natural contraceptive?

Contrary to what's been believed for many years, breast-feeding is not reliable as a natural contraceptive. In its initial stages, nursing may prevent conception from taking place, but that protection rapidly vanishes. Studies indicate, in fact, that up to 10 percent of nursing mothers become pregnant and that the percentage rises significantly for women whose menstrual cycles have resumed.

A nursing mother who wants to prevent a new pregnancy should, first of all, refrain from sex until after having a six-week checkup. It's very important that postdelivery healing has been successfully completed before contraceptive measures are begun and normal sexual activity is resumed.

Diaphragms and condoms are considered by many specialists to be the best methods of contraception for nursing mothers. Neither method causes any interference with the breast-feeding process. The IUD doesn't affect the quality or supply of the mother's milk either, but the increased risk of pelvic inflammatory disease makes it a less attractive choice.

Most doctors advise against using the birth-control pill because some studies indicate that it can cause hormones to pass into the mother's milk, possibly endangering the baby's health. There is, however, some dispute on how great the danger may be.

Discuss your concerns about contraception with your doctor. The available methods can then be considered in a way that takes your individual needs into account.

Once a Caesarian, always a Caesarian?

It ain't necessarily so. A year-long clinical study at Kaiser Foundation Hospital in San Diego has helped to turn the tables on traditional medical wisdom. Eight out of ten women studied, all of whom had delivered previously by the Caesarian method, subsequently gave birth vaginally, without complications.

This finding, as well as twenty-five other major studies, reversed a seventy-five-year-old policy of the American College of Obstetricians and Gynecologists. Repeat Caesarians are no longer standard medical procedure. And a National Institutes of Health panel now recommends that, in cases where the doctor believes the mother can have a natural delivery, it should be done.

Doctors used to perform repeat Caesarian operations routinely because they felt that the surgical scar from the original operation increased the risk of the uterus's rupturing during labor. But now surgeons are using incisions that are smaller, horizontal, and located lower in the uterus. These three factors have reduced the risk of rupture.

Whether or not you can deliver naturally depends upon the reason for your Caesarian in the first place. If it was caused by bleeding during pregnancy, breech position, toxemia, or fetal distress, chances are you're a good candidate for vaginal delivery, since these problems will not necessarily appear in another pregnancy.

If you've had one Caesarian and you're pregnant again, consult your obstetrician about vaginal delivery. Your new baby could arrive naturally.

Can a mother nurse an adopted infant?

Yes. According to recent studies, some adoptive mothers are able to partly nurse the infants—an obvious emotional benefit for both mother and child.

The key is preparation. Several weeks before the baby is received, the woman begins special breast exercises involving nipple stimulation aimed at increasing her supply of milk-producing hormones. The exercises are continued throughout the nursing period.

Dietary supplements can assist the process. Doctors recommend that adoptive mothers increase their fluid intakes and add brewer's yeast or B-complex vitamins to their menus. In some cases, hormone supplements are effective in increasing milk supply.

Nearly all the women studied used bottle feedings in addition to the nursing. Scientists say these supplemental feedings are important to normal growth. All the mothers reported that what mattered to them was not the amount of breast milk they were able to produce, but the warm, close bond they were able to create with their adopted newborn. No one looked upon the need for supplemental feeding as a failure in any way.

What should you eat if you're on the pill?

For one thing, you probably should be supplementing your diet with vitamins. An oral contraceptive has definite nutritional effects on all women. This holds particularly for those who have recently given birth, or who already have nutritional deficiencies, or who have had a recent illness or surgery. Teenagers who use the pill are also susceptible to vitamin deficiencies.

Recent studies on the effects of the pill on nutrition show that women are especially susceptible to decreased levels of certain vitamins—folic acid, riboflavin, and vitamins C, B_6, and B_{12}—because the pill prevents their complete absorption.

Besides those vitamins, eat plenty of vegetables, fortified cereals, and whole-grain breads. And if you decide after several years to go off the pill to get pregnant, that's an important time to discuss your nutritional needs with your doctor.

What do contact lenses and the pill have in common?

They sometimes interact, and the consequences can be serious. If you are one of the nearly 9 million women who wear contact lenses and are considering the use of a birth-control pill, you should be aware that the pill can seriously affect the ability of the lenses to correct your vision problems.

Contact lenses have to fit perfectly. It's not a hit-or-miss proposition. The pill can alter hormonal balance. Ophthalmologists have discovered that use of the pill can also change the shape of the cornea, the part of the eye on which the contact lens rests. The cornea remains out of shape throughout the month without fluctuation but will revert to its original shape once the pill is dropped and entirely out of the body's system.

This doesn't mean that taking an oral contraceptive will impair your vision. But the pill can affect the fit of your contacts, resulting in eye discomfort, increased tear production, redness, and constant irritation.

If you notice any problems with your lenses when you're going on, or even coming off, the pill, consult your eye doctor immediately and be sure to tell him or her you're using the pill. Don't waste time using eye drops; they won't help at all. There's only one solution: The doctor will have to adjust the lenses to conform to the changes in the shape of your eyes.

Is there any risk in using an IUD?

Yes. Some 6 million women in America use an intrauterine device (IUD) for birth control. Although most of them never run into any problems, the latest research indicates women using IUDs are far more susceptible than women using other forms of contraception to pelvic inflammatory disease—an infection of the uterus, ovaries, or fallopian tubes that can cause sterility.

In 1978, Dr. David Eschenbach, an infectious-disease specialist, published research demonstrating that IUD users were about four times likelier to suffer pelvic inflammatory disease than nonusers. Moreover, young, childless women using IUDs were at least nine times more apt to develop pelvic infections than other women. Frequency of intercourse and the number of sexual partners were not factors in developing the disease.

Not all members of the medical community, however, agreed with Dr. Eschenbach. Some doctors pointed to earlier studies showing no link between IUDs and pelvic inflammatory disease. A Swedish study argued that patients who selected IUDs were likely to have more sexual partners than women choosing other methods of contraception, and thus pelvic infections were transmitted sexually.

Nevertheless, it is true, and significant, that prior to the widespread marketing of IUDs in the United States, few doctors had cause to treat pelvic inflammatory disease. Doctors saw its incidence mainly among poor and minority patients, and the infections were caused primarily by gonorrhea bacteria.

228

The Food and Drug Administration was impressed enough with Dr. Eschenbach's findings that it subsequently issued an advisory bulletin to doctors suggesting they warn patients using IUDs about the possibility of sterility. "Election of intrauterine contraception clearly carries with it some risk of pelvic inflammatory disease and possible infertility," the FDA declared.

The culprit may be the tail of the IUD. It apparently provides a conduit for bacteria moving between the vagina and the uterus. Once the bacteria infect the uterus, which is susceptible to infection because its lining is irritated by the IUD, the infection can spread to the fallopian tubes and ovaries.

The following are symptoms of pelvic inflammatory disease:

- [ ] Increased bleeding when menstruating
- [ ] Bleeding between periods
- [ ] Increased menstrual cramps
- [ ] Abnormal or foul-smelling vaginal discharge
- [ ] Abdominal pain or tenderness
- [ ] Pain during intercourse
- [ ] Fever

If you wear an IUD and have any of these symptoms, see your doctor immediately. A quick blood test to check for pelvic inflammatory disease may prove helpful.

When you want to conceive do you just drop the pill?

No, that's not enough.

It seems that becoming pregnant after going off a birth-control pill requires a little *extra* family planning.

The latest advice from physicians is that women who have been using oral contraceptives should not attempt to conceive for three months after they have discontinued the pill. Those who become pregnant earlier have higher rates of miscarriage, probably as a result of changes in hormone levels caused by the pill. The body needs time to return to its normal hormone condition. While you're waiting for your reproductive system to reregulate itself, you can use mechanical birth-control devices such as the diaphragm, condom, or foam.

229

Even after waiting three months, many women still cannot become pregnant because the hormonal imbalance has not been fully resolved. A recent study of more than 3,000 former users of oral contraceptives disclosed that these women had lower rates of conception for more than a year after stopping the pill than did women who had used other forms of birth control. Nearly 25 percent of former pill users had to wait thirteen months or longer before they conceived; only about 10 percent of other women had that long a delay.

So if you're on the pill and want to have a baby, be prepared to be patient.

What's quicker than a rabbit?

A newly available pregnancy test called the BSU.

The BSU (Beta Sub Unit) is an extremely sensitive yet simple blood test that can be performed within eight to nine days of conception. The test has an accurate record in diagnosing pregnancies and the results are ready within hours. It represents a marked advance over the more commonly used urine test, which isn't accurate until two weeks after a missed period (four weeks after conception).

The BSU works by isolating a hormone known as HCG that is found only in pregnant women.

The test can also help identify potential tubular pregnancies and miscarriages. Smaller quantities of HCG are often associated with unhealthy embryos. The HCG level shown in the test may, therefore, indicate a problem pregnancy. Early detection of a tubular pregnancy is critical because, if the problem progresses too far, there is the danger of a burst tube and serious hemorrhage. And, in cases of staining or bleeding early in pregnancy, the test can help the doctor monitor the problem and take early action to prevent a possible miscarriage.

Ask your doctor about the BSU test. Often physicians are reluctant to perform it because it costs from $10 to $15 more than the urine test. But it may well be worth the added expense, and it may be covered by your medical insurance.

230

How curable is cervical cancer?

One hundred percent, if detected early enough. And radiation therapy is not necessary for the most common form of cervical cancer.

The key to detecting cervical cancer before it's too late is a regular visit to your gynecologist for a Pap smear, a short, painless, inexpensive test for any cellular changes in the cervix. If the smear is positive, the doctor will immediately do another smear to verify the first one. If the initial result is confirmed, the gynecologist must then determine how much the cells have changed by performing a biopsy, another painless office procedure that involves snipping off some cervical tissue for further analysis. To get tissue from the most affected part, gynecologists now use a sophisticated instrument called a colposcope, which provides a magnified, well-lit view of the suspicious area of the cervix.

If the examination discloses an early stage of cancerous tissue in a relatively well-defined area of the cervix, doctors can now destroy it completely with a procedure called cryosurgery, during which the abnormal cells are frozen and slough off. Like a simple biopsy, both the examination and the freezing procedure can be done in the doctor's office.

The Pap smear is the crucial step in preventing cervical cancer. Every year 10,000 women in this country die from cervical cancer, too many of them because they failed to visit a gynecologist regularly for a smear. That is especially tragic because the test is effective, and cervical cancer is totally curable.

Is a hysterectomy always necessary?

Not at all. There are alternatives available—methods that allow a woman to save her uterus and her ability to conceive and bear children.

One out of every five women over thirty will develop fibroid tumors of the uterus. These tumors are rarely cancerous; yet many women undergo needless hysterectomies that remove the uterus and, as a result, they can no longer bear children.

A less radical alternative is a surgical procedure called myomectomy. With this technique, the benign tumor is removed and the uterus remains intact, allowing for pregnancy at some future date.

Myomectomies are not new. They were first performed in the mid-nineteenth century. At that time, the lack of surgical techniques and technology made the operation a dangerous and difficult one. But these obstacles no longer exist and the operation is now routine.

The operation is particularly important for young women who are in the prime of their child-bearing years, although chances of conceiving and bearing children after a myomectomy are slightly reduced.

Fibroids are most common in black women, in fact three times more common than in white women. But 99 times out of 100, fibroids are benign. Some of them also shrink with time and often disappear after menopause.

Many women can avoid surgery altogether by having these fibroids watched carefully by their doctor. If there is no change in size, and they are not causing any problems—excessive bleeding, pain, urinary or bowel pressure—then there is no reason to remove them at all.

The point is there are alternatives to a hysterectomy. More than 800,000 hysterectomies are performed each year and at least 20 percent of them are unnecessary. So question your doctor carefully about these options. If he or she recommends a hysterectomy, insist on a second or even a third opinion. Most health insurance plans routinely pay for second opinions, and some even pay for third opinions.

What's a good nightcap for cystitis?

A glass of cranberry juice.

At some time, more than half of all women suffer from cystitis. It occurs when bacteria enter the bladder, causing irritation that can be extremely uncomfortable. Symptoms include frequent urination, a burning sensation while urinating, cramping or pain in the lower abdomen, and urine that is cloudy and sometimes bloody. Because 95 percent of the bacteria can't live in an acid environment, drinking a glass of cranberry juice in the morning and another at night may aid in protection.

There are other ways to fight cystitis. One is proper hygiene. It's important for women to wash and rinse the vaginal and rectal areas, wiping from front to back to discourage infection from foreign bacteria. Urinating before and after sexual intercourse is important, too. An attack of cystitis is often related to the beginning of frequent sexual activity, which is why the infection is also known as "honeymoon cystitis."

If you suspect you have cystitis, see your gynecologist as soon as possible. But until your appointment you can help treat the symptoms at home. Drink lots of clear fluids—at least eight to ten glasses a day, to flush bacteria out of your system. Try soaking in a hot tub two or three times a day. Rest with a heating pad on your stomach or back to help alleviate discomfort. Above all, avoid coffee, tea, alcohol, and spicy foods because they tend to irritate the bladder.

Most doctors will take a urine sample and probably prescribe antibiotics or sulfa drugs. If necessary, the prescription will be adjusted once the specific bacteria causing the infection are isolated. Symptoms will clear up almost immediately. Keep drinking that cranberry juice as a preventive.

Can you get rid of those annoying lumps in the breast?

Yes, there's a simple solution for many women—diet.

One out of every two women develops fibrocystic breast disease, which causes noncancerous nodules to form in usually both breasts. According to new research, such women, if they are under thirty-five years old, should give up caffeine for six months and other substances that contain a chemical compound called methylxanthine. Women over thirty-five should stay away from them for a longer period of time—at least a year.

Until recently, no one was certain what caused the cysts. But now research undertaken at Ohio State University College of Medicine has found that fibrocystic breast disease may be the result of ingesting methylxanthines including caffeine, theophyline, and theobromine. Coffee, tea, colas, chocolate, and other caffeine-containing foods as well as common over-the-counter

233

painkillers and some asthma and allergy medications contain methylxanthines.

In the study, women with fibrocystic disease were asked to stop taking methylxanthine, either in coffee or other forms. (The average coffee consumption of the group was four cups daily.) The results were encouraging. The breast nodules completely disappeared in most of the women over a twelve-month period, and in half of the women within one to six months.

In addition to dietary changes, doctors recommend that if you have such nodules in your breasts you should give yourself a monthly breast examination. If you discover any change other than a reduction in the size of the nodules, report it immediately to your doctor.

Even if you don't have nodules, you should examine your breasts every month. It's a simple, worthwhile precaution.

Is a D and C the only way?

Until recently there was little reason to doubt that a D and C (dilatation and curettage) was necessary to stop abnormal bleeding. Now there are two new alternatives that are safer, take less time, and are far less expensive. In more than four out of five cases the alternative procedures, performed in a doctor's office, are as effective as an operation performed in a hospital.

Abnormal bleeding is so common that almost a million women a year now have a D and C. In fact, it's the most common operation women have. The most frequent cause of abnormal bleeding is hormonal imbalance, and the problem is usually corrected by this procedure, though why is unknown.

In a D and C, after the patient receives a general or spinal anesthetic, the surgeon dilates her cervical canal so that the uterus can be scraped and cleaned out. In many cases the procedure is also used to take a sample of tissue for a biopsy to see if there is any possible malignancy.

Both alternative procedures are usually done under a local anesthetic, and, instead of a full day at the hospital, take less than an hour to complete.

One is called a tissue aspiration or suction curettage. The doctor vacuums out the uterus with a small plastic straw. This

234

procedure is often used when there's reason to believe that the problem is a hormonal imbalance. Inexplicably, the aspiration itself often cures the problem without hormonal therapy.

The other procedure is an endometrial biopsy. The doctor uses a tiny forceps to extract a small sample of tissue from the uterus. Because the lining of the uterus has no pain receptors, it doesn't hurt at all. An endometrial biopsy is particularly useful if a woman has a fertility problem. The cells of the tissue remain intact and can be carefully studied under a microscope.

Either of the two procedures can be used if there is any reason to suspect that abnormal bleeding may be caused by cancerous cells, but the vacuum aspiration is more complete and accurate for diagnosis. For some women a regular D and C may still be necessary, but in the majority of cases, the new alternatives should be considered.

Guess who's the new plumber in town?

If you're a woman who's not interested in traditional work, and you want a higher paying job, new possibilities are opening up every day—and are rewarding in more ways than one. Women are joining the ranks of painters, plumbers, truckers, mechanics, typesetters, electricians, miners, welders, landscapers, and other craftspersons. And they're finding out that earnings in these fields can be twice as high as in traditional female job categories such as secretary and file clerk.

Some women have been led to believe that many nontraditional jobs required the strength of a Hercules, but this is not true. Recent studies in the skilled trades, for example, indicate that there is no significant sex difference in the ability to carry out the majority of the essential tasks.

Barriers to employment of women in the skilled trades and other customarily all-male jobs have been falling since the passage of the Civil Rights Act in 1964. Although females account for only a small percentage of the total number of workers in such jobs, it is estimated that by 1990 7 million women will be on these payrolls.

Women who have taken such jobs emphasize that of course they use their heads as well as their hands in their work. They have more independence and freedom than in traditional jobs, and they're not cooped up indoors all day. Many create a finished product and feel a sense of pride and achievement in their occupation.

Of course, there are some negatives: teasing or outright harassment by co-workers, family disapproval, exposure to environmental hazards, danger of accidental injury.

A woman interested in a nontraditional job must usually obtain training. Some companies—including many in the aerospace industry, for example—offer on-the-job instruction with a low starting salary while you learn. Some jobs, such as several of the construction crafts, require a formal period of apprenticeship that often includes classroom work. It may take months or years before an individual becomes fully qualified.

If you'd like to know about jobs and job training, contact:
Women's Bureau,
U.S. Department of Labor,
200 Constitution Avenue NW,
Washington, D.C. 20210.

―――――――――――

Should a woman mind her own business?

There's no reason not to. There is now help available from two organizations that, between them, make loans, provide training, and offer vital information about business matters such as how to price goods, how to market them, and how to keep books.

Because it may be the best path to a satisfying career, or just a good way to earn money, women in recent years have been finding that, despite what they may think, they can successfully start and run their own businesses, either part- or full-time.

A large basement can become a studio for teaching art, drama, dance, or exercise. Cakes and other baked goods can be sold to neighbors or local food shops. Part-time child-care service is another possibility, as is a home-based catering business. Some women have set up typing and telephone services.

The federal government's Small Business Administration, created specifically to help small businesses, encourages women to use its services. The SBA arranges substantial loan money for qualified persons—and the qualifications are not as stiff as you might think. In fact, if you're turned down by two banks, they might step in and help. For details, write the Small Business Administration, Women's Business Enterprise Division, 1441 L Street NW, Washington, D.C. 20416, or the regional office of the SBA listed in your phone directory.

Women can also get expert counseling from the American Woman's Economic Development Corporation, or AWED. This is a federally funded, rapidly expanding organization that trains women to run their own businesses or start new ones. You send in an application, and, for a small fee, you can participate in a telephone training service in which you are matched with an expert in your field.

AWED has helped women get started in businesses as diverse as carpet clearning, public relations, and a sailing school. And if you already have a business, it'll help you improve it. One woman, a sportswear designer, was totally at sea when it came to the financial and record-keeping side of her enterprise. AWED stepped in, showed her how to figure break-even points and the cost on each garment made by outside contractors—and her business blossomed.

More than 7,000 women have already received AWED counseling, and follow-up research has found that 95 percent of them benefited from it. For further information, write to AWED, 1270 Avenue of the Americas, New York, N.Y. 10020.

The IRS siding with working mothers? No catch?

Under the new tax law that took effect January 1, 1982, a working mother, whether married or single, is entitled to a tax credit of up to 30 percent of what she spends on employment-related child-care costs. Her deductions can include almost any payments made for child care—cost of day-care centers, housekeepers, nursery school, after-school programs, even live-in relatives who serve as baby-sitters.

The amount of credit a working mother is entitled to depends upon her adjusted gross income, which includes her salary, interest from bank accounts, dividends, or any additional taxable monies. For example, a working mother with one child who has an income of $10,000 or less can take 30 percent of her child-care expenses as credit against her tax bill. For every $2,000 more she earns up to a maximum of $30,000, there's a reduction of one percentage point.

This means that if she has a total income of $10,000 and spends $1,000 on child care, she's entitled to a 30 percent tax credit, or $300. If her income is up to $12,000 and she spends $1,200 for child care, she's entitled to a 29 percent credit, or $348. The higher her income (up to a maximum of $30,000), the smaller percentage deduction she's allowed. (At $30,000 and upward the deduction is fixed at 20 percent.) The formula is complicated, so check with your local IRS office for details.

Can two persons share a job and be happy?

Absolutely—especially when they are two working mothers who want to work as well as to have time at home with their young children. Two innovative concepts—job sharing and flexitime— provide opportunities for working mothers to better balance the often conflicting demands of job and family.

Flexitime—a system now in use by some 16 percent of the nation's businesses—allows workers to break up their schedules in a way that provides them with more time to spend with their children. It does away with the rigid nine to five workday, allowing for earlier or later arrivals and departures, extended lunch periods, and time off in the afternoon. The employee is still expected to put in a certain number of hours on the job each month, and there is a specified time span, usually four hours a day, during which the worker must be on the job.

Studies indicate that most workers' morale and productivity increase in those institutions—mostly banks, large insurance and real-estate firms, and some government agencies—that have adopted flexitime.

Job sharing entails the employment of two part-time workers to fill one full-time position. The hours and salary are split between them. Studies point to reduced absenteeism, lower employee turnover, and increased productivity in businesses and government agencies where job sharing is in effect.

The concept is making particular headway in the field of education. Teachers, teacher aides, and librarians are successfully

238

sharing positions in school districts across the country with few of the anticipated fears—lack of communication, poor follow-through, lack of job commitment—developing.

Workers involved in job sharing stress that the key to the system's success lies in the selection of compatible partners. Job sharers must show flexibility in arranging schedules and in relating to their colleague's strengths and weaknesses.

Is marriage healthy?

Physically speaking at least, the state of matrimony is good for you. Many studies conducted in recent years at university and hospital medical centers have found that married persons live longer than those who do not have a mate. They also suffer fewer chronic illnesses and physical disabilities. Of course, we all know that, fairy tales notwithstanding, married couples often live neither happily nor ever after. And many persons who live on their own do live to ripe old ages. But if you're married, the odds are with you.

Divorced and separated individuals have a greater risk of dying early than any other group. Divorced men are especially vulnerable: Their chance of dying between the ages of thirty-five and fifty-five is more than three times that of their married peers.

Widowed women and men are next on the mortality tables. With this group, however, there is one particularly dangerous period: Death rates skyrocket in the first year of widowhood. A British study found that during the first year after the death of a mate, the survivor was ten times more likely to die than a person of the same age and sex who was still married.

Nonmarried individuals in general have particularly high death rates from causes related to smoking, drinking, and driving. It's as if they have less stake in prolonging their lives—or insufficient encouragement to do so. In any event, married persons take better care of themselves, and of one another.

Perhaps the most striking statistic of all comes from the National Institute of Mental Health: Men who are married are up to seven and a half times *less* likely than single males to be burdened by severe emotional problems or breakdowns that require hospitalization.

Does love at first sight have to wilt?

If a true, enduring love is what you're after, one glance isn't nearly enough. Tonight's Prince Charming may easily become next week's Freddy the Frog.

A major study of one thousand couples—some married, some divorced—discloses that relationships based on instant physical attraction are almost all doomed to fail. Often, a powerful sexual attraction is misinterpreted as "love at first sight." But couples who considered themselves happily married said that their first impressions of their mates were only mildly positive, at best. More intense feelings came much later, along with a better sense of "being understood" by their partners. Furthermore, the better they knew each other, the more attractive they perceived their partners to be.

Psychologists define love as a relationship, not a feeling or a form of behavior. Persons who love each other can also feel occasional anger or irritation toward their mate, but such feelings do not necessarily mean that their love is over.

Experts assure us that love cannot be realized "some enchanted evening across a crowded room," nor is it a by-product of intense physical attraction. "Love" is strengthened as the relationship unfolds. It involves trust, respect, and, above all, understanding of one's partner.

Whirlwind courtships and marriages based on "love at first sight" have trouble withstanding the pressures of time—unless compatibility of intellectual interests and life-styles is part of the relationship as well.

If you think you've found true love, marriage counselors recommend a courtship of at least one to three years before you decide to tie the knot.

Sources for Further Information and Help

ADOLESCENCE

BOOKS

Adelson, Joseph. *Handbook of Adolescent Psychology*. New York: John Wiley & Sons, 1980.

Bloss, Peter. *The Adolescent Passage*. New York: International Universities Press, 1979.

Conger, J. *Adolescence: Generation Under Pressure*. New York: Harper & Row, 1980.

Gallagher, J. Roswell, and Harris, Herbert I. *Emotional Problems of Adolescents*. New York: Oxford University Press, 1976.

Ginott, Haim G. *Between Parent and Teenager*. New York: Avon Books, 1971.

Gordon, Sol. *The Teenage Survival Book*. New York: Times Books, 1981.

Gross, Leonard H. *The Parent's Guide to Teenagers*. New York: Macmillan Publishing Co., 1981.

Schowalter, John E., and Anjan, Walter R. *The Family Handbook of Adolescence*. New York: Alfred A. Knopf, 1979.

ORGANIZATIONS

American Society for Adolescent Psychiatry
24 Green Valley Road
Wallingford, PA 19086
(215) 566-1054

Society for Adolescent Medicine
P.O. Box 3462
Granada Hills, CA 91344
(213) 368-5996

AGING

BOOKS

Anderson, Barbara G. *The Aging Game: Success, Sanity and Sex After Sixty*. New York: McGraw-Hill, 1981.

Hurdle, J. Frank. *A Medical Doctor's Home Guide to Arthritis, Muscle and Bone Ailments*. Englewood Cliffs, NJ: Parker Publishing, 1980.

Lake, Alice. *Our Own Years*. New York: Random House, 1979.

Silverstone, Barbara, and Hyman, Helen Kandel. *You and Your Aging Parent*. New York: Pantheon Books, 1976.

Stonecypher, D.D., Jr. *Getting Older and Staying Young*. New York: W. W. Norton & Co., 1980.

Uris, Auren. *Over 50*. New York: Bantam Books, 1981.

ORGANIZATIONS

American Association for Geriatric Psychiatry
230 North Michigan Avenue
Chicago, IL 60601
(312) 263-2225

American Geriatrics Society
10 Columbus Circle
New York, NY 10019
(212) 582-1333

Gray Panthers
3635 Chestnut Street
Philadelphia, PA 19104
(215) 382-3300

National Council of Senior Citizens
1511 K Street, N.W.
Washington, D.C. 20005
(202) 347-8800

National Council on the Aging
600 Maryland Avenue, S.W.
Washington, D.C. 20024
(202) 479-1200

ALLERGIES

Books

Burns, Sheila L. *Allergies and You.* New York: Julian Messner, 1980.
Golos, Natalie. *Coping with Your Allergies.* New York: Simon & Schuster, 1979.
Norback, Craig T. *Allergy Encyclopedia.* Edited by Asthma and Allergy Foundation. New York: New American Library, 1980.
Rapp, Doris J. *Allergies and Your Family.* New York: Sterling Publishing Co., 1980.
Silverstein, Alan, and Silverstein, Virginia B. *Allergies.* New York: J. B. Lippincott Co., 1977.
Zamm, Alfred V., and Gannon, Robert. *Why Your House May Endanger Your Health.* New York: Simon & Schuster, 1981.

Organizations

American Academy of Allergy
611 E. Wells Street
Milwaukee, WI 53202
(414) 272-6071

American Allergy Association
P. O. Box 7273
Menlo Park, CA 94024

American College of Allergists
2141 14 Street
Boulder, CO 80302

Asthma and Allergy Foundation of
America
19 West 44 Street
New York, NY 10036
(212) 921-9100

BABIES

Books

Baumgartner, Leona. *The Parent's Book of Baby Care.* New York: Grosset & Dunlap, 1978.
Better Homes and Gardens Baby Book. New York: Bantam Books, 1982.
Castle, Sue. *The Complete New Guide to Preparing Baby Foods.* New York: Doubleday & Co., 1981.
Cohen, Jean P., and Goirand, Roger. *Your Baby: Pregnancy, Delivery and Infant Care.* Englewood Cliffs, NJ: Prentice-Hall, 1981.
Consumer Guide: The Complete Baby Book. New York: Simon & Schuster, 1979.
Hagstrom, Julie, and Morrill, Joan. *Games Babies Play and More Games Babies Play.* New York: Pocket Books, 1982.
Jones, Sandy. *Good Things for Babies.* New York: Houghton Mifflin Co., 1980.
Samuels, Mike, and Samuels, Nancy. *The Well Baby Book.* New York: Summit Books, 1981.
Spock, Benjamin. *Baby and Child Care.* New York: Pocket Books, 1982.

ORGANIZATIONS

American Academy of Pediatrics
180 Hinman Avenue
Evanston, IL 60204

American College of Obstetricians
and Gynecologists
600 Maryland Avenue, S.W.
Suite 300
Washington, D.C. 20024
(202) 638-5577

American Association for Maternal
and Child Health
P.O. Box 965
Los Altos, CA 94022
(415) 964-4575

La Leche League International
9616 Minneapolis
Franklin Park, IL 60131
(312) 455-7730

BIRTH CONTROL

BOOKS

Mayle, Peter. *Congratulations! You're Not Pregnant.* New York: Macmillan Publishing Co., 1981.

Sala, Andre, and Duxler, Margot. *Expectations: A Completely Unexpected Guide to Planned and Unplanned Parenthood.* New York: G. P. Putnam's Sons, 1981.

Shapiro, Howard I. *The Birth Control Book.* New York: Avon Books, 1981.

Tucker, Tarvey. *Birth Control.* New York: Dell Publishing Co., 1981.

ORGANIZATIONS

Health and Human Services
Department Office of Family
Planning
5600 Fishers Lane
Rockville, MD 20857
(202) 443-2430

Planned Parenthood Federation of
America
810 Seventh Avenue
New York, NY 10019
(212) 541-7800

CANCER

BOOKS

Brody, Jane. *You Can Fight Cancer and Win.* New York: Times Books, 1977.

Levitt, Paul. *Cancer Reference Book.* New York: Dell Publishing Co., 1980.

McKhann, Charles F. *The Facts About Cancer: A Guide for Patients, Family and Friends.* Englewood Cliffs, NJ: Prentice-Hall, 1980.

Morra, Marion, and Potts, Eve. *Choices: Realistic Alternatives in Cancer Treatment.* New York: Avon Books, 1980.

Salsbury, Kathryn, and Johnson, Eleanor L. *The Indispensable Cancer Handbook.* New York: Seaview Books, 1981.

ORGANIZATIONS

American Cancer Society
777 Third Avenue
New York, NY 10017
(212) 371-2900

Breast Cancer Advisory Center
P.O. Box 224
Kensington, MD 20795

CAREERS

BOOKS

Berman, Eleanor. *Re-Entering.* New York: Crown Publishers, 1980.
Catalyst. *Marketing Yourself.* New York: Bantam Books, 1981.
————. *What to Do With the Rest of Your Life.* New York: Simon & Schuster, 1981.
Jawin, Ann J. *A Woman's Guide to Career Preparation, Scholarships, Grants and Loans.* New York: Doubleday & Co., 1979.
Pletcher, Barbara A. *Saleswoman: A Guide to Career Success.* New York: Pocket Books, 1978.
Schrader, Constance. *Nine to Five.* Englewood Cliffs, NJ: Prentice-Hall, 1981.
Summer Employment Directory of the U.S.: Where the Jobs Are and How to Get Them. Cincinnati: Writer's Digest Books, 1981.

ORGANIZATIONS

American Women's Economic
Development (AWED)
1270 Avenue of the Americas
New York, NY 10020

Catalyst
14 East 60th Street
New York, NY 10022
(212) 759-9700

Council for Career Planning
310 Madison Avenue
New York, NY 10017
(212) 758-2153

Small Business Administration
Women's Business Enterprise
Division
1441 L Street, N.W.
Washington, D.C. 20416

CONSUMER RIGHTS

BOOKS

Consumer Reports 1982 Buying Guide. Mount Vernon, NY: Consumers Union of the U.S., 1982.
The Consumers Union Report on Life Insurance: A Guide to Planning and Buying the Protection You Need. New York: Holt, Rinehart & Winston, 1981.
Feinman, Jeffrey. *Freebies for Kids.* New York: Wanderer Books, 1979.
Free Stuff for Home and Garden. Wayzata, MN: Meadowbrook Press, 1981.
Hullinger, Robert, and Grosch, Robert. *Move Yourself and Save!* St. Louis: Clayton Publishing House, 1980.
Jorpeland, Elain. *The Freebies Book.* New York: Holt, Rinehart & Winston, 1981.
Porter, Sylvia. *Sylvia Porter's New Money Book.* New York: Doubleday & Co., 1981.

ORGANIZATIONS

American Movers Conference
P.O. Box 2303
Arlington, VA 22202

Consumers Federation of America
1012 14 Street, N.W. Suite 901
Washington, D.C. 20005
(202) 387-6121

Consumers Research
Bowerstown Road
Washington, NJ 07882
(201) 689-3300

Consumers Union of the United
States
256 Washington Street
Mount Vernon, NY 10550
(914) 664-6400

Council of Better Business Bureaus
1150 17 Street
Washington, D.C. 20036
(202) 862-1200

244

U.S. Department of Defense
Surplus Sales
P.O. Box 1370
Battle Creek, MI 49016

The National Center for Citizen
Involvement
P.O. Box 4179
Boulder, CO 80306

Public Citizen
P.O. Box 19404
Washington, D.C. 20036
(202) 785-3704

DEPRESSION

BOOKS

Flach, Frederic F. *The Secret Strength of Depression.* New York: Bantam Books, 1979.
Kline, Nathan. *Factors in Depression.* New York: Raven Press, 1974.
———. *From Sad to Glad.* New York: Ballantine Books, 1975.
Sturgeon, Wina. *Depression: How to Recognize It, How to Cure It, and How to Gain From It.* Englewood Cliffs, NJ: Prentice-Hall, 1979.
Wonokur, George. *Depression: The Facts.* New York: Oxford University Press, 1981.

ORGANIZATIONS

American Psychiatric Association
1700 18 Street, N.W.
Washington D.C. 20009
(202) 797-4900

American Psychological Association
1200 17 Street, N.W.
Washington, D.C. 20036
(202) 833-7600

Health and Human Services
  Department
National Institute of Mental Health
Mental Health Clearinghouse
5600 Fishers Lane
Rockville, MD 20857
(202) 443-4513

National Mental Health Association
1800 N. Kent Street
Arlington, VA 22209
(703) 528-6405

DRUGS: PRESCRIPTION AND OVER-THE-COUNTER

BOOKS

Editors of Consumer Reports Books. *The Medicine Show.* New York: Pantheon Books, 1980.
Graedon, Joe. *People's Pharmacy—Two.* New York: Avon Books, 1980.
Long, James W. *The Essential Guide to Prescription Drugs.* New York: Harper & Row, 1980.

ORGANIZATIONS

American Pharmaceutical Association
2215 Constitution Avenue N.W.
Washington, D.C. 20037
(202) 628-4410

Food and Drug Administration
5600 Fishers Lane
Rockville, MD 20857
(202) 872-0382

Public Citizen Health Research
  Group
200 P Street, N.W. Suite 708
Washington, D.C. 20036
(202) 872-0382

EDUCATION

Books

Jawin, Ann J. *A Woman's Guide to Career Preparation: Scholarships, Grants and Loans.* New York: Doubleday & Co., 1979.
Kranes, Judith Ehre. *The Hidden Handicap.* New York: Simon & Schuster, 1980.
Lovejoy, Clarence E. *Lovejoy's College Guide.* New York: Simon & Schuster, 1982.
Miller, Mary Susan, and Baker, Samm Sinclair. *Straight Talk to Parents: How You Can Help Your Child Get the Best Out of School.* Briarcliff Manor, NY: Stein & Day Publishers, 1977.
Smith, Sally L. *No Easy Answers: The Learning Disabled Child at Home and at School.* New York: Bantam Books, 1980.

Organizations

American Association for Higher Education
1 Dupont Circle, Suite 780
Washington, D.C. 20036

The College Board
888 Seventh Avenue
New York, NY 10019

Elderhostel
100 Boylston Street Suite 200
Boston, MA 02166

National Education Association
1201 16 Street, N.W.
Washington, D.C. 20036

Scholarship Search
800 Huyller Street
Peterboro, NJ 07608

U.S. Department of Education
Office of Public Affairs
400 Maryland Avenue, S.W.
Washington, D.C. 20202

For Learning Disabilities or Gifted Children

Council for Exceptional Children
1920 Association Drive
Reston, VA 22091

Gifted Education Specialist
Office of Elementary and Secondary Education
Donohoe Building Room 1725—A
400 Maryland Ave., S.W.
Washington, D.C. 20202

U.S. Department of Education
Learning Disabilities Program
Office of Special Education and Rehabilitation Services
Washington, D.C. 20202

ENVIRONMENT

Books

Eckholm, Erik P. *The Picture of Health: Environmental Sources of Disease.* New York: W. W. Norton & Co., 1977.
Mackarness, Richard. *Living Safely in a Polluted World.* Briarcliff Manor, NY: Stein & Day Publishers, 1980.

Organizations

Environmental Action
1346 Connecticut Avenue, N.W. Suite 731
Washington, D.C. 20036

U.S. Environmental Protection Agency
Office of Public Affairs
Washington, D.C. 20460

EXERCISE

BOOKS

Cooper, Kenneth. *Aerobics*. New York: Bantam Books, 1972.
Jacobson, Howard. *Racewalk to Fitness*. New York: Simon & Schuster, 1980.
Kuntzleman, Charles T., and Editors of Consumers Guide. *Rating the Exercises*. New York: William Morrow & Co., 1978.
————. *The Complete Book of Walking*. New York: Pocket Books, 1982.
Sheehan, George. *This Running Life*. New York: Simon & Schuster, 1980.

ORGANIZATIONS

American Alliance for Physical Education, Recreation and Dance
1900 Association Drive
Reston, VA 22091

American College of Sports Medicine
1440 Monroe Street
Madison, WI 53206

Athletic Institute
200 Castlewood Drive
North Palm Beach, FL 33408

National Association for Girls and Women in Sport
1900 Association Drive
Reston, VA 22091

National Senior Sports Association
1900 M Street, N.W.
Washington, D.C. 20036

FINANCE

BOOKS

Kirsch, Charlotte. *A Survivor's Manual*. New York: Doubleday & Co., Anchor Press, 1981.
Mackevich, Gene. *The Woman's Money Book*. New York: Bantam Books, 1981.
Porter, Sylvia. *Sylvia Porter's New Money Book*. New York: Doubleday & Co., 1979.

ORGANIZATIONS

Federal Trade Commission
Bureau of Consumer Protection
633 Indiana Avenue, N.W.
Washington, D.C. 20580

National Foundation for Consumer Credit
1819 H Street, N.W.
Washington, D.C. 20006

Social Security Administration
P.O. Box 57
Baltimore, MD 21203

Women's Credit Rights Project
University of Southern California
University Park
Los Angeles, CA 90007

GYNECOLOGY

BOOKS

Cherry, Sheldon H. *For Women of All Ages*. New York: Macmillan Publishing Co., 1979.
Lauersen, Niels, and Whitney, Steven. *It's Your Body: A Woman's Guide to Gynecology*. New York: Playboy Press, 1977.
Madaras, Lynda. *Womancare: A Gynecological Guide to Your Body*. New York: Avon Books, 1981.

247

American College of Obstetricians
and Gynecologists
600 Maryland Avenue, S.W. Suite 300
Washington, D.C. 20024

National Women's Health Network
224 Seventh Street, S.E.
Washington, D.C. 20003

HEALTH

BOOKS

American Red Cross. *Family Health and Home Nursing.* New York: Doubleday & Co., 1979.
Consumers Union. *The Medicine Show.* New York: Pantheon Books, 1980.
Eiseman, Ben. *What Are My Chances?* Philadelphia: Saunders Press, 1980.
Foster, Daniel W. *A Layman's Guide to Modern Medicine.* New York: Simon & Schuster, 1980.
Galton Lawrence. *The Complete Book of Symptoms and What They Can Mean.* New York: Simon & Schuster, 1978.
Haessler, Herbert. *Bodyworkbook.* New York: Avon Books, 1980.
Johnson, Timothy G., and Goldfinger, Stephen E. *The Harvard Medical School Health Letter Book.* Cambridge, MA: Harvard University Press, 1981.

ORGANIZATIONS

American Academy of Ophthalmology
P.O. Box 7424
1833 Fillmore Street
San Francisco, CA 94120

American Dental Association
211 East Chicago Avenue
Chicago, IL 60611

American Diabetes Association
2 Park Avenue
New York, NY 10016

American Heart Association
7320 Greenville Avenue
Dallas, TX 75231

American Medical Association
535 North Dearborn Street
Chicago, IL 60610

American Public Health Association
1015 15 Street, N.W.
Washington, D.C. 20005

American Society of Clinical
Hypnosis
2400 East Devon Avenue Suite 218
Des Plaines, IL 60018

The Arthritis Foundation
Lenox P.O. Box 1888
Atlanta, GA 30326

Food and Drug Administration
Re: X-Rays
HFX-28
Rockville, MD 20857

Society for Clinical and Experimental
Hypnosis
129-A Kings Park Drive
Liverpool, NY 13088

World Health Organization
Room 2424
United Nations
New York, NY 10017

HOMES AND APARTMENTS

BOOKS

Blumberg, Richard E., and Grow, James R. *The Rights of Tenants.* New York: Avon Books, 1978.
Diamond, Stuart. *No-Cost Low-Cost Energy Tips.* New York: Bantam Books, 1980.
Raimy, Eric. *Shared Houses, Shared Lives.* Los Angeles: J. P. Tarcher, 1979.

Robinson, Steven, and Dubin, Fred S. *The Energy-Efficient Home*. New York: New American Library, 1978.

ORGANIZATIONS

National Homeowners Association
1906 Sunderland Place, N.W.
Washington, D.C. 20036

National Tenants Union
380 Main Street
East Orange, NJ 07018

Shared Housing Resource Center
6344 Green Street
Philadelphia, PA 19144

U.S. Department of Housing and
  Urban Development
Office of Consumer Affairs
HUD Building
Washington, D.C. 20410

U.S. Department of Housing and
  Urban Development
Rehabilitation Management Division
Office of Urban Rehabilitation,
  Community Planning and
  Development
Washington, D.C. 20110

HYPERTENSION

BOOKS

Galton, Lawrence. *The Silent Disease: Hypertension*. New York: New American Library, 1974.
Rees, Michael K. *The Complete Family Guide to Living with High Blood Pressure*. Englewood Cliffs, NJ: Prentice-Hall, 1980.

ORGANIZATIONS

American Heart Association
7320 Greenville Avenue
Dallas, TX 75231

American National Red Cross
17th and D Streets, N.W.
Washington, D.C. 20006

Citizens for the Treatment of High
  Blood Pressure
1101 17 St., N.W.
Washington, D.C. 20036

High Blood Pressure Information
  Center
National Institutes of Health
7910 Woodmont Avenue
Bethesda, MD 20014

MARRIAGE

BOOKS

Berman, Claire. *Making it as a Stepparent*. New York: Bantam Books, 1981.
Dreikurs, Rudolf. *Challenge of Marriage*. New York: E.P. Dutton, 1978.
Gathorne-Hardy, Jonathan. *Marriage, Love, Sex and Divorce: What Brings Us Together, What Drives Us Apart*. New York: Summit Books, 1981.
Napier, Augustus Y., and Whitaker, Carl A. *The Family Crucible*. New York: Bantam Books, 1980.
Ryglewicz, Hilary, and Thaler, Pat Koch. *Working Couples*. New York: Sovereign Books, 1980.
Satir, Virginia et al. *Helping Families to Change*. New York: Jason Aronson, 1976.
Singer, Laura J. *Stages: The Crises That Shape Your Marriage*. New York: Grosset & Dunlap, 1980.
Wallerstein, Judith S., and Kelly, Joan Berlin. *Surviving the Breakup: How Children and Parents Cope with Divorce*. New York: Basic Books, 1980.

249

American Arbitration Association
140 West 51 Street
New York, NY 10020

American Association for Marriage
and Family Therapy
924 West Ninth
Upland, CA 91786

Family Mediation Association
2380 S.W. 34 Way
Fort Lauderdale, FL 33312

National Council on Family Relations
1219 University Avenue, S.E.
Minneapolis, MN 55414

The Office of Child Support
Enforcement
6110 Executive Boulevard Room 900
Rockville, MD 20852

NUTRITION

BOOKS

Brody, Jane. *Jane Brody's Nutrition Book*. New York: W. W. Norton & Co., 1981.
Deutsch, Ronald M. *Realities of Nutrition*. Palo Alto, CA: Bull Publishing Co., 1976.
Jacobson, Michael F. *Eater's Digest: The Consumer's Factbook of Food Additives*. New York: Doubleday & Co., 1980.
Robertson, Laurel et al. *Laurel's Kitchen: A Handbook for Vegetarian Cookery and Nutrition*. New York: Bantam Books, 1978.
Slattery, Jill S. et al. *Maternal and Child Nutrition*. New York: Appleton-Century-Crofts, 1980.
Smith, Lendon. *Feed Your Kids Right*. New York: McGraw-Hill Book Co., 1979.
White, Alice, and the Society for Nutrition Education. *The Family Health Cookbook*. New York: David McKay Co., 1980.

ORGANIZATIONS

American Dietetic Association
430 North Michigan Avenue
Chicago, IL 60611

American Institute of Nutrition
9650 Rockville Pike
Bethesda, MD 20014

U.S. Department of Agriculture
Science and Education
Administration
14th Street and Independence
Avenue, S.W.
Washington, D.C. 20250

PARENT/CHILD

BOOKS

Behrstock, Barry. *The Parent's When-Not-To-Worry Book*. New York: Harper & Row, 1981.
Gregg, Elizabeth, and Knotts, Judith. *Growing Wisdom, Growing Wonder*. New York: Macmillan Publishing Co., 1980.
Hanson, Jerome K. *Game Plans for Children*. New York: Perigree Books, 1981.
McDermott, John F. *Raising Cain (and Abel, Too): The Parent's Book of Sibling Rivalry*. New York: Wyden Books, 1980.
Maslow, Arthur. *Family Connections: Parenting Your Own Grown Children*. New York: Doubleday & Co., 1982.
Sutton-Smith, Brian, and Sutton-Smith, Shirley. *How to Play with Your Children (And When Not To)*. New York: Hawthorn Books, 1974.

American Academy of Child
  Psychiatry
1424 16 Street, N.W.
Washington, D.C. 20036

American Academy of Pediatrics
1801 Hinman Avenue
Evanston, IL 60204

PREGNANCY

BOOKS

Borg, Susan, and Lasker, Judith. *When Pregnancy Fails.* Boston: Beacon Press, 1981.
Brewer, Gail Sforza. *What Every Pregnant Woman Should Know.* New York: Penguin Books, 1979.
Cherry, Sheldon. *Understanding Pregnancy and Childbirth.* New York: Bantam Books, 1980.
Eastman, Nicholas J., and Russell, Keith P. *Expectant Motherhood.* Boston: Little, Brown & Co., 1970.
Ewy, Donna, and Ewy, Roger. *The Cycle of Life: Guide to a Healthy Pregnancy.* New York: E. P. Dutton, 1981.
Fleming, Alice. *Nine Months: A Practical Guide for Expectant Mothers.* New York: Harper & Row, 1974.

ORGANIZATIONS

American College of Obstetricians
  and Gynecologists
600 Maryland Avenue, S.W.
Washington, D.C. 20024

American Fertility Society
1608 13th Avenue S. Suite 101
Birmingham, AL 35205

American Foundation for Maternal
  and Child Health
30 Beekman Place
New York, NY 10022

American Society of Childbirth
  Educators
P.O. Box 16159
7113 Lynnwood Drive
Tampa, FL 33687

American Society for
  Psychoprophylaxis in Obstetrics
1411 K Street, N.W.
Washington, D.C. 20005

Childbirth Without Pain
20134 Snowden
Detroit, MI 48235

U.S. Department of Health and
  Human Services
National Institute of Child Health
  and Human Development
9000 Rockville Pike
Bethesda, MD 20205

PSYCHOLOGY—ADULT

BOOKS

Branden, Nathaniel. *The Psychology of Self-Esteem.* New York: Bantam Books, 1969.
Calhoun, James F., and Acocella, Joan. *Psychology of Adjustment and Human Relationships.* New York: Random House, 1978.
Hightower, Howard J. *Psychology for Parents.* New York: William Frederick Press, 1981.

American Psychological Association
1200 17 Street, N.W.
Washington, D.C. 20036

American Psychotherapy Association
P.O. Box 2436
West Palm Beach, FL 33402

Community Guidance Service
140 West 58 Street
New York, NY 10019

National Psychological Association
P.O. Box 2436
West Palm Beach, FL 33402

PSYCHOLOGY—CHILD

BOOKS

Adelson, Joseph, ed. *Handbook of Adolescent Psychology*. New York: John Wiley & Sons, 1980.

Angrilli, Albert, and Helfat, Lucile. *Child Psychology*. New York: Harper & Row, 1981.

Azerrad, Jacob. *Anyone Can Have a Happy Child*. New York: M. Evans & Co., 1980.

Bean, Reynold, and Clemes, Harris. *How to Raise Children's Self-Esteem*. Sunnyvale, CA: Enrich, 1980.

Kohl, Herbert. *Growing With Your Children*. Boston: Little, Brown & Co., 1978.

Smart, Mollie S., and Smart, Russell C. *Development and Relationships*. New York: Macmillan Publishing Co., 1978.

Stone, Joseph L., and Church, Joseph. *Childhood and Adolescence: A Psychology of the Growing Person*. New York: Random House, 1979.

ORGANIZATIONS

American Academy of Child
  Psychiatry
1424 16 Street, N.W.
Washington, D.C. 20036

American Psychological Association
1200 17 Street, N.W.
Washington, D.C. 20036

Association for Child Psychoanalysis
4524 Forest Park
St. Louis, MO 63108

National Psychological Association
P.O. Box 2436
West Palm Beach, FL 33402

SAFETY

BOOKS

Accident Action: The Essential Family Guide to Home Safety and First Aid. New York: Viking Press, 1979.

The American Medical Association Handbooks of First Aid and Emergency Care. New York: Random House, 1980.

American Red Cross. *Standard First Aid and Personal Safety*. New York: Doubleday & Co., 1979.

Florio, A.E. *Safety Education*. New York: McGraw-Hill Book Co., 1979.

McGrath, Ruth E. *Developing Concepts of Safety in Early Childhood*. Buffalo, NY: DOK Publishers, 1977.

Olson, Nancy Z. *Personal and Family Safety*. New York: Holt, Rinehart & Winston, 1981.

ORGANIZATIONS

American Red Cross
17th and D Streets, N.W.
Washington, D.C. 20006

Child Safety
American Academy of Pediatrics
P.O. Box 1034
Evanston, IL 60204

Consumer Product Safety
Commission
1111 18 Street, N.W.
Washington, D.C. 20207

Food Safety Council
1725 K Street, N.W. Suite 306
Washington, D.C. 20006

National Burn Federation
3737 Fifth Avenue Suite 206
San Diego, CA 92103

National Highway Traffic Safety
Administration
400 Seventh Street, S.W.
Washington, D.C. 20590

National Office of Lifeline Systems,
Inc.
400 Main Street
Waltham, MA 02254

National Poison Center Network
Children's Hospital of Pittsburgh
125 DeSoto Street
Pittsburgh, PA 15213

National Safety Council
444 N. Michigan Avenue
Chicago, IL 60611

Physicians for Automotive Safety
Communications Department
P.O. Box 208
Rye, NY 10580

SEX

BOOKS

Brecher, Ruth, and Brecher, Edward, eds. *An Analysis of Human Sexual Response.* New York: New American Library, 1966.

Comfort, Alex, and Comfort, Jane. *The Facts of Love.* New York: Crown Publishers, 1979.

Hass, Aaron. *Teenage Sexuality.* New York: Macmillan Publishing Co., 1979.

Karasu, Toksoz B., and Socarides, Charles W. *On Sexuality.* New York: International Universities Press, 1979.

Money, John. *Handbook of Human Sexuality.* Edited by Benjamin B. Wolman. Englewood Cliffs, NJ: Prentice-Hall, 1980.

Uslander, Arlene S. et al. *Sex Education for Today's Child.* New York: Association Press, 1977.

ORGANIZATIONS

American Association of Sex
Educators, Counselors and
Therapists
1 East Wacker Drive Suite 2700
Chicago, IL 60601

American Venereal Disease
Association
Box 385
University of Virginia Hospital
Charlottesville, VA 22901

Center for Reproductive and Sexual
Health
424 East 62 Street
New York, NY 10021

Council for Sex Information and
Education
Box 23088
Washington, D.C. 20024

Sex Information and Education
Council of U.S.
84 Fifth Avenue Suite 407
New York, NY 10011

SINGLE PARENTING

BOOKS

Baruth, Leroy G. *A Single Parent's Survival Guide: How To Raise the Children.* Dubuque, IA: Kendall/Hunt Publishing Co., 1979.
Bosco, Antoinette. *Successful Single Parenting.* Mystic, CT: Twenty-Third Publications, 1978.
Davenport, Diana. *One-Parent Families.* North Pomfret, VT: David & Charles, 1979.
Gardner, Richard. *The Boys and Girls Book About One-Parent Families.* New York: G. P. Putnam's Sons, 1978.
Klein, Carole. *The Single Parent Experience.* New York: Avon Books, 1978.

ORGANIZATIONS

Committee for Single Adoptive Parents
P.O. Box 4074
Washington, D.C.

Mothers Without Custody
P.O. Box 76
Sudbury, MA 01776

Parents Without Partners
7910 Woodmont Avenue Suite 1000
Washington, D.C. 20014

Single Dad's Hotline
P.O. Box 4842
Scottsdale, AZ 85258

SKIN CARE

BOOKS

Schoen, Linda A., ed. *The AMA Book of Skin and Hair Care.* New York: Harper & Row, 1976.

ORGANIZATIONS

American Academy of Dermatology
820 Davis Street
Evanston, IL 60201

Skin Care Association of America
16 West 57 Street
New York, NY 10019

SLEEP

BOOKS

Hartmann, Ernest. *The Sleeping Pill.* New Haven, CT: Yale University Press, 1978.
Maxman, Jerrold S. *A Good Night's Sleep: A Step-by-Step Program for Overcoming Insomnia and Other Sleep Problems.* New York: W. W. Norton & Co., 1981.
Silverstein, Alvin, and Silverstein, Virginia. *Sleep and Dreams.* New York: J. B. Lippincott Co., 1974.
Spiegel, Rene. *Sleep and Sleeplessness in Advanced Age.* Jamaica, NY: Spectrum Publications, 1980.

ORGANIZATIONS

Association of Sleep Disorders Centers
c/o Dr. Merrill M. Mitler
Department of Psychiatry, T-10, HSC
State University of New York
Stony Brook, NY 11794

Sleep Disorders and Research Center
Henry Ford Hospital
2799 West Grand Boulevard
Detroit, MI 48202

STRESS

BOOKS

Ainsworth, Stanley. *Positive Emotional Power: How to Manage Your Feelings.* Englewood Cliffs, NJ: Prentice-Hall, 1981.
Antonovsky, Aaron. *Health, Stress and Coping: New Perspectives on Mental and Physical Well-Being.* San Francisco: Jossey-Bass, 1979.
Benson, Herbert. *The Relaxation Response.* New York: Avon Books, 1976.
Cooper, Cary L. *The Stress Check: Coping with the Stresses of Life and Work.* Englewood Cliffs, NJ: Prentice-Hall, 1980.
McGuigan, F.J. *Calm Down: A Guide to Stress and Tension Control.* Englewood Cliffs, NJ: Prentice-Hall, 1981.

ORGANIZATIONS

American Academy of Stress
  Disorders
8 South Michigan Avenue
Chicago, IL 60603

International Stress and Tension
  Control Association
P.O. Box 8005
Louisville, KY 40208

SURGERY

BOOKS

Crile, George. *Surgery: Your Choices, Your Alternatives.* New York: Delacorte Press, 1978.
Denny, Myron K. *Second Opinion.* New York: Grosset & Dunlap, 1979.
Melluzo, Paul J., and Nealon, Eleanor. *Living with Surgery: Before and After.* Philadelphia: W. B. Saunders Co., 1980.
Schrock, Theodore. *Handbook of Surgery.* Greenbrae, CA: Jones Medical Publications, 1982.
Schultz, Richard C., ed. *Outpatient Surgery.* Philadelphia: Lea & Febiger, 1979.

ORGANIZATIONS

American College of Surgeons
55 East Erie Street
Chicago, IL 60611

American Surgical Association
c/o Dr. W. Gerald Austen
Department of Surgery
Massachusetts General Hospital
32 Fruit Street
Boston, MA 02114

Association of American Physicians
  and Surgeons
8991 Cotswold Drive
Burke, VA 22015

WORKING WOMEN

BOOKS

Berman, Eleanor. *Re-Entering.* New York: Crown Publishers, 1980.
Catalyst. *What to Do with the Rest of Your Life.* New York: Simon & Schuster, 1980.
Norris, Gloria, and Miller, Jo Ann. *The Working Mother's Complete Handbook: Everything You Need to Know to Succeed on the Job and at Home.* New York: E. P. Dutton, 1979.
Schlayer, Mary E., and Cooley, Marilyn. *How to Be a Financially Secure Woman.* New York: Ballantine Books, 1978.

Wallace, Phyllis A. et al. *Women in the Workplace.* Boston: Auburn House Publishing Co., 1981.

ORGANIZATIONS

Catalyst
14 East 60th Street
New York, NY 10022

National Commission on Working
   Women
Center for Women and Work
1211 Connecticut Avenue, N.W.
Washington, D.C. 20036

Network Directory
Working Women
600 Madison Avenue
New York, NY 10022

U.S. Department of Labor
Office of the Secretary
Women's Bureau
200 Constitution Avenue, N.W.
Washington, D.C. 20210

FYI PRODUCTION STAFF

Producer	YANNA KROYT BRANDT
Coordinating Producer/Writer	MARY ANN DONAHUE
Director	MICHAEL GARGIULO
Head Writer	LINDA KLINE
Director of Research/Writer	JOE GUSTAITIS
Researchers/Writers	ELAINE BROWN, ROBIN WESTEN
Field Producers	ANDREW COMINS, JANE CHAPLINE
Photography Editor	NANCY BRENNER
Staff Photographer	GIL ORTIZ
Business Manager	GREG MASON
Production Staff	SHARON FISHER, SAL MANIACI, NEIL O'DONNELL, DELPHINE SNIPES
Logo Design	ELINOR BUNIN

FYI CONSULTANTS

Child and Adolescent Psychiatry   DR. WILLIAM ELLIS. Child psychiatrist. Associate Professor of Child Psychiatry, Columbia University—Harlem Hospital affiliate.

Dentistry   DR. STEPHEN J. MOSS. Practitioner in pediatric dentistry, New York City. Professor and Chairman, Department of Pedodontics, New York University Dental Center. Past President, American Academy of Pedodontics.

Economics   REVA CALESKY. Financial counselor/accountant, tax specialist. Frequent lecturer on business and personal financial management.

General Medicine   DR. JACK GEIGER. Arthur C. Logan Professor of Medicine, City College of New York. Director, Program in Health, Medicine and Society, School of Bio-Medical Education, City College of New York.

257

Nutrition	RUTH LOWENBERG. Program Development and Training/Supervisor, Nutrition Education Specialist, Cornell University, Cooperative Extension. Registered dietitian and Master of Science, Nutrition.
Obstetrics and Gynecology	DR. SHELDON H. CHERRY. Associate Clinical Professor of Obstetrics and Gynecology, Mount Sinai School of Medicine. Author of *Pregnancy and Childbirth* and *For Women of All Ages.*
Ophthalmology	DR. ROBERT WARD KLEIN. Director of Ophthalmology, Goldwater Memorial Hospital. Clinical Instructor, Ophthalmology, New York University School of Medicine.
Pathology and Laboratory Medicine	DR. RAYMOND GAMBINO. Director of Laboratories and Chief Pathologist, St. Luke's-Roosevelt Hospital Center. Editor, *Lab Report for Physicians.*
Pediatrics	DR. RAMON MURPHY. Assistant Professor, Clinical Pediatrics, Mt. Sinai School of Medicine. Director, Pediatric Poison Control Program. Fellow of the American Academy of Pediatrics.
Psychology	DR. MAGDA DENES. Clinical Professor, Adelphi University and New York University Faculty, and Supervisor, Mt. Sinai School of Medicine, Department of Psychiatry. Author of *In Necessity and Sorrow: Life and Death in an Abortion Hospital.*
	MRS. PEGGY PAPP. Family therapist, marriage counselor, Ackerman Institute.
Sexual Help	LORNA SARREL. Assistant Clinical Professor of Social Work in Psychiatry, Yale University School of Medicine. Contributing editor to *Redbook* magazine.
	DR. PHILIP SARREL. Associate Professor of Obstetrics and Gynecology and Psychiatry, Yale University School of Medicine. Contributing editor to *Redbook* magazine.

258

About the Editor

Nat Brandt's extensive career as a journalist has included work in radio and television and for newspapers, magazines, and a book company. He was a writer for CBS News in New York before entering the newspaper field, first as a reporter on several newspapers in Connecticut and New Jersey, then as an editor on the National News Desk of *The New York Times*. He subsequently was the managing editor of *American Heritage* magazine and the editor-in-chief of *Publishers Weekly*.

Mr. Brandt has edited books by, among others, William Saroyan and S. L. A. Marshall. Photographs from his travels around the world have appeared in *Life International, Horizon,* and numerous books and encyclopedias. His articles have appeared in *American Heritage, The New York Times Sunday Magazine, Redbook, Reader's Digest,* and other publications.

In addition to his current freelance activities, Mr. Brandt is an adjunct professor of communications at St. John's University, where he teaches journalism and lectures on the mass media.

Index